Living in Tin

Also by Linda Wells and published by
Ginninderra Press *Kultitja*

Linda Wells

Living in Tin
The Bungalow, Alice Springs
1914–1929

With heartfelt thanks to the descendants of the Bungalow who shared, with grace and generosity, their family stories; Emily Potter and Paul Venzo, surely the most switched-on and supportive PhD supervisors there could ever be, along with other brilliant scholars from the Deakin School of Communication and Creative Arts; Marly the Barly, who offers real and honest insights as well as fun and love; fellow doctoral candidates who shared the experience; and family and friends, you know who you are, who provided material and emotional support throughout those PhD years. Thanks also to Stephen and Brenda of Ginninderra Press for supporting new and emerging authors as well as works that push boundaries.

Warning: This book contains images of people who have died.

Living in Tin: The Bungalow, Alice Springs, 1914–1929
ISBN 978 1 76109 516 0
Copyright © text Linda Wells 2023
Cover image from PRG-1365-1-248, Laver Collection,
State Library of South Australia

First published 2023 by
GINNINDERRA PRESS
PO Box 3461 Port Adelaide 5015
www.ginninderrapress.com.au

Contents

Introduction	9
Walking the History of Mparntwe	17
The Immense Possibilities	22
The Poetics of Dust	25
The Police Journals	28
Introduced Species	31
Stuart – The Statue	37
Topsy	40
Up the Track	46
The Smiths of Arltunga	50
Archival Portrait of Half-castery	52
The First Schoolteacher	56
Mparntwe	73
The Early Years	74
The Photos	91
Sergeant Stott on Trial	99
Removal	118
Solid Rock	120
In Their Place	123
Sarah Breaden: 'a refined and splendid kind of girl'	143
The Sacrifices	159
Iron and Squalor 1	160
Being a Kid	169
Iron and Squalor 2	180
Maggie Plenty	188
Back in the Alice	195
Iron and Squalor 3	197

The King	206
This is How Freeman do to Me	209
How Emily Made History	216
Ida and Topsy	226
Algebuckina	239
Jay Creek	240
Appendix: The Interconnectedness	244
Notes	247
References	255

For the descendants of the Bungalow survivors

Introduction

I set out to research and write the story of the first Bungalow in Alice Springs. It was a tin shed home in the centre of the burgeoning town between 1914 and 1929. The home was set up for children of dual Indigenous/Anglo heritage who had predominantly been removed from their families. They were cared for by a few key women, including Topsy Smith, the mother of the first seven children who lived at the Bungalow after their Welsh-born father Bill had died, some other mothers of children of the Bungalow, ands Ida Standley, who was Alice Springs' first schoolteacher. The operation was overseen by the police officer in charge of the district – Sergeant Stott and his wife.

I have had a long association with Alice Springs. I moved there as a recently graduated schoolteacher myself in the late 1980s and stayed for more than three decades. My awareness of the Bungalow began with the names of streets and services around the town: Ida Standley Pre-School, Topsy Smith Hostel, Stott Terrace. There is a sign about Ida Standley and her work on display outside the original heritage school of the town. The story of the Bungalow and its main players gets a few paragraphs, even the odd chapter, in local history books. I heard it mentioned too, by the people whose ancestors were most directly affected. All of those snippets, in the contemporary landscape of Alice Springs, piqued my interest and led eventually to a doctoral-sized fascination.

My doctoral research about the Bungalow and the context in which it existed came from a variety of sources. They include original archival materials such as letters, reports, memos, scribbled notes, architectural plans, visitor book entries, newspaper articles and the like, from the early years of the twentieth century. These documents have all been carefully classified and stored in various archive collections around Australia. They are a valuable source of information about Australia's history and cultural development. At the same time, archival collections, particularly as they relate to our colonial origins, largely reflect the dominant viewpoint of the time. The documents were, on the whole, created and selected for preservation by colonial forces. They are an embodiment of the old adage that history belongs to the victors. To gain more than a colonial and mostly patriarchal understanding of the times those documents represent, we read across the grain and pay as much attention to what is missing as to what is there.

To wrestle our history out of the victors' hands and share it amongst all the people, we must, as well, measure the information of the archives, against any other sources that are available. Fortunately for this particular story, there are oral histories of four of the people who grew up in the Bungalow that were made in the later years of their lives. Those people include Ada Wade (née Smith), Clarence Smith, Milton Liddle and Emily Liddle. The transcripts of these recordings, stored in the office of the NT Archives in Alice Springs, offer insights from the lived experience of the, shall we say, inmates: the Bungalow survivors.

Some books, too, offer first-hand accounts. They include *Man From Arltunga: Walter Smith, Australian Bushman*. This is a biography of Topsy and Bill Smith's oldest son, as told to Alice Springs historian Dick Kimber. There is also *Racial Folly: A Twentieth Century Aboriginal Family* by Gordon Briscoe, whose mother was an inmate of the first Bungalow and who himself was born at a later version of the institution.

The Bungalow is a foundational story of Alice Springs. Living in the town today, and radiating out to other parts of Australia, are descendants of the people who feature in this story. I spoke with several of these children and grandchildren. They shared memories of their ancestors and the stories they had been told of their experiences. Not only did those descendants have stories and material artefacts from the past, they are an expression of what the past has become. The past is all around us in Alice Springs and beyond, the history expressed in myriad ways. The people of the Bungalow era live on through their ongoing families. (Due

to time constraints, there are many other Bungalow descendants I missed out on speaking to. Perhaps one day we can create a website of the Bungalow where everyone who wants to can share their story.)

As I gathered the information from those three key sources and allowed the process of writing the story to take place, sometimes pieces of writing emerged that were based on the historic material I was working with, but detoured from regular referenced history. I found myself creating scenes and conversations, both embodied into people and also at times disembodied, floating in the ether. Things obviously wouldn't have happened exactly as I have written them into these fragments of speculation. At the same time, they are my best guesses, my creative channelling, of the information at hand. Where I have deviated into such historic speculation, I clearly acknowledge that, so as not to deceive or confuse the reader. This technique of laying bare the act of historic speculation and sharing it with the reader is well established in a genre of history writing known as speculative biography. Central to the genre is the straightforward declaration of the author's interpretation in the process of creating the historic narrative (Donna Lee Brien, 2018, p. 4). This differs from historic fiction, in which we are presented with a work of fiction based on historic research but it is not made clear which parts of the story are historically accurate and which have been constructed by the author in their attempt to entertain and to bring the story to life. Speculative biography strives to bring the stories to life of people whose pasts are not well documented. It is also offers a way 'of putting the blood and bone back into the inquiry process while retaining an allegiance to the evidence' (Miller, 2008, p. 93).

At times, this story I have written based on our recent past veers into the present. The Bungalow is not something that happened in the past that bears no relation to the present. The past from which the Bungalow comes is alive and well in the people, in the attitudes, in the social fabric of the town. Introducing the lived experience of contemporary Alice Springs into the story has enabled me to draw those connections between the past and present.

I have written myself into the story in two ways. One is through sharing experiences of my research journey. Written histories always, to some extent, include the author. We interpret and express stories through our own eyes. We choose what to write about, what to include and what to leave out. By writing myself into the story, I am making transparent my authorial presence.

The other way I have written myself into the story is autoethnographic. I have spent nearly three decades living in Alice Springs and broader Central Australia, experiencing and thinking through issues of racism, whiteness, oppression and intercultural relations. I have lived, learnt and felt the stories of the history of the place and spent much time considering how the dominant social forces in play around the time of the Bungalow continue to operate at both personal and systemic levels. I have felt it as a schoolteacher; as the white mother of a child whose father was Warlpiri; as the friend, ally and colleague of people whose ancestors only one or two generations earlier, lived the story of frontier Central Australia and who go on living it in a variety of ways. I have also lived in Central Australia as a woman of white privilege who sometimes, inadvertently, has supported the colonial project.

When I started to write the story of the Bungalow, I started to appear in it and, when I thought about it, my presence made sense. A 'characteristic that binds all autoethnographic work is the use of personal experience to examine or critique cultural experience' (Jones, Adams & Ellis, 2013, p. 22). This contrasts with the places in the writing where I have included stories of my own experience but not interrogated the nuances of those experiences in light of general cultural phenomena. That writing is autobiographical.

Autoethnography enables us to express personal experience in research and to illustrate why the personal is important in our cultural life (Jones, Adams & Ellis, p. 33). Ideas for research projects are usually guided by the thoughts, feelings and experiences we have in and about our lives. Rather than silencing or disguising the personal reasons we have for research, through autoethnography we can make use of this personal experience.

In an autoethnographic sense, I appear in my work as a person who is giving her own personal perspective on the history and society of Central Australia from an informed outsider's perspective. I am informed because I have been immersed in Central Australian culture and society and am deeply affected by the social and cultural forces at play. I am an outsider because I did not experience this history first-hand, nor am I a First Nations person who suffers from the racist and discriminatory policies and practices that came with the colonial project. At the same time, you cannot live in Central Australia, or Australia more broadly, without being affected by those policies and practices. We are all affected by the brutal and unresolved history of Australia whether we know it, or like it, or not. My intention is to provoke an intellectual and affective engagement with this story of our nation's history. With its essential combination of the personal and critical, autoethnography can play a role in helping support that engagement.

Living in Tin is not your regular work of academic, referenced history. Rather, it deliberately blurs the distinction between literature and literary-critical commentary and as such could be classified as a work of fictocriticism. It features a compositional approach, a unique mix of archival research, biography, geography, autoethnography, Indigenous and settler-colonial studies, poetry and techniques of fiction. Intercultural Central Australian history is presented from a range of viewpoints, through the information presented as well as through the structural aspects of the work: in the variety of linguistic registers presented; the hybridisation of genre; the discontinuous narrative, reflective of that character of memory (Prosser 2009); and a disruption of the linearity and coherence that we have been taught to expect from texts focused on information rather than knowledge (Hecq, 2005, p. 187). Such techniques, all features of fictocritical works, became relevant to my work because they addressed the aims of my project.

The Bungalow is a story that is integral to intercultural relations in Alice Springs. It is about First Nations people, white people and the smattering of other ethnic groups who were present in Central Australia at that time, including Middle Eastern cameleers and Chinese.

I have deeply considered the ethics of this project: was it my story to explore and, if so, how could I do it in ways that were ethical and constructive? In these deliberations, I have drawn guidance and inspiration from First Nations scholars, writers and associates, including a range of people most closely connected to this story.

I have also been buoyed in these deliberations by the words of Jennifer Martiniello, writer, visual artist and academic of Arrernte, Chinese and Anglo-Celtic descent, who points out that 'for many issues there is also a white story, not just a black story – after all, we didn't create the last 200 years of crap all by ourselves' (Martiniello, cited in Heiss, 2002, p. 200).

The story of the Bungalow has elements that are unique to its particular time and place. 'The occupation of Australia varied from colony to colony, region to region, district to district' (Krichauff, 2017, p. 7). The Bungalow story also has elements that are emblematic of Australian history as a whole: rich, nuanced, intercultural relations that have been too easily reduced to us and them, black and white, good and bad; the obsession with Indigenous children 'who had some white blood', their removal from families and subsequent institutionalisation and brutalisation in attempts to manipulate and 'whitewash' them; massive state control over the movements of First Nations people; and an archival representation of these stories that highlights male, and particularly white male, achievement.

My intention was to write a story of the Bungalow as a yarn, full of atmosphere and imagery.

I wanted to capture the expansive arid lands of Central Australia, the societies that inhabit them and the ideologies that underpin those societies. It would be a work of non-fiction, drawing on scholarly and historic research as well as personal experiences.

The result is a multi-genre work of creative nonfiction that incorporates techniques of speculative biography, fictocriticism, autoethnography and archival poetics. I offer this story first and foremost as a contribution to understandings of the Bungalow and the formative years of Central Australian society. More broadly, I offer it as a contribution to the decolonisation of our written history, the advancement of a more comprehensive view of the Australian experience, and 'the unlearning of the inherent dominative mode' (Said, 1995, p. 28). Truth-telling, recognition, justice for First Nations Australians: it is in the spirit of such that I offer this work.

Brien, D. 2018, 'Conjectural and speculative biography: convict and colonial biographies', *Offshoot: Contemporary Life Writing Methodologies and Practice*, D. Brien and E. Quinn (eds), UWA Publishing, Crawley WA, pp. 13–30.

Briscoe, G. 2010, *Racial Folly: A Twentieth Century Aboriginal Family*, ANU Press, Canberra.

Hecq, D. 2005, 'Autofrictions: the fictopoet, the critic and the teacher', *UTS Epress*, vol. 11, no. 2, retrieved 12 March 2020, <https://epress.lib.uts.edu.au/index.php/csrj/article/view/3667>.

Kimber, R. 1986, *Man from Arltunga*, Hesperian Press, Western Australia.

Krichauff, S. 2017, *Memory, Place and Aboriginal-Settler History: Understanding Australians' Consciousness of the Colonial Past*, Anthem Press, NSW.

Miller, A. 2008, 'Personalising ethnography: on memory, evidence, and subjectivity. the writing & learning journey', *New Writing: The International Journal for the Practice and Theory of Creative Writing*, vol. 5, no. 2, pp. 89–113.

Prosser, R. 2009, 'Fragments of a fictocritical dictionary', *Outskirts: Feminisms Along the Edge*, vol. 20.

Said, E. 1995, *Orientalism*, revised edn, Penguin, London.

Walking the History of Mparntwe

We are walking the history, through the streets of Alice Springs (Mparntwe); soaking it in through our pores, feeling it scrunch underfoot. History is all around us here: in the landscape, the built environment, the people of the place. I know of nowhere else on earth where the history is so evident. Then again, I have developed such a passion for the history of this place that maybe it's just me, and others with a similar penchant, who see it everywhere. Maybe all the rest just see people and places and goings-on but they don't join the dots.

The history of this place can bite you on the bum. It can trip you up so you fall flat on your face. I've seen it time and time again. The aggrieved jump up. Furious. Who was that, they demand to know. Where's that bastard who just tripped me up? Looking all around, spoiling for a fight, dazed and confused. But they can't see the history for looking.

It's not the First Nations people who are spoiling for those fights. They know about the history and its effect on the present; know it all too well. If anyone should be spoiling for a fight, it's them.

I am the tour guide on this jaunt around town; complete with Akubra, walking shoes and a folder full of maps and photos to highlight the points I am making. It's a tour I have put together and delivered for the last ten years; to share my passion for this place and help others understand this history that defines us. I enjoy this venture very much but also see it as a responsibility: part of the national truth-telling that's required if we are ever to become more than, as Xavier Herbert has put it, 'a community of thieves'.[1]

My small business venture is called Foot Falcon Walking Tours. Foot Falcon is an Aboriginal English expression for walking. As in,

Where are you going?

To visit my uncle.

How are you getting there?

Foot Falcon.

It's like Ford Falcon but when you don't have a car. It's a pun. A playful twisting of the English language by people who are less likely to have a car, by nature of their position in Australian society.

Foot Falcon is just one of the many clever things I have learnt from Central Australian Indigenous people across the decades I have lived amongst them, on their country.

Another of those things is to introduce and position yourself by way of introduction. I do that for the guests on my tour, as follows.

> I am a white Australian. I grew up on Wurrundjeri country to the east of Melbourne (narm). My ancestors on both sides migrated to Australia in the mid-1800s, from England. I came to Alice Springs in 1989 and have lived here, more or less, ever since; in remote Indigenous communities and in Alice Springs. Many years ago, I had a relationship with a Warlpiri man from the Tanami Desert, about three hundred kilometres to the north-west of Alice Springs, and together we had a beautiful daughter.

Introductions over, the tour begins with an acknowledgement that Alice Springs was built on the lands of the Mparntwe people. They are a subgroup of the Arrernte. The original name for the land upon which Alice Springs was built is Mparntwe (M-parnt-wa). I show the guests the first item in my folder, the AIATSIS[2] map of the Aboriginal languages of Australia.

I point to where we are in the Arrernte section and explain that going out into the desert in all directions are Indigenous people who live on their own homelands and speak their own languages as their first language. People from all those communities come into Alice Springs for the goods and services on offer as do folk from pastoral stations and mining settlements. That's the way this town has always been: a regional centre, smack bang in the heart of the continent, set up to service the activities of a vast, outlying area.

Halfway through the tour, we detour from the streets, down into the predominantly dry river bed beside which the town was built. There Mparntwe is the Arrernte name for this section of the river or, in colonial terms, the Todd River. Here on the creamy, crunchy sand, with the breeze blowing and birds singing out, we sit and soak up the ambience, and I prepare my guests for a piece of prose-poetry I am about to perform.

'Many years ago,' I tell them, 'a woman moved to Alice Springs to work for Greening Australia. One day, I overheard her say the river is disgusting. I wrote this piece in defence of the river.'

> I am the river, the river that runs through the town. The desert river, the desert town. Significantly dry. There's nothing wrong with me, nothing that is, that isn't wrong with the whole town and all the people in it. I'm a part of the people, the people are a part of me.

And on it goes. (See Appendix for the full version.)

It's an evocative piece that moves people, sometimes to tears, and has led, over the years, to discussions of a deep and philosophical kind that are not generally part of your average tourist package.

One day at the completion of my reading, a French traveller asked me, 'Why don't Australians like Aboriginal people?'

The question was a kick in the guts. Even though I am all too familiar with that situation, to have it laid out quite so plainly, and by an outsider, was confronting. Inherent in the question also was the notion that Aboriginal people weren't Australian. I still recall it years later as if it was yesterday, parked in the tranquillity of the river, beneath that dome of beautiful blue sky, collecting my thoughts and giving my answer with all the truth I could muster. The Frenchman and his family listened. He then asked me to repeat my speech so he could record it to include in the film he was making about their travels. I did my best.

I told those travellers that the colonists have done a damn good job in what they set out to do. To justify their behaviour in the takeover of this entire country, the British men in charge needed to paint a picture of the original people as simple and barbaric; as people who neither belonged to nor cared for country. They needed to present them as people who were not evolved much beyond apes, who you could neither trust nor associate with.

By contrast, the worldview and way of being of the First People of this land was underpinned by communality and a deep respect for the natural order which they knew to be intrinsically linked to their own survival. This way of being could hardly have been in greater contrast to the predilection of the English colonisers for competition, individualism and the conquering of natural resources for their own, immediate gain. With their guns and germs, the colonisers imposed their order on this place and its people, all the time controlling the narrative to suit their own purposes. As part of their need to present the first people in objectionable ways, the colonists also left the stories of cooperation and intercultural humanity out of the dominant narrative. It is that storytelling and associated myth-making that has been so successful in creating the 'us and them' disdain he had observed.

In reality, Australia's intercultural history abounds with all kinds of engagement. Which brings me to the story that stole my heart and grew ever larger in my imagination across the years I presented it, towards the end of each of my tours. It's the story I never grew tired of telling, the one that kept nagging at me until I turned to give it my full attention. This story features children of dual Aboriginal and settler heritage, similar to that of my own daughter, except that those sixty or more children had been removed from their mothers and culture and land to grow up in a collection of dilapidated tin sheds in a burgeoning settler town. It features the biological mother of some of these kids, of dual heritage herself, who ended up living with and caring for them all, for the fifteen years of its existence. It also features an outback schoolteacher, much like myself, except that she was the very first schoolteacher in Central Australia and her name was Ida, like my favourite old great, great aunty, also a schoolteacher, who died in the 1970s. The story features, too, the police officer in charge who oversaw this ramshackle home that he had been instrumental in creating. This is a story from the frontier that has, at its heart, the women, children and Indigenous people who were an integral part of such early Australian settings but have repeatedly been sidelined in the narratives that the colonists so carefully constructed. The story speaks of frontier contact and intercultural relations and seems as pivotal to the social foundations of the town that I have called home for many years, as the original arterial roads and planning documents do to its material establishment. As with so many of this nation's foundational stories, it also speaks of brutality, resistance and resilience.

This is the story of the Bungalow.

The Immense Possibilities

No one seems to know what time Topsy Smith got to town. It's a trifling detail really, compared to so many of the others. It's just that I want to know everything.

I want to go there and live amongst the ruckus that was frontier Central Australia, early last century, when Alice Springs was just getting going.

'No you don't,' my daughter insists. 'Imagine the racism. Imagine the sexism.' She's got a point there, no doubt.

But it's more than that. It's the simplicity of that outback life: wide open spaces, time to be. It's the immense possibilities for Central Australia, at those earliest times of cultural interface. It's the potential for understanding how what went on back then has shaped our present. I don't want to go there because I think it's any better. I want to go there because it unsettles me.

Imagine it now: Topsy and the younger children on the truck, the older ones with the herd of goats bringing up the rear. Jolting along rough desert tracks that were cut by wear and tear through the semi-arid landscape: of mulga bush, spinifex grass, dry sandy river beds and bushflies.

Crunch. Buzz. Crack.

Penetrating light.

Craggy ranges of solid, sun-baked rock.

The whole scene overlaid by that vast dome of pure blue sky.

Imagine those bush kids with their groundedness and goats. Were they wearing shoes? Did they brush their hair? Did they call the goats by name as they herded them along towards a shared and unknown future?

Their time of arrival will depend on whether they camped along the way or made the journey in one fell swoop, from Arltunga to Stuart in a day. You can do it these days in an hour and a half, along those sleek outback highways, with the windows of your Prado firmly sealed and the air conditioner pumping. Or you can wind your windows down, let the desert air toss your hair, Warumpi Band pounding from the playlist.

Either way, there's a lot more choice these days than when Topsy was around. There was no state-administered stipend. No compassionate leave. *Get to a town and get some help with the kids or starve.* That's pretty much how they rolled back then.

Topsy wasn't always Smith. She married a Smith, name of Bill. He was of Welsh descent, gold mining at Arltunga, providing for his wife and kids. He was a decent man, Bill, doing the right thing. Plenty of those other settler blokes back then used Aboriginal women for one thing then ditched them.

'Gins' they called them. And 'lubras'. They fucked them, dispensed with their men, then took for the hills. It would seem by 1914 that the worst of the killing times was over.

Bill Smith (1866–1914) died of a mining-related illness and was buried at the crossroads at Arltunga.[3] In its heyday, about ten years earlier, the little gold-mining town with the eastern Arrernte name had supported about two hundred people. By 1914, most of them had moved on.[4]

It was dangerous and back-breaking tough at the mines. Availability of water was one of the defining features of life and there certainly wasn't enough to spare on separating out the gold, as is the preferred method in rainier lands. In this desert version of gold mining, the ore was crushed by battery and livings were squeezed out.

Once in town, Topsy was met by Sergeant Stott. He was a short, burly Scotsman with enough responsibility for ten. He had been expressing official concern about those who were commonly referred to as the 'half-caste'[5] children that were springing up in numbers around the region. In line with colonial thinking of the time, Stott believed those children needed a place to grow up, away from the influence of the full blacks, where they could be taught and trained up to be half useful.[6]

> In my opinion one of the first works to be undertaken is to gather in all half caste children who are living with aborigines.
> The police could do most of this work. No doubt the Mothers would object and there would probably be an outcry from well-meaning people about depriving the Mother of her child but the future of the children should I think outweigh all other considerations. (Administrator, Northern Territory 1911)[7]

Topsy's arrival, with her children of both Aboriginal and European heritage, gave Stott some live subjects to work with. He erected a tent as crisis accommodation, on a plot of land across from the police compound that had been set aside for 'government purposes'. He then wrote to the administrator in Darwin, recommending that the block be used for the 'half-castes'. Permission was granted for a permanent shelter to be built. That took the form of a tin shed that became known as 'the Bungalow' or 'the Bungalow for half-castes'.[8] Stott ordered that all the kids in the district with Aboriginal Mothers and white Fathers should be brought in to live at the Bungalow.

If they had known what we know now, would they have done things differently? If they could come here, or we could go there, would that change the course of what has become? What do we know now that they didn't know then and what difference does that make?

No one seems to know what time Topsy Smith got to town. The police journal with its version of that event has gone missing. It was sometime in late May 1914. But there's a lot about what went on that we can know.

The Poetics of Dust

There may in fact be a veritable paradise adorning the interior. Nobody can say. But I am inclined to believe, Mr Voss, that you will discover a few blackfellers, a few flies, and something resembling the bottom of the sea.[9]

At dawn, a pale aqua slips along the horizon[10]

The sense of space
Clear bright limitless space

The riverbed is wide for miles down
A swath of white sand and smooth pebbles
Where tall gums and delicate acacias cast deep cool shadows

River red gums shed thin bark
The sweet honey drips

Thirsting sun and thirsting earth drink deep
This hard-baked desert glows like a rose
Everything has evolved to survive the heat

Sparse needled foliage, burled bark and skewed stances
A silver belt of mulga scrub, the weird kingdom of the white ants
Tall graceful weeping desert oaks
Like sentinels guarding the landscape
Their needle-fine fingers dangling, grey plumes swaying in the breeze

A shine in the distance, an old bloodwood tree
Two *arleyel* emus ambling through the ironwood

Rich, red cliffs glisten in the sun
Ridges of the most extraordinary shape and appearance
Tossed up in all directions
The cliffs change colour during the day
From purples in the early morning to deep red at noon and to crimson at the setting of the sun

Ghost gums cling precariously to the cliffs
Almost bonsaied by the effort of staying alive
Delicate ferns from a time when the desert was much wetter, and native fuchsias and figs grow in the moister, sheltered regions
Rare mountain hakeas and fragile central flannel flowers grow exposed on mountain ridges where water is really scarce

And birds. Everywhere birds. black cockatoos, sulphur-crested, swallows, Major Mitchells, willy-wagtails, quarrian, kestrels, budgerigar flocks, bronze-wings, finches
Rainbow bee-eaters are often spotted as they grab insects and dragonflies mid-air
The spinifex pigeon prefers to walk, taking to the air only if disturbed
Whistling kites circle

The weather is hotter still, the country very dry
Great angry thundering clouds swarmed and bustled out of nowhere, and it hailed and poured a deluge

As rain transforms the countryside, green grasses and colourful wildflowers emerge
Dry sandy riverbeds became raging torrents
In the ranges rain is captured and held in waterholes and gorges

The water seeps away, leaving small shimmering pools, until eventually these disappear

Late afternoon. The day going down in flames
The ranges lit up like burning embers
Orange fading into dusty blue
The rich light of dusk
Evening shadows burn and fade across the bluebush
A secret billabong of the ranges, streak of quicksilver in the dusk, with the first stars reflected

Darkness envelops the ranges and thousands of stars twinkle overhead
In the still of the night
Silence echoes

The Police Journals

The old police journals are hard and hefty tomes. There is no need to wear white cotton gloves, the archivist explains, but please handle the volumes with care and view them in the reading room.

The reading room is ghostly clean and silent. Would noise rearrange the words, I wonder, or shatter the thin threads that hold these old tomes together? Would turning up the heat dissolve the history? This archival research seems like a solemn business where it is best to remain calm and discreet at all times.

Even when you want to scream and shout, you don't. Even when you want to kiss the custodian of the documents and throw a party for the darling scrap of history you've just travelled halfway across Australia on the off chance of finding, you must contain yourself. Even when you want to rampage and tear apart the brutal system that is at the core of the pain of our nation, you hold it in.

I was thrilled to discover the existence of the Alice Springs police journals. Between 1911 and 1927, Stott showed up for work practically every day, seven days a week, and etched the details of his day into the journal. On the rare occasion he was elsewhere, someone else made the entry.

The following excerpts are presented as they appear on the pages of a range of the journals that are stored in the archives in Alice Springs. I have selected them to show a typical cross-section of entries as well as issues of particular relevance to the Bungalow story:

The daily recording always began with who was on duty for the day:

15th February 1918
    MC Sherman Stn duty Tkr Sam acting Gaol warder. Sgt Stott, Tkr Tom absent on duty…[11]

Followed by the activities of the day:

18th February 1918
Sherman & Tkr Sam & 5 prisoners carting firewood for station.

March 7 1918
Station Master Oodnadatta desires procure service half-caste girl. Recommend Katie Hill for position age about 14 years.

Patrols undertaken:

28th April 1917
... MC Kelly. Tracker Tom returned to station 4.P.M. from Patrol Western District, found all quiet. Stages as follows. Left Alice Springs 10. Am. 19th April 1917. To Jay 28 Miles. 20th Jay to Jeremiah 28 Miles. 21st Jeremiah to Hermannsburg Mission stn 24 Mile. 22nd Hermannsburg to Glen Helen 22 Miles. 23rd Glen Helen to Mt Razorback (Meyers) 20 miles. 24th Mt Razorback to Through's Yard 28 Miles. 25th Throughs yds to Craudale. 26 Miles. 26th Craudale to Harris & Staines. 26. 27th Harris & Staines to Birt Plain. 16 Miles. 28th Birt Plain to Alice Springs. 4 p.m. 18 Miles. Total distance 236 miles.

Correspondence in and out:

Friday May 4th 1917
... Received wire. Did Plew leave my little boy with you for Bungalow or do you know what became of him? G Hayes Jnr.

And the names of the horses in use:

Sunday January 27th 1918
Johnson, Boomerang, Whitefoot, Starlight, Burrundi, Norman, Flint, Ambrose, Granite, Fox, Jackson, Fez, Tully.

So many of the volumes are catalogued now and available for public access, so many except 1914. It was a pivotal year in Alice Springs and fundamental to the story of the Bungalow. Whatever happened to that journal? Was it lost? Stolen? Destroyed? I've searched high and low and asked everyone who might know. They all shrug sympathetically and tell me it's not there and there's nothing more they can do.

Oh well. Historical debris can be found in all manner of places. We work with what we have and make best possible estimates about the rest.

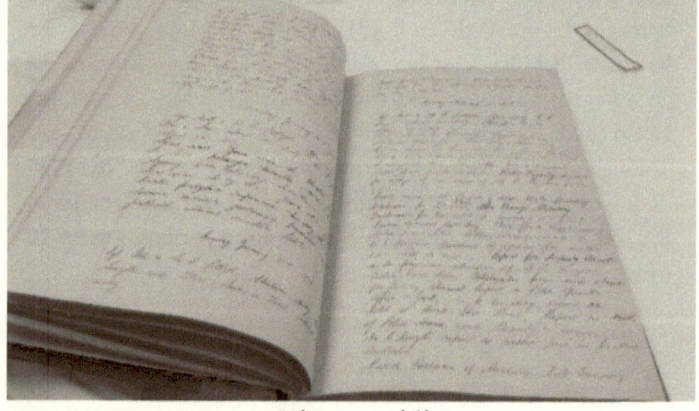

Police journals.[12]

Introduced Species

I climb up in Central Australia and look out, and beyond, to the people who have been cradled by these lands in the thousands of years until now.

I see dark figures stalking prey, women grinding seeds for home-baked bread, kids digging yams in the creek.

The time I have spent with the descendants of those first people stirs my imagination and forms the basis of my understanding of the human foundations of the country that is my home.

The Indigenous population spread out across the desert wilderness.[13] It was like a gigantic patchwork quilt of nations laid across rolling terrain, with a new patch every couple of hundred kilometres. There were, and still are in Central Australia, the Warlpiri people who speak the Warlpiri language and belong to Warlpiri country, the Anmatyere people who speak the Anmatyerre language and belong to Anmatyerre country, the Arrernte, the Luritja, the Pintubi, Pitjantjatjara, Kaytete, Waramungu, Mardi, Nganantjarra, Yankunjatjara and so on.

One of the most charming and vital aspects of Central Australia is that many of these languages live on. They are the oldest living languages on earth. You can hear them on the radio and bouncing around the streets. They are written these days too, through collaborations between linguists and native speakers.

For thirty thousand…fifty thousand…who knows how many thousand years, these people were shaping their creativity and continuity around the contours of their homelands, ensuring that their propriety was not at odds with their perpetuity. Across an ice age, a ten-thousand-year drought, standing shoulder to shoulder with megafauna, they made it work. There wasn't much, when they put their collective minds to it, that these people couldn't figure out or find a use for. They're not the oldest living culture on earth for nothing.

From my understanding, each language group was divided into smaller family groups, much like the turn-out you'd expect at an extended Christmas gathering. There was old Great-aunt Kinyariya and her second husband; Grandad and Uncle Jarnpu, withered and wise like old seeds in an acacia pod; Mum and all her cousin-sisters who collected the yams, berries, sugar bag, juicy lizards and grubs that made up the majority of the feast. There's Jungarrayi with his new sweetheart from the neighbouring tribe and the plethora of second cousins twice removed who, in the authentic Central Australian way, you know as your brothers and sisters.

Dad's over there. Standing on the sand dune. Watching over.

It was in 1862, fifty-odd years before the Bungalow began, that John McDouall Stuart rode his sorry arse into the party. Perhaps that is unfair. Despite his scurvy and his gammy hand, his trachoma and his penchant for the hard stuff, Stuart was remarkable. He became one of Australia's great explorers for a reason. He pushed on…just a little bit further… just a little bit harder…half-starved…in tatters…parched and pain-ridden. Most of us white people, long before, would have put our tails between our legs, carved our initials into the trunk of a tree and turned back for Adelaide, perhaps fading back into the earth along the way.

Not our Stuart. As if in some ultimate cross-country challenge, he traversed the continent from south to north, tagged the top-end coast, then retraced his footsteps to fall across the finishing line. First place.

While his capacity to go where white man had not been before was exceptional, Stuart's attitude to the people who had been there before was not. 'The Black' was how he referred to the man who travelled with him on the first leg of his journey and camped with him at the end of each long day. Or sometimes with just a slightly greater twinge of proprietal familiarity, he wrote 'Our Black'. There is nowhere, it seems, in the annals of Australian history where 'Our Black's' name or identity is recorded. This too, on the basis of colonial behaviour, is unexceptional.

Stuart showed no interested in making contact with the Indigenous people whose land he was (tress)passing through. Earlier explorers such as Sturt, Grey and Mitchell stressed the value in engaging with First Nations peoples at each stage of the journey and securing the services of a local guide to negotiate entry to the next section of country. They also urged the importance of picking up at least a smattering of local Indigenous language. Stuart showed no such interest.

Samples of the explorer's journal entries illustrate his attitude:

> About three-quarters of an hour afterwards I came suddenly upon another native, who was hunting in the sand hills. My attention being engaged in keeping the bearing I did not observe him until he moved, but I pulled up at once, lest he should run away, and called to him. What he imagined I was I do not know; but when he turned round and saw me, I never beheld a finer picture of astonishment and fear. He was a fine muscular fellow, about six feet in height, and stood as if riveted to the spot, with his mouth wide open, and his eyes staring. I sent our black forward to speak with him (Friday 25 June 1858 Yarraout Gum Creek).[14]

Presumably, Stuart thought all blacks were more or less the same. Such is the impression he creates in his account of the one 'black' on the expedition up and leaving him.

> Our black fellow left us during the night; he seems to be very much frightened of the other natives… He was of very little use to us, and I wish I had sent him off before, but I thought he might be useful in conversing with the other natives when we should meet them (Tuesday 3 August 1858 Good Country).[15]

Stuart revealed a distinct ignorance of how Indigenous Australian societies worked. The 'blacks' have never been one conglomerate mass, one big happy family. There are separate nations, separate languages, a complexity of protocols and customs, of allegiances and trespass laws. I suppose Stuart never made privy to that information and nor did he ever think to ask. Interpersonal relations weren't one of his strong suits.

Stuart battled his way across the Great Southern Land…

Through drought:

The journey today has been very rough and stony. Not a drop of water have we passed to-day, nor is there the appearance of any on before us. I shall be compelled to fall back to-morrow to the water of last night (Friday 26 April 1861 Morphett Creek).[16]

Through flooding rain:

At about 8 p.m. it began to rain, and continued the whole night, coming from the east and east-south-east. It still continues without any sign of a break. The ground has become so soft that when walking we sink up to the ankle, and the horses can scarcely move in it. At sundown there is no appearance of a change. It has rained without intermission the whole of last night and today. I do not know what effect this will have on my further progress, for now it is impossible to travel. The horses in feeding are already sinking above their knees (Tuesday 4th June 1861 Chain of Ponds).[17]

Through horseplay:

It is late before we can get a start to-day, in consequence of one of the horses concealing himself in the creek. He is an unkind brute, we have much trouble with him in that respect; he is constantly hiding himself somewhere or other (Tuesday, 23rd April 1861 Bishop Creek).[18]

And general hardship:

The horses look very bad today; I shall therefore give them three or four days' rest. It is very vexing, but it cannot be helped. The water here will last about ten days. I shall cause another search for more to be made; I myself am too unwell to assist. Yesterday I rode in the greatest pain from the effects of my fall, and it was with great difficulty that I was able to sit in the saddle until we reached here. Scurvy has also taken a very serious hold of me; my hands are a complete mass of sores that will not heal, but, when I remain for two or three days in some place where I can get them well washed, they are much better; if not, they are worse than ever, and I am rendered nearly helpless. My mouth and gums are now so bad that I am obliged to eat flour and water boiled. The pains in my limbs and muscles are almost insufferable. Kekwick is also suffering from bad hands, but, as yet, has no other symptoms (Tuesday 15 May 1860 Centre).[19]

When he finally limped back into Adelaide in December 1863, Stuart offered up the journal into which he had recorded, in pencil, the details of the journey and a chart of his path through the country:

> In conclusion, I beg to say, that I believe this country (i.e., from the Roper to the Adelaide and thence to the shores of the Gulf), to be well adapted for the settlement of a European population, the climate being in every respect suitable, and the surrounding country of excellent quality and of great extent....I see no difficulty in taking over a herd of horses at any time.[20]

There is an Arrernte term, *interteke-irreme*. It refers to following along in one line and stepping in each other's footsteps, thus minimising your collective impact on the land.[21] In a sense, that's what the newcomers did, following Stuart's tracks into Central Australia and beyond.

Of course, minimising collective impact was far from their intentions. They came with cattle and sheep, the precious flesh of colonial cuisine, crashing their way across the desert floor, sucking the substance out of waterholes. They came with camels, the ships of the desert, loaded down with all that is required and desired by people from a culture that is invested in living beyond its means.

They came with a book that they held as gently as the old folk held the *tjuringa*, the rock art and the stories. The book held stories too, of a new deity, determined to be heard above all others.

They came with guns: essential vocabulary in the language of domination.

And rations to subdue the natives.

And seeds; they spread their seeds.

Dick Kimber, whose knowledge of the Central Australian story has been recognised as unrivalled, and whose approach is measured and generous, estimates that until the beginning of World War II, there were generally less than a thousand white people and Afghans (most of them men) in an area of one million square kilometres, across Central Australia. There were also probably four thousand or so Aboriginal people in relatively close contact with the newcomers, and an equal number again of bush folk who had little or no contact with the whites and Afghans.[22]

That's up until the beginning of World War II. In the first decades of contact, from the 1870s, there would have been less than a couple of hundred white people and Afghans as well as a handful of Chinese spread out across that vast brown land. Between 1860 and 1895, it is estimated that the native population fell by nearly forty per cent due to introduced diseases, internal conflict and murder at the hands of white man's shooting parties.[23] The only women around were Indigenous women, going about their business as best they could.

It was a vast and sparsely populated frontier with its very own rules of engagement.

Stuart – The Statue

On my way to the State Library of South Australia, one wintery Monday morning, bustling along with all the other folk in the city, out of the corner of my eye I spy a statue. I gasp. It's John McDouall Stuart, with whom I have been in a conflicted historical relationship for years. The library can wait; there is a research topic right here: history holding hands with the present, in the contemporary landscape.

Mr Stuart towers over me, aloft a plinth that proclaims in bold, gold capitals,

> JOHN MCDOUALL STUART
> EXPLORER
> ADELAIDE TO INDIAN OCEAN
> 1861–2

It's on the corner of an irregular-shaped patch of parkland at the intersection of King William and Flinders Streets, Adelaide.

John, you old bastard, fancy bumping into you here.

I stop, put down my backpack , examine the representation with curiosity. How have they chosen to portray this character of our imperial foundations? He made it through the heart of the country, to claim and name where others had failed, then staggered back into Adelaide amidst the hip-hip and hoorays of a public holiday announced in his honour, pissed his reward up against fetid laneway walls then faded into oblivion to later die, broke and alone, in London where only seven people attended his funeral. As a bold explorer of course.

The detail in this statue is impressive. Stuart's legs are parted with his left leg stepped out in front – the long stride forward. Was he left-handed, left-footed, I wonder? Held in Stuart's left hand and clasped to his chest is a scroll of parchment, perhaps the map he drew. A water canteen is slung across his body. Water was such an issue for Australia's early explorers; a defining feature of their survival. It is appropriate to have included this in the depiction. A cloak is draped over Stuart's left shoulder that tumbles down his back, his blanket perhaps. It suggests a soft, human touch I find surprising. The Stuart story is generally one of uncompromising toughness. He's sporting the thick explorer's beard he has in any image I have ever seen of him. I am struck by the buttons in a line down the sides of his trousers. That's how explorers' trousers must have been back then, of substantial fabric, canvas perhaps, wrapped around the legs and buttoned up. A hard hat lies on the ground at his feet.

Stuart's right arm is outstretched and comes to rest on a cut-off log, standing upright, against which his rifle rests. It reminds me of the larger-than-life bronze version of this bloke that was planted in a park in Alice Springs a few years back, on the hospital lawns where lots of First Nations people and others go to sit and meet up with countrymen. Then there was Stuart, towering over us all, with his rifle ever at the ready. There were objections aplenty. Long-term Alice Springs resident and artist Dan Murphy and I were on the ABC News the night that statue was erected, talking about why we found it so offensive. A local journalist had plucked us out of a small protest at the site. Deputations were made to council and the issue was pushed around a bit but Stuart stayed. Years on, I still have to fight the urge to run the damn thing down. Plenty of the residents of Alice Springs had no issue whatsoever with an effigy of their great colonial hero, armed and looming, over the place where Indigenous people come to sit.

There are other, alternative versions of our history that can be told. In his journal, Stuart recorded an exchange he had with an older native man who came into his camp with two younger men, early one morning, in country north of what became Alice Springs.

> After some time and having conferred with his two sons, he turned round and surprised me by giving me one of the masonic signs. I

looked at him steadily, he repeated it and so did his two sons. I then returned it, which seemed to please them much, the old man patting me on the shoulder and stroking down my beard (Saturday 23 June 1860, Kekwick Ponds).²⁴

What a fine statue could be constructed from that scene; the two men exchanging a hand gesture that would have meant wildly different things for each of them. Masonic Lodge meets wild bush blackfella: communication across the chasm. It seems a far more suitable image for the moving forward we'd like to do than the solitary white man looming over the rest of us with a rifle.

This Adelaide version I'm looking up at now is a mighty tribute that was erected by public subscription and presented to the city of Adelaide on 4 June 1904 by the South Australian Caledonian Society. I think more people have noticed it today than have done so for a long time, due to the attention I have drawn to it. If one person is looking at something in a populated place, the gaze of others will be drawn there as well, even as they rush on by.

It's John McDouall Stuart, I want to tell them. I don't revere him, that's not why I've been standing here, examining and noting down the features of this public representation. But he's an important part of our history, from whence we have come. Wouldn't you like to know some more about it?

*John McDouall Stuart.*²⁵

Topsy

Amidst the dust and stars that had swirled for aeons, on the land of the Arabana, a baby slipped into the world. For those of us whose arrivals are hailed on birth certificates and increasingly captured on film or pixel, it was rather a different approach to the welcome of a human life. You can bet your bottom dollar that baby was graced with a name that came from the dust and the stars but she scored another name too, which she shared with the new order that was moving in. Mary, the holy mother; Mary, daughter on the cusp of a brave new world – circa 1860.

The Arabana lands cover an area across what is also known, these days, as north-central South Australia. Features include Kati Thanda (Lake Eyre), which at ten thousand square kilometres is the largest lake on the continent; and Pangki Warruna (Strangways Springs), a series of artesian springs that support an outburst of desert life. Beyond that, the Arabana lands are a pastiche of the stone plains, shrublands, grass plains, dune fields, salt lakes, riverbeds and oases that are the mainspring of inland Australia.[26]

It's a land of solitude, marked by unexpected treasures and the distance between things. Temperatures range from winter nights that plummet below zero to fifty degrees Celsius during the height of summer. Indigenous people have called this place home for millennia, and been sustained by the birds and mammals, reptiles, fish, foliage, roots, berries, seeds, nectar and water of the region; plentiful if you know where and when to look.

If you don't know where and when to look, you might run the risk of considering these lands 'perfectly worthless' and 'incapable of feeding even a bandicoot'. Such was the impression of twenty-nine-year-old Alfred Howitt, explorer and so-called 'natural scientist' who was sent up from Melbourne in 1859 to examine the pastoral potential of the region.

There was land. There were seasons. There was day and sky and star-filled nights and fires and sacred bodies of water that held the key to life. There was food and shelter. There were trade routes across the whole broad continent that criss-crossed Arabana country. There were the neighbouring Diyari and Thirrari and Kuyani and Wangkangurru peoples with whom the Arabana came together to worship and socialise. And at the heart of the Arabana lands were its own people, getting on with it.

There were no boutiques then, no Best and Less, nor online catalogues from which you ordered your garments. There was little in the way of garments. People generally went naked. Then along came the curious white men: clothed, armed and on horseback.

The frontier is the zone at which Indigenous people and colonisers come face to -face. It is a place where morality is suspended, or at least new rules of engagement emerge.[27]

Mary's mother was Arabana. Her father, or sperm donor at least, was one of the very first white men in the district, George Benfield.[28] What language did that young mother-to-be and George use to communicate in that zone in which they stood so close and yet so very far apart? A look? A gesture? An ultimatum? An exchange?

Perhaps the young mother-to-be spoke some words of faltering English.

Yes.

No.

If you like.

Although at that stage, so early in the piece, perhaps not.

Did they do it on the comfort of a bed roll or up against a tree?

Did it happen more than once?

Did they snuggle together afterwards and savour that post-coital murmur of flesh against flesh?

Or did he buckle up and jump back on his horse, still dripping?

Intimate details aside, it would appear that, from one of the first parties of white men to ever stamp their footprints on that dusty inland floor, came intercultural relations of the kind that resulted in Mary, one of the very first, perhaps the first, child of such inheritance, in inland Australia.

In 1862, white men erected their first buildings near the great water source, Pangki Warruna. In the next year, they brought their first herds of strange animals (three thousand ewes, three hundred rams, forty cattle and twenty horses); the likes of which the Arabana had never encountered.

From the settlers' perspective, they had laid claim to five hundred square miles of pastoral land and named it Strangways Station. Throughout the 1860s, half a dozen other stations were set up across that region too, thus commencing the great mutual projects of occupation and economic exploitation of the inland.

The introduced stock, along with dogs, cats, foxes, rabbits and goats, ran riot over the landscape. They trampled the native vegetation and reduced native animal populations, some to extinction. They damaged the water sources too; crushing some, turning some putrid, causing others to no longer flow.

The Arabana continued on as best they could. They built shelters according to the seasons and lived in camps, spread out across the land. With the environment changing rapidly around them, locals soon started working on the stations, in exchange for flour, sugar, tea, tobacco, blankets and cloth. Their employment included sheep and goat herding, controlling horses and bullocks, cooking, lambing, washing the freshly shorn wool, construction, translation, tracking and delivery of messages. Each station was a network of sites over the massive area of the pastoral lease. Station work was generally seasonal and sporadic. The Arabana who chose to get involved could continue with their own ways of living and graft the activities of station life onto that.

A few local people scored a personal mention in the station records as workers of the 1860s. They include Tilbrook, Camp Oven Jacky,

Winkie, Kalli Kalli, Sambo, Annie, Mary Ann, Judy, Lucy and Billy Rowdy.

Other Arabana people avoided contact with the settlers and their ways. 'Wild blacks', was the term commonly used by settlers to refer to native people that they either viewed as a threat or were simply not engaging with the new order.

> Wild blacks came to Strangways and disrupted the work of wool washing to conduct a ceremony including the Arabana boy Kalli Kalli.

> The Emu is dead. I think it was stolen by some wild blacks.

> A wild black came to Francis Springs and guided Jeffreys to water.[29]

I wonder what terms the 'wild blacks' were using to refer to the white men and their shenanigans.

Between 1863 and 1866, everyone, wild or not, struggled through the worst drought on record. Large amounts of stock were lost, as illustrated by station manager Julius Jeffreys in a letter to one of his fellow station owners, of November 1865:

> My dear Warren
>   I am sorry to have to tell you very bad news by this mail. We had no deaths amongst the sheep until a few days after we commenced shearing. The weather suddenly changed to a most intense heat; for days the thermometer was 102 in the store and 135 upon a post and rail fence that I put around the front of the store to keep the horses from eating the thatch. 500 sheep died in a few days, principally out of one flock, the first flock shorn... The horses are dying as well. Matheson has totally abandoned [the station] and the families Duncan and Lockhart are living in his deserted huts. The Duncans and the Lockharts are going to leave next week – they say they will never return. The whole of the cattle at Chambers Creek and Finniss Stations that numbered 8500 will be dead in one month – about 8000 are dead. [Ferguson's] cattle are dying twenty and thirty a day... After the end of next week there will be no occupied stations except Ferguson's...

Flooding rains followed.

The next significant encroachment onto Arabana country began in 1872 with the construction of the Overland Telegraph line. This three-thousand-kilometre strand of galvanised wire traversed the continent from south to north, strung along telegraph poles and connected by a series of repeater stations, about a hundred and fifty kilometres apart. At Port Darwin the cable connected with a line that crossed the seafloor to London. The Overland Telegraph line was a major feat of civil engineering that facilitated communication across the continent and also with the motherland.

The site for one of the twelve repeater stations fell in the proximity of Strangways Springs. This brought a new wave of workers, many of whom passed through during the construction phase and a handful who stayed on to keep the messages flowing up and down the line. Known as the Angle Pole Telegraph Station because of the sharp turn to the north the line took at this point, this settlement also became a stop-off point and refuge for white travellers.

By 1875 when young Mary gave birth to her own daughter Topsy, all of the shepherds on Strangways Station were Aboriginal and, in the opinion of telegraph station operator turned ethnographer Francis Gillen, they did just as well as the whites. Topsy had been sired by Police Trooper White in circumstances we know nothing about. How did he and Mary come together? What common language did they speak? Presumably in the fifteen or so years since Mary's conception, the English language had spread, like other introduced species, across the arid lands. Mary must have been about fifteen when she conceived Topsy. Again, how did that come to be? On his bedroll or up against a tree? Once or on several occasions? How many other Arabana girls did Police Trooper White have on his card and how many little Whites did he leave behind?

Topsy grew up on the threshold of two or more cultures colliding. She would have learnt about station life as well as the more traditional Arabana ways. She would have been exposed to increasing numbers of outsiders who came to stay and those who were passing through including pastoralists, surveyors, telegraph workers, builders, bush workers, cameleers and then, from 1887, prospectors heading up to the Central Australian gold rush.

Presumably Welsh-born Bill Smith, of a similar age to Topsy, was one of those prospectors passing through. Or perhaps he'd been working in the region before deciding to head north for gold. Either way, Bill and Topsy met, somewhere in the vicinity of her birthplace, around 1890, and decided to make a go of it together.

Said their eldest son Walter, when telling the story of his life, 'Bill and Topsy fell in love.'[30]

Said their granddaughter Christine, when telling the story of their lives, 'Bill and Topsy fell in love.'[31]

They married. Then they followed the track to Arltunga.

Up the Track

Topsy was leaving the place of her childhood. Bill was continuing on his nomadic way; from Wales, to the shores of Australia, and now into its heartland. From the occasional published account of the Track, recollections from their descendants and my own encounters in that country, I have reimagined the journey of Bill and Topsy.[32]

*

They headed north, up the Track.

My wife, Bill called her proudly, with no regard for what anyone else might have thought. She was strong and skilled and sweet.

My husband, Topsy called him. He was kind and determined with a song in his voice.

There were things that mattered and the colour of one's skin wasn't one of them, even though others tried to make it matter.

Bill and Topsy knew about the Track; what to look and look out for.

It was the path that Topsy's ancestors on the Arabana side had set as a trading route.

The track trod by Stuart with his horses and men.

The Track that the Overland Telegraph line followed.

The obvious route, the one that followed water.

There was traffic enough. With the gold rush going on, it was never long before someone else passed by. More of them heading north than south. Most of them with just what they could carry or push in a wooden barrow. Some of them whistling under the desert sky. Others trudging so hard you wondered if you'd have to bury their bones around the bend. The occasional train of camels trekking, north or south. A few, like themselves, with horse and buggy.

Crunching over stony plains.

The sun beating down.

Flies and prickles. Glare and wind. The heat throwing mirages in the distance. Bill and Topsy had some supplies they'd brought with them: flour, tea and the like. They supplemented that with food they found along the track: a goanna roasted in the coals of the campfire, some berries Topsy picked from a bush.

On day three, with the sun dropping low in the western sky, they arrived at the riverbed they'd had in their line of vision all afternoon. It was a sprawling expanse of sand dotted with river gums.

'Two big waterholes,' Bill nodded. 'This must be Bloods Creek.'

Topsy grinned and dropped onto the cool sand. 'Mwenangkenh tula,' she said, calling the place by its original name. 'Let's camp here.'

On day four, the track converged briefly with the telegraph line at the Charlotte Waters Telegraph Station.

Topsy had only seen a few such constructions in her life and this, along with its twin at Pangki Warruna, were the largest. Bill had seen many and had grown up looking into them, in his homeland and then in Adelaide.

'White fella building,' Topsy announced and Bill laughed. He enjoyed Topsy's perspective on the world.

They passed the white fella building on their left.

The stony plains gave way to soft, sandy floor as the Track entered the floodplains of the vast Finke River system. It brought welcome relief for horse and humans. More food, more shade, another welcome camping spot.

At night, they heard the dingoes howl.

The next morning, they came across a simple homestead and a shepherd tending to flock.

'You gotta walk along creek, riiight along, big walls too much,' he said, pursing his lips to indicate the great red gorge up ahead. 'Come up on bank, other side… You be right,' he added, perhaps at their apprehension. Looking towards this young woman on the move but without making eye contact, he asked, 'Who your mob?'

'Arabana,' she replied. 'Mary my mum.'

He raised his eyebrows knowingly then indicated Bill. 'Dis your *wati*?'

'Yeah, he my husband.'

The man smiled. 'Good luck to you,' and went back to what he was doing.

The thick river sand was hard going so they stopped halfway to boil the billy and rest the horse; rock walls towering on either side.

Ghost gums and wild figs grew on the slopes of the ranges. A soft breeze blew. A flock of red-tailed black cockatoos screeched overhead.

Topsy, sitting on the sand and gazing up, watched until they were out of sight. 'We're on the right track,' she told Bill.

He smiled and leaned over to wipe the strands of hair from her face.

It was a relief when they finally left the thick sand and walked on firm ground for a while.

At the base of a sandhill, there was a grave with no name.

'Perished,' Topsy said. 'He didn't know about the water up ahead.'

Sure enough, just a few hundred metres around the sandhills from the grave, was a small gorge shaped like a horseshoe with a waterhole at its base. The horse had gulped it up and Bill and Topsy filled their bags. The cattle station was up to the left.

They wound their way up through the gorge, where the river gums made a rim of green along the creek. Then it was back onto river flats until they reached the Depot Sandhills. A sea of shifting sand dunes of powdery red sand. It felt like it would never end. The wind howled through relentlessly, erasing the prints of those who'd gone before.

They made it up, step by step, guided by the telegraph line. The horse needed coaxing and in places Bill and Topsy laid down a mat of spinifex grass to ease the buggy wheels over.

Finally, they looked out and down to the river bed again; a snaking path of white sand lined with trees. They tumbled down into its shade to stretch and rub each other's aching muscles. Rest over, they continued, through one river crossing after the next; stopping to eat, camp and dig for water.

Beyond the Ooraminna Range, they reached a fork in the road; Alice Springs or Arltunga? More of the same stretched either way but they knew their destination was almost within range. Bill hooted and Topsy laughed.

On day fifteen, they passed through the hilly outskirts of the settlement and pulled up in the village that had grown up on eastern Arrernte country. It was abuzz with hope from recent finds.

The rhythms Bill and Topsy had developed on their journey became the refrain of the next twenty-five years they spent carving out a life together at Arltunga.

One of the miner's huts at Arltunga.[33]

The Smiths of Arltunga

Topsy and Bill presumably built one of the huts of stone, iron and thatch that their son Walter later remembered growing up in and whose remains you can walk around to this day.[34] The children started to arrive: Walter around 1893, Maude in 1902, followed in order, although we don't know all the years, by Rosie, Jim, Ruby, Fred, Willie, then Emily in 1903, Ada in 1909, Jean 1910 and Clarrie in 1914.

Some of the children died in childhood. As Ada told it, later in life looking back,

> One swallowed a bead, one broke its neck on the swing and I don't know what happened to the boy, he died when he was quite young.[35]

Those children were buried in unmarked graves.[36]

Bill was a miner with interests in the Great Western and Joker mines. He worked hard to provide for his wife, children and mother-in-law, Mary. 1903 was the boom year on the goldfields. At that stage, there were tents up every gully, and six hundred men on the fields. As the gold became harder to find, the population was more often just a few dozen.[37]

Ah Hong arrived once a week with fresh produce to sell, from his market garden in Alice Springs. It formed a vital part of the Smiths' diet, supplemented by their own supply of goats, poultry, rabbits and seasonal bush foods. Water came from wells and soakages, dug into the ground.

Walter was born and raised in Arltunga. As he told it to his biographer later on in life, there was no school but there was always plenty to do. The children learnt by observation, practice and encouragement. There were a couple of water sources, including Paddy's Rockhole and Akura-ala soakage, where you could go to climb rocks and trees and watch horses and cattle being watered. There was plenty of activity around town with the mining and extraction operations and bullock drays coming and going. There was the weekly arrival of the camel train too, that brought supplies including wine and beer, flour, tea, sugar, salt and ointments such as Condy's Crystals, Balsam's Salve and turpentine that 'stung like blazes' and was used to treat cuts, scratches, blisters and other wounds.

There were plenty of other kids around to play with. They made their own games and fashioned their own wagons out of jam tins with long wire handles. Older kids rode goats and horses, with horses being the main form of transport into and out of the goldfields. By the age of about twelve, the boys would be going with their fathers, starting on the men's work. Presumably, girls had a similar, gendered trajectory in life.

In 1914, the Smiths had six living children and another on the way. Bill was worn out and unwell. Topsy's eldest daughter Maud was twelve. She later told of how, on his deathbed, Bill asked Topsy to take the children to Oodnadatta, to her relatives, where they might receive a proper education.[38]

Oodnadatta was, by then, a thriving town at the railhead, where travellers congregated on their ways north and south and a resident population was in force. The schoolhouse was a large room with a porch and one teacher where the thirty-five or so students of various heritages and combinations were educated together.

Topsy wanted to honour Bill's wishes and the relatives were keen to have her but, according to Maud, Sergeant Stott, who had a long reach over much that went on in the district, wouldn't let them go. He communicated via telegram with the Inspector of Police in Darwin as well as the 'Protector of Aborigines', who agreed with Stott's suggestion that he 'take charge of the children'. Stott arranged with police at Arltunga for the Smith family and their herd of several hundred goats to be brought to Alice Springs.[39]

Archival Portrait of Half-castery[40]

The colour problem

A most difficult problem
What shall be done with the half-castes?
Intermingling of the white blood with that of the untutored savage
Little outcasts of society
A kind of helot class

The tragedy

Backward children and adults
Much inferior to the full-blooded Aboriginals

The solving of the half-caste problem

Enquire into the half-caste problem
Report on the half-caste question
Enquire into the half-caste problem
Report on the Half Castes and Aboriginals of the Southern Division of the Northern Territory

Proposals for the housing, care and instruction of half-castes in the Alice Springs District

Training of the half-castes
A home for half-castes
A suitable building for half-castes
A kind of preparatory home and school for the very young half-castes
A self-supporting home for all half and three-quarter caste females

Protection of half-caste native girls
Under reasonable conditions of seclusion from the rest of the community
Complete segregation
They should be treated as children in law
Unless they are educated and Christianised
All Territory half-castes and possibly those of the Northern part of South Australia sent to southern orphanages
Some of the most intelligent half caste youths
Raise them to the status of their white parents
Positions in the ordinary life of the community

Removal from the bush

Fully fifty half-castes still remain to be collected in Central Australia
The earlier this is done the better for them
The bush blacks
The natural tendency, unfortunately, is to drift to the Aboriginal
Revert to bush conditions of life
The half-caste of 50% or more aboriginal blood, no matter how carefully brought up, will drift back to the aboriginal
Wild bush brothers
And it will take some time to eradicate

Removal from the town

It was necessary to remove the half-castes from the town
It was essential that the half-castes should be removed from the town of Stuart

Gross immorality

Malicious scandal
Infamous debauchery
Lubras
Concubines

Black gins

Half-caste progeny

A number of the surnames were identical with those of settlers in the Territory

Out of the forty or fifty children in the Bungalow, only about four are being maintained by their fathers

Prevent the employment of Aborigine and half-caste females by white men unless under the care and protection of a respectable married white woman

The increase of white women in the community shall greatly assist in solving the problem

Crossbreeds

Three-quarter-caste aboriginals

Half-caste aboriginals

Quadroons

Octaroons

There are cases here where half-caste girls have three-quarter-caste children

Seven half-caste women with thirteen quadroon and octaroon children

Seven quadroons under thirteen years of age

Four quadroon women with three octaroon children

Quadroons and octaroons under ten or twelve years of age

A half-caste from Central Australia

Shows no indications of Aboriginal blood

Eventual absorption in the white population

What a valuable asset can be made of what is now a difficult problem

An eminent authority on the Aborigines of Australia

Chief protector of Aborigines

Sub Protector of Aborigines

In dealing with these people one is often perplexed and the longer you are with them the better you realise how little you understand them

The First Schoolteacher

On a day uncommonly grey and damp for that part of the world, I imagine her stepping down onto crunchy earth and into the mayhem that erupted with the arrival of the fortnightly train.

I imagine languages and luggage being hurled in all directions by the unlikely mix who gathered in Oodnadatta and made that place their history.[41]

Oodnadatta was one of those outback settlements that gave the impression it had landed, holus bolus. As if someone in 1890, with a pre-assembled town, lost control of it six hundred miles north-west of Adelaide, three hundred and five down from Alice Springs, a couple of hundred up from Kati Thanda/Lake Eyre, and thump, down she went.

Oodnadatta: the blossom of the mulga, which the great Lutheran missionary Carl Strehlow (1871–1922) would have preferred to see spelt Utnadata. Strehlow had been running Hermannsburg Mission, three hundred and fifty miles up, on Western Arunda country, since 1894. His interest in spreading the good word amongst the natives led to his development of a way of writing their language so as to translate the bible. It was the first Arunda anthology.

Oodnadatta lay scattered about the plains. Houses and trees grew huddled in clumps, reliant on each other for survival. Denuded expanses of sandy red earth lay in between, where feral species, captained by the goats, had mowed it dry.

Beyond the town and across the desert plains, the land and sky intersect at the horizon that you can pretty much see in its entirety by spinning full circle.

In those early years of the twentieth century, when Mrs Standley was passing through, Oodnadatta hosted three general stores, the

Transcontinental Hotel, several butchers, a blacksmith, two bakeries, two boarding houses, a fruit shop that opened for two days after the train arrived each fortnight, a police station, a carpentry shop and the railyards but no platform. There was a school too, with an enrolment in 1912 of thirty-five students.

A mile from the railway station was the Ghantown, where the cameleers camped in small tin shacks. This village was surrounded by open space where their camels were free to graze. Collectively known as 'the Afghans', the cameleers were mainly from the arid hills and plains of Afghanistan and British India, today's Pakistan. They wore distinctive headwear and tunics, fasted for the month of Ramadan and prayed in Arabic to Mecca. From the Ghantown emanated the exotic aroma of curried goat mingled with hashish smoke from water-cooled pipes.

Four miles south at Hookey's Hole, Cherry Ah Chee tended his market garden. He was married to Mini, of Arrernte/European descent, and they had four children. The crops included watermelon, rockmelon, peaches, cabbages, carrots, sugar cane and garlic.

Ida Standley, the picture of matronly discretion, would have seen and heard and smelt it all as she stepped down into it on 9 May 1914. Was she nervous? Appalled? Excited? Did she falter, thinking, What on earth am I doing? Or, more in fitting with what else we know of her, take it in her stride – duty-bound and committed?

Sergeant Stott had entrusted his offsider Harry Kunoth as well as Bill Fox, a linesman from the Alice Springs Telegraph Station, to greet the first schoolteacher. They were to bring her, by police horse and buggy, as well as telegraph station wagon, up the track.[42]

We can suppose the constable stepped out of the throng to greet her.

'Welcome, ma'am, Harry Kunoth at your service,' tipping his hat.
She would have recognised him, known in advance of the arrangement.
'Pleased to meet you, constable. So good of you to collect me.'
'It's a pleasure, ma'am. Can I give you a hand?'
The trip from Oodnadatta to Stuart took fourteen days. Normally

a land of clear blue sky, on this occasion the heavens opened up and progress slowed to a crawl. The party spent days sheltering under a tarpaulin from torrential rains that mucked up the track and made the journey, particularly through the depot sandhills, hard going.[43]

*

Ida Standley had been born forty-five years earlier, in 1869, to Hanson and Bethia Woodcock (née Frankland) of North Adelaide. Hanson was a butcher and Ida was the youngest of their six children.[44]

Ida was born into a city just a few decades old. It was a well-designed grid, of parklands and squares. Of bluestone and limestone and iron lacework civility. Of settlers who had fled their homelands to a new place where they were welcome to practise their marginal Christian beliefs and build as many churches as they pleased, hence Adelaide: the city of churches. It was a progressive and cultured corner of Australia where people promenaded and promoted democracy and the advancement of women. Where horses clip-clopped along wide, paved streets.

Streets that had been freshly laid upon the hunting grounds, the smallpox scars and the blood-stained earth of the Kaurna, the original inhabitants.

On a clear night, if you listened, you could hear the cries and whispers of those who'd either died before their time or been transported to Poonindie, the native (un)settlement on the Eyre Peninsula; the heartbreak hotel such a long way from home.

Ida's mother died when she was three, her father fourteen years later. Ida's schooling was completed at Misses Lucy and Florence Tilley's Hardwick House Ladies College. Established in 1883 to provide an education for Methodist girls, Hardwick House was one of several private girls' schools in Adelaide at that time, leading the way with the education of girls.[45]

At the age of eighteen and newly graduated, Ida Woodcock took up a position as governess at the Standley family property on the Eyre Peninsula, at a place called Mount Wudinna. That name seems to come from the local word for a granite monolith with a commanding presence in the area, said to be the second largest rock in Australia. That's *weedna*. Twenty-five years earlier when Robert and Sarah Standley had moved in as the first permanent European settlers of the district, Indigenous people were allegedly numerous and hostile.[46] It is curious then, that the Standleys adapted a local word for their own imposition of labels on the landscape instead of importing the name of some foreign dignitary or piece of turf as was so much more the done thing.

Robert and Sarah went on to have eleven children of which George was their oldest surviving. Who Ida's charges were at Mount Wudinna is not clear. However, in 1887 when Ida arrived, George Standley was thirty-five years of age and had two teenage sons, Charles and Joseph Franklin. Charles and Joseph Franklin, the son of George Standley: what was this about? Why weren't they also called Standley? Had they taken their mother's name? Did anyone do that back then? Was it before she died? After she died? Had she died? Who was she?

As a researcher, I had turned over all the usual stones in an attempt to unearth any more about Charles and Joseph and their mother. I tried standard internet searches: births, deaths and marriages; genealogy sites. On a visit to South Australia, I had pored over the family history volumes at the State Library. They are time-worn volumes of solidly bound, wafery, discoloured paper that bear lists of the names, birth and death dates, occupation, residence and offspring of practically every person, it seems, who has been born or died or lived in South Australia. Practically every person, except for Charles and Joseph Franklin and their mother.

I had become a bit obsessed by this, perhaps given it too much time. Engrossed in the archives, you can tumble down a rabbit warren that leads to a series of tunnels. You take one tunnel and then another and another until eventually you have become hopelessly awash in a sea of details, fascinating but utterly excessive for your purposes, and taken page after jotted page of dates and places and tenuous links that are of no interest to anyone but you, the infected researcher. It doesn't really matter that much, I tried reminding myself; get out of the warren and back to the matter at hand. It's about the Bungalow and Central Australia and Ida, not her husband's earlier sons and their mystery mother.

It was late in the afternoon of my last day of researching. I was due to fly home the next day and was satisfied with the fruits of my labour. I'll just have one more look for Charles and Joseph, I decided, as well as anything else I might find, and typed 'Standley' into the general catalogue.

That brought hits aplenty. There were the resources about Ida Standley with which I was already familiar, books and documents about other Standleys, books by other Standleys and amidst all that, a result that was new to me:

Standley [compiled and written by Else Wauchope, Tom Hynes]
Wauchope, Else, 1923–
Book/pamphlet | 2008
Available at S Australiana Pamphlets (929.2099423 S785.W) see all

I had no idea what this was about. Perhaps it was unrelated, but it couldn't hurt to check it out; my last little enquiry before calling it a day. I scribbled down the details and bowled over to the long desk behind which the librarians sat with their computers, their knowledge, their processes and advice, their patience and dedication and an extraordinary willingness to be of assistance.

'Can I see this?' I asked hopefully.

They were used to me. I'd been badgering them for days now; in early, there until late.

'Yes, sure.'

Of course!

'It will be in the reading room. You're registered, aren't you?'

I nodded. That had happened earlier when they copied details down from my driver's licence, issued me with a temporary pass and made me feel welcome and of import.

'We'll have to order it. It'll take a couple of hours. Will that be all right?'

Of course it would. The wait added to the air of importance, like when a pharmacist makes you wait for your prescription even though what you need is sitting right there on the shelf.

I went for a wander, had my daily fix of tea and cake at the library café, all part of the ritual of research. An enforced break was good. I got so caught up in the dig sometimes that I ignored my physical needs until I couldn't.

On my way back into the main library area, I stopped off at the cloakroom and produced the numbered tag I'd been issued with earlier. The attendant moved to retrieve my items.

'I'm going to the reading room,' I told him.

He nodded knowingly and brought my backpack so I could put my pens and purse in it – things that weren't allowed where I was going – and he issued me with a large, plastic ziplock bag. He knew I knew the ropes, he had explained them to me earlier – whatever you take into the reading room you take in the ziplock bag, no pens, phone on silent, if you want to photograph documents you ask.

Normally up for circumventing rules and pushing the boundaries, here I happily complied. I am one with the whole ritual of archival library research; its solemn purposefulness and performance. Here were documents, rare and precious, protected by law, safeguarded by librarians and stored, with care and a respect for their fragility and public proprietary. Here the shrapnel that can take us to our history is treated with the value and respect it deserves.

I made my way to the glass sliding door in a corner of the main library room and pressed the green button. The curator of the reading room, a no-nonsense woman who could see me from behind her desk just within the inner sanctum, granted access. I presented my ziplock bag, she nodded her assent.

'Linda, is it?' and as I nodded she handed me a large document envelope that contained the brochure in question.

We were the only two in the reading room. The researchers from earlier in the day must have had homes to go to, dinners to prepare.

I sat at a researcher's table, opened the envelope, removed the brochure. To my delight, it was all about the Standleys, the Robert and Sarah of Mount Wudinna Standleys, my Standleys! An eight-page local history, family brochure. Bingo. Rabbit warren, here we come. I wanted to hoot, to hug the curator. I remembered where I was, contained myself. Solemn. Discreet. I hooted inwardly.

'Robert and Sarah Standley settled at Mt Wudinna,' I read. 'Born Norwich, England. Eleven children.' Things I knew.

I turned the page, read on. 'George was a sheep farmer, wheat grower, labourer and a prospector. George and his aboriginal partner had two sons – Charles and Joseph Franklin.'

I savoured the polite postmodern reference to 'George and his Aboriginal partner.' I bet that's not how they put it at the time.

At last, here they were: Charles and Joseph. Their father was George Standley. Their mother was an Aboriginal woman, presumably a Franklin, still unnamed by history, still with no greater identity, no greater claim to fame than that her sons were fathered by a white man who went on to marry Ida Standley, who went on to become the first schoolteacher in Alice Springs and was awarded an MBE.

The penny finally dropped. A woman who goes unnamed, who barely rates a mention in the archives in the history of our country, for whom all research trails lead to a dead end, whose sons don't warrant their father's name; of course she was Aboriginal.

Franklin Harbour is a hundred miles from Mount Wudinna, on the north-eastern edge of the Eyre Peninsula. It was named after Sir John Franklin, rear-admiral of the blah-de-blah and lieutenant something or other at some stage. One of the origins of First Nation people's European surnames, bestowed on them by people who insisted they have such a name, was the area around where they lived. Maybe that is from where the Franklin boys got their name.

I read on.

> When George married Ida Woodcock they lived near Poolalalie Hill. He brought his two sons to live with them.

In spite of his nomadic instincts he was fairly well read, and a likeable man. He became blind in his final years of life… He would talk of the Indigenous people with whom he was familiar. He spoke several Aboriginal dialects…

Towards the end his two sons, Charles and Joseph never forsook him and saw that he did not want.

George and Ida married within a year of her arrival and went on to have four children of their own whose names and years of birth were Marian 1889, Clarence 1892, Carmen 1894 and Vivian 1896. On account of her husband's 'nomadic instincts', Ida was on her own to some great extent, to care for that unique, late-nineteenth century Eyre Peninsula version of the Brady Bunch: three boys and three girls, from a white dad, a white mum and a black mum.

When Ida was offered a position to teach the children of the families of the Boothby district, one hundred kilometres north-west, she accepted. Lessons commenced in the year 1900 in the dining room of the Foulds' family home and Joe Way built a small cottage for Ida and her children to live in. Later, when the Boothby school was built, Ida became the first teacher for up to twenty-four pupils.[47]

According to a later reflection of one of her pupils, the school under Ida's care was very well organised, the flag was flown regularly, and all subjects and grades were thoroughly taught including music and singing.

In 1911, Ida transferred to Buchfelde, another rural, one-teacher school but this time much closer to Adelaide. By then, her children were aged twenty-two, nineteen, seventeen and fifteen but it is not clear who, if any of them, went with her. By 1914, after eighteen years of service, Ida's annual salary had risen from sixty-five to one hundred pounds.[48]

In the March of 1914, Ida was, let's say, flipping through the current edition of the *Education Gazette* of South Australia, keeping abreast of developments in education, when the following box caught her eye:

TEACHER FOR ALICE SPRINGS NORTHERN TERRITORY

Applications are invited from women teachers for the above-mentioned position. The salary will be 150 pounds per annum. A free passage and travelling expenses to Alice Springs will be given. At the end of two years' service travelling expenses and a free passage to Adelaide will be paid. Applications are to reach The Director of Education Adelaide, not later than Wednesday, March 31st.

Was she excited in an instant: *Right then, that's where I'm going?*

Or did the notion take hold slowly, tossed around by Ida like pikelets in a pan and discussed with her nearest and dearest, especially her own offspring?

She was self-sufficient and resourceful, Ida, and accustomed to running one-teacher schools. Vivian, her youngest, was eighteen, in the days when girls were grown-up and possibly married by then. It would be exciting and original. The first schoolteacher for the Red Centre – that had a certain ring to it. Ida was, presumably, keen to step up, to be of further use, and the increase in wages would be welcome.

*

The settlers of the Alice had been wanting a schoolteacher for some time. Discussion began appearing in the public records in July 1913 in a report from Senior Constable Stott to the Department of Home & Territories. 'Want of a Public School at Alice Springs', wrote Stott, was a great 'obstacle against permanent settlement of desirable married settlers with families.'[49] He listed a number of settler families whose Central Australian lives had been disrupted by lack of access to schooling for the children:

> During 1910 Mr Meyers [stockowner] was obliged to send his wife and four children to Adelaide. Since then Mr Meyers has been obliged to live apart from his family. The extra expense of having to keep family in Adelaide has, and is, proving a great impediment to Meyers in stocking Permit country. May last Mr. S. Nicker, holder of Permit No. 319, sold his sheep (1450) has temporarily abandoned Permit country. Went to Adelaide with wife and four children. Ru-

mour says Mr Nicker and family intend returning to MacDonnell Ranges whenever there is school accommodation at Alice Springs.

May last Mr Freer with wife and family (2) left Alice Springs for South Australia.

During 1911 Mr Kennear of Arltunga, Labourer, with wife and four children, left for South Australia.

May last Mr McKay, Postmaster of Alice Springs, sent his only son to Adelaide. During 1909, Mr Bradshaw ex Postmaster of Alice Springs, with wife and 6 children was obliged to get transferred to Adelaide.

1908 C.R. South, Ex Licensed Victualler and Storekeeper of Alice Springs was obliged to sell out. With wife and 3 children went to Adelaide.

1910 the Rev. Strehlow of Hermannsburg Mission Station, took 5 of his children to Germany to be educated.

In almost every instance the primary reasons of migration of residents and their children, referred to, is want of school for children at Alice Springs.

I beg to point out the nearest school to Alice Springs is Oodnadatta state school, in the State of South Australia, distance 340 miles.[50]

In September 1913, Mr and Mrs Hayes of Undoolya Station presented their case for a school to the Reverend Steele of the Presbyterian Church of Australia, who then took it to the Minister for External Affairs in Melbourne:

> Yesterday I saw in Adelaide a Mr Hayes of Undoolya Station, Alice Springs. He, on behalf of the residents, pressed for a school. Mrs. Hayes said that there are at least two houses available and suitable, and that at least ten pupils would attend...
>
> Corporal Stott would have three children, Mrs. Crooks (government assistant) three, and Mr. Johansson would send a child from Deep Well on the border of Alice Springs. Mr. Nicker, near Ryan's Well, about 80 miles north of Alice Springs, in the event of a school being established, would send his wife and three children to Alice Springs.
>
> Mr Stott guarantees a temporary suitable place for the school.[51]

The secretary to the Minister for External Affairs followed up with a letter to Mrs Hayes:

Madam,
    With reference to the proposed establishment of a school at Alice Springs, Northern Territory, I have the honour, by direction, to inform you that the Minister has given this question consideration, but has decided to take no action in the matter for the present.[52]

In a letter to the Reverend Steele, the secretary went further, explaining that the cost could not be justified. It was however hoped that within a year the policy of connecting with the MacDonnell Ranges by railway would be sanctioned and then 'a great deal of the difficulties of pioneering settlement mitigated'.[53]

The Northern Territory wasn't settled by people who took things lying down. On 20 January 2014, the Northern Territory Administrator wrote to the Minister for External Affairs, arguing for a school in the centre.

The administrator's letter also highlights colonial beliefs of the time about race and interracial breeding. Such beliefs dominated scientific and political thinking in the late nineteenth and early twentieth centuries. They formed the basis of the governmental response to the First Nations people of the great southern land. Although such views have since been disproven and rejected, they form the basis of the ignorance and racial prejudice upon which Australia was built and has proven so very difficult to dismantle.

The scientific theories, based on a line of thinking known as eugenics, supposed that there were races and groups of people across the world with superior and, by corollary inferior, genetic traits. By rigorous supervision of breeding, less desirable traits could be bred out of the entire human family. Of course, white aristocrats were superior and miscegenation was regarded as one of the greatest dangers faced by any society, particularly those that were white-dominated.[54] It was generally believed, across the European-dominated world, including in Australia, that the 'full blood' was inferior and therefore dying out, and that people of mixed race were morally and physically defective, biologically dangerous and a threat to racial purity and national interests.[55]

For example, in an official report in 1915, the Administrator of the Northern Territory declared that 'all half-castes were morally worthless, that the taint was in them and that it must inevitably manifest itself'.[56] Reverend Carl Strehlow of the Hermannsburg Mission considered those of mixed race to be 'a hopeless people and much inferior to the full blooded aboriginals'.[57]

By the administrator's reckoning, in early 1914, eleven white children and four 'quadroons' (the offspring of half-caste mothers and white fathers) could be taught together, for several hours, each morning. The twelve–fourteen 'half-castes' and twenty-five 'aboriginal children' could then attend school for two or three hours in the afternoon.

The teacher should be 'a man with personality'. His wife could 'teach the female aboriginal and half-caste children sewing and such useful work'. The administrator's letter read as follows:

Sir,
    1. With reference to the proposed school at Alice Springs, I looked into this question fully while at that township, and there appears to be no doubt that it is incumbent upon the Government to provide a school and schoolteacher for the children there.
    2. Shortly there will be eleven white children of school age at Alice Springs, this is, if a school be guaranteed. Two are at present kept at Oodnadatta for the purposes of education. There are four quadroons, the children of a half-caste mother by one or more white fathers: These are living in the black's camp close to the township. For all practical purposes these should be included as white children.
    3. There are a number of half-castes in the camp – 12 or 14 in all – who should receive education of some sort.
    4. In addition to these there are about 25 aboriginal children who should receive some educational attention.
    5. Leaving the aboriginals out of the question, one may calculate on from 25 to 30 children – whites, quadroons and

half-castes – to whom it is imperative some education should be offered. You are aware how anxious the parents of the white children are to have a teacher. Corporal Stott has communicated very fully in regard to the matter.

6. To meet this pressing necessity I would propose, if funds can be made available, to erect a teacher's residence with school room attached, as per accompanying sketch. The teacher should be a married man, and in addition to his ordinary scholastic duties, he should be placed in charge of the native camp adjacent, so as to keep full control over the native and half-caste children.

7. The whole of the aboriginals and half-castes could all be taught in one class as none have received any education whatever hitherto. The mornings might therefore well be given to the education of the white children, and two or three hours in the afternoon devoted to the aboriginals and half-castes.

8. The cost of the school house building complete with ten foot verandah would be about 600 pounds, judging from a rough estimate I received in Alice Springs from a man who would be willing to take the contract. This would be a stone building.

9. I think it would be possible to secure an efficient teacher for 250 pounds per annum, but perhaps it would be necessary to increase it to 300 pounds. It is imperative that the teacher be a man with personality, able to take charge of the camp efficiently. It is also important that his wife should be able to teach the female aboriginal and half-caste children sewing and such useful work.

10. I am dealing more fully with the question of the large number of blacks at present at the camp at Alice Springs. For some considerable time where will always be a fair number of aboriginals with their children close to the township.

I shall be glad to be advised as soon as possible of your decision regarding the school.[58]

The administrator continued pressing, with follow up letter to the minister in March. By his calculations, there were, by that time, eleven white children, four quadroons who were 'practically white', at least twelve 'half-castes', and twenty-five 'aborigines' of school age. The administrator was now thinking a single female teacher might be suitable. She could be paid less than a man and could bunk in with the Stotts. Stott's wife and children were making plans to move to Sydney for schooling if a teacher was not appointed. Rather than having a man separated from his wife and family under such circumstances, the administrator explained, he would prefer to transfer Stott to Pine Creek and replace him with a single man, a transfer he considered to be costly and unwise.[59]

By March, the money had been allocated. The Director of Education in South Australia was enlisted to identify a suitable teacher. The Northern Territory would undertake the transport and establish a school. The teacher was to be paid a hundred and fifty pounds per annum, be allowed return passage after two years and, if a woman, would board with the Stotts. Up to thirty-five pounds could be spent on converting a small room adjacent to the police station and jailhouse, currently used for storing the Aboriginal rations, into a temporary schoolroom. Stott would oversee the construction as well as arrange for the loan of some furniture until the timber arrived from Oodnadatta for school furniture to be made. According to the Minster for External Affairs, the school would be 'for white children, including perhaps quadroons, to commence with'.[60]

Imagine the excitement around town! Stott shot off the following, in a telegram to the administrator:

> Teacher can reside with us. Building for school unavailable. Suggest room where I supplied aboriginals rations from time Your Excellency visit Alice be converted into temporary schoolroom by adding two additional windows or doors erecting front verandah width ten feet. Estimated costs additions verandah school fittings about thirty two pounds.[61]

The selected applicant declined to proceed because the salary was too low. Perhaps it was Ida Standley but nowhere in the documents is it stated. With residents agreeing to provide free board and washing, estimated to be worth one pound per week, Ida Standley accepted the deal. Her appointment was from 6 May 1914, the day she left Adelaide, and she requested her salary be paid into the English, Scottish & Australian Bank Adelaide.

*

Did she question her sanity? Pine for her children? With each rattly passing mile, did she feel herself slipping further and further from the life she knew? Was she moving away from or going towards?

A diary would have helped. It could have saved us from a lot of this wonder and speculation. But she didn't seem to be the diary-keeping kind. The men did: Stuart and Giles, for example, and Stott with his daily police journal – the pioneering men who prised open the centre. We can read their diaries and see the new world through their eyes. Did Ida not think her journey mattered enough? Did she not have time? Couldn't be fagged?

Had Ida kept a diary, it might have gone something like this:

> *The little town of Stuart isn't entirely dissimilar to Oodnadatta. It's a small settlement set on a dry and ancient land, with an abundance of wide-open space and distance to be traversed.*
>
> *Surrounding the little town are the most majestic mountain ranges. These are sheer rock with brave little plants way up high that seem to root in the absence of soil. On the way, we passed through much country that is scarcely more than gibber plain and herbaceous little species that struggle for life in the harsh, dry soils. As we grew closer to our destination, the land became richer, with more undulating country and vegetation along with dry riverbeds that criss-cross the land.*
>
> *One enters the town through a great chasm in the Mac-Donnell Ranges, on a track beside the town's own dry river bed.*
>
> *The constable assured me that the river flows after a big rain. The whole place appeared as dry as an old boot, with no evidence here of the rains which had so impeded our progress further south.*
>
> *About a mile before reaching the town itself, we passed by the native camp. This was a shambolic looking affair with huts of bark and grass and people looking unkempt and uncomfortable in ill-fitting, mismatched clothes. I glimpsed dark children and half-castes alongside their parents. I cannot bear the thought of children growing up in such conditions and hope they will soon all be removed for their own good, or the half-castes at least.*

Although I have been recruited here to teach the white children, of whom there are eleven, there was some talk of me seeing what I can do with the half-castes et cetera as well. Surely their lives would also be enhanced by some education. Experience shows that they can be taught, at least the basics.

There were the white children of the town, too, waving gaily as we rode in, or peeking out from behind their parents' shirt tails. They appear to have neither shoes nor coats. It must be a big thing for those white children who have been running almost as wild as the natives to now be facing the prospect of a schoolteacher and school. Hopefully it is not just daunting but exciting for them as well. Let's see what I can do!

The town centre is a grid of dusty streets. There are a few buildings of solid stone: the police complex, the Stuart Arms Hotel, the gaol, and then a range of shacks that appear as if a good gust of wind would level them to the ground.t

Sergeant Stott and his wife gave me a warm welcome me and showed me to my lodgings. I shall board with them to begin with, they and their brood, who have shown me every kindness, complete with he best room in the house and all the food I could desire. There is goat meat aplenty, some beef and a surprising amount of fresh fruit and vegetables, provided largely by the Chinese market gardener, Ah Hong. My school room is to be the old warder's residence, in the vicinity of the gaol and the police station. It is a solid little structure of local stone, just one small room with two windows. Sergeant Stott has had to borrow furniture from around town until the material comes up from Oodnadatta for school furniture to be made.

It is all quite an adventure and I feel full of hopes and plans for the challenges that lay ahead.

*

The new schoolteacher has arrived.
What's she like?
She's boarding with the Stotts.
Yes, that was the agreement.
She looks strict.

She looks kind.
She's not young.
No, she has grown-up children apparently.
And experience in one-teacher schools.
She'll need it up here with our lot.
They don't know what they're in for.
Will we be allowed to go to school too?
I think it's just for the whites. That's why I wanted to take you to Oodnadatta.
Mrs Standley, welcome. How wonderful to finally have you here.
Thank you. You are too kind. I am pleased, at last, to be here.

Mparntwe

The town grew up on an area of land known as Mparntwe, the traditional lands of the Mparntwerinye people. They are a subgroup of the Arrernte. They have lived with and cared for this land for as long as anyone can remember. They know it like the backs of their hands.

The area chosen for the initial site of the town was a flood plain, between the junction of two rivers. The rivers are predominantly dry, sandy beds that have been carved by flood waters through the desert plain: tranquil when dry, imposing in flow. The chosen portion of floodplain was divided into a hundred and four urban lots and auctioned off in Adelaide in 1888–9.[62]

Settlers have been complaining ever since that when the rivers flow, the town is flooded. That is what you get for building your town on a floodplain. Any Mparntwerinye could have told you that!

View of Lhere Mparnte/the Todd River, 1921.[63]

The Early Years

Ada remembered coming in from Arltunga. She was five years of age. 'I had no shoes,' she said. 'We didn't know what shoes was at the Bungalow'. Then Ada laughed.[64] People laugh for all kinds of reasons.

Ada was in her senior years by 1981, when her memories were recorded and then archived:

> Our father died early in 1914. He had the Great Western mine at Arltunga and also he was buried at the crossroad at Arltunga. My father's name was William Smith. We had a herd of goats; that's five or six hundred we brought in from Arltunga. Constable Dowdy brought us in, also a black tracker called Sam who was driving. Constable Dowdy and two native women helped my mother to drive the goats in. We was on the dray. My brother Walter Smith drove the dray with seven children on it.
>
> We got two, three days later to Williams Well and was met by John Hayes. He had Undoolya Station at that time and bought us some lollies, cakes, biscuits and fresh milk. We got to Undoolya the next day. He made us stay there the night; we have to spell. We arrived into Alice Springs and he had the day off.[65]

Big brother Walter remembered the coming in too:

> Topsy drove the dray, which carried as many belongings as possible including some hens. Behind her followed the rest of the family, ranging from young men to very young children for they needed to drive the family's herd of several hundred goats. Even little Jean and Ada, respectively four and five years old, did their best, although they spent considerable times on the dray. They were always grateful to Mrs John Hayes of Undoolya station; she drove a wagon out with food and plenty of water when they were still 50 km east of Alice Springs.[66]

Walter was the oldest of Topsy and Bill's children, aged twenty-one at the time.

> He was still so upset at his father's death that he wished to…remain with the family and keep everyone together, but gruff old Sergeant Stott…pointed out that he was a man and needed to provide for the family.[67]

The Bungalow began as one tin shed with wooden benches for beds and hard, earthen floors, made from a mixture of tar, sand and gravel.

It was more like a stable, recalled Clarence, the youngest of Topsy's kids. He was *in utero* when they came in and in his senior years when his memories were recorded in 1988. He was born, he thought, in a bough shelter under a gum tree in the Todd River, in October 1914.[68]

Walter went to work for Charlie Sadadeen, one of the Afghan cameleers. From then on, he travelled extensively and only saw his family sporadically. There was little way of keeping in touch in those days, except for turning up. You were where you were and with who you were with, I suppose.

Alice Springs was a tiny outpost of a town, just twenty-five years into its existence and crawling along slowly. In 1914 when the Smiths came in, there were, according to Clarrie, 'about four or five houses… and a couple of shops and the Stuart Arms and the police station,' along with plenty of wide-open space'.[69]

Clarrie's perception of the town at the time he was born is confirmed, more or less, by official records which show that in 1914 there were three houses, three stores, the police complex, a big vegetable garden and the Stuart Arms Hotel.[70] The hotel was

> A modest structure of stone and iron, about the size of an average house, with a post and rail hitching fence around the veranda. Buggies and wagons parked outside [in what was then] a forest of gums.[71]

Out from the fledgling town were the main population and activity centres of the region: Arltunga, Hermannsburg Mission, the Alice Springs Telegraph Station, cattle stations.

Clarrie also remembered,

> Looking south there [were] great big saltbushes between where the hospital is there, right down to The Gap; they'd grown to about six or eight feet in height. You couldn't see anything that was coming through The Gap at that time, whether it was a buggy or a wagon or a team of camels – all you could see was dust between the saltbushes – you knew there was something on the way in. The saltbushes were so high that you couldn't see nothing, only the dust, till they came out of the scrub or whatever you'd like to call it – the saltbushes that was growing there.[72]

It's all suburban build-up these days and you can't see the dust for the development.

Down amidst that saltbush country, Clarry recalled the native camp:

> There was a big camp there behind that little hill opposite the hospital there where the Shell service station is. Probably three or four hundred Aboriginals lived there…
>
> It's only just wurlies built up about oh, four to five feet high, I suppose, with brushes, like branches, off trees. And they'd get under these windbreaks.[73]

When Topsy and the kids arrived, Stott put up a tent for them and, as was reported later,

> informed the Administrator in Darwin that there was no accommodation for [Topsy's] children, and suggested that two township allotments near the Police Station should be reserved for half castes. The Administrator agreed to this and authorised the building of an iron shed. This was done, and Topsy Smith placed in charge of it under the supervision of Sergeant Stott. Rations were supplied from the general Aboriginals grant.[74]

It cost just twenty-five pounds to build the first tin shed, an economy that impressed the administrator who reported that

> The economy exercised has been mainly due to the efforts of Senior Constable Stott who with trackers, and aboriginals, has cut timber, put down ant bed floors, erected bunks etc.[75]

The trackers were, of course, also Aboriginal, and employed for their extraordinary powers of observation. On days when those powers weren't specifically required, the trackers undertook all manner of other duties, as directed. As reported later by a journalist,

> Upon a rectangular frame sheets of iron were nailed. A few sheets were left out to allow a door to be inserted on each of the long sides of the building. On each side of the door sheets were left out to make windows. There is no glass in the windows; they have iron shutters, and when the doors and windows are closed no air can possibly enter the buildings…
> There are three rough bunks…no verandahs, so that the heat or the cold or the rain must beat directly on to the walls of the buildings.[76]

Ida watched as the Smiths arrived and the Bungalow went up. She had been in town for just a few weeks herself and was boarding with the Stotts, across the road and down a bit. Mr Crook was watching too. He got wind of an idea that there were plans to teach all the children together and decided to make his views on that idea very clear. In a lettergram to the Minister for External Affairs in Melbourne, in August 1914, Crook wrote,

> Sir I respectfully wish [to] call your attention following: of 26 children attending public school here 13 are half-castes. At present whites are instructed in mornings – coloured in afternoons, but I understand all are to be taught together through lack educational facilities. White children are already years behind city children and in view this fact I consider they should have all teachers attention. I also strongly protest against having place my two little girls with coloured children from Blacks' camps. When i promised [to] contribute 12.10.0 per annum towards teacher's support no mention was made of half-castes receiving tuition, and therefore consider I should now be exempt from paying this fee. Respectfully ask your careful consideration this matter. W Crook[77]

There is no information about where Crook's idea of co-schooling came from. From a drinking session down the pub perhaps or a conversation held under one of the store verandas. Wherever the idea came from,

Crook's outpouring prompted a flurry of correspondence between departments that culminated in an urgent telegram from the Northern Territory Administrator to the Department of External Affairs in Melbourne

> Have communicated with teacher and have now arranged white children to attend from nine to twelve-thirty six days a week coloured Monday to Friday three to four thirty stop this should meet objection made by Crook and seems best arrangements possible in circumstances.[78]

Next, as told by Ada, 'the police[man] named Stott got the children from the native's camp and put them in the Bungalow'.[79] By the end of the year, six such children had, as reported by Stott 'been removed from Aboriginals camp within the vicinity of Alice Springs'.[80]

Been removed.

Were they plucked off like fruit from the native plum tree? Was it more like the dislodging of wildcat kittens from their mother? Or were they given, with resignation as in *Go get a good feed and learn about the whitefella ways then come back and tell us?*

In his letter to the Department of External Affairs in Melbourne of December 1914, Stott reported that fourteen children from the Bungalow were receiving tuition as well as eleven Europeans. He enclosed a photo entitled *Group of European and Coloured Children attending Public School at Alice Springs.*

Stott also advised of 'other coloured children living with the Aboriginals in outlying portions of this District, who are likewise in need'. There was not sufficient accommodation at present to receive more children into the building, he said, a matter he had brought to the attention of the Chief Protector of Aboriginals in Darwin.[81]

The Chief Protector passed that on to the Administrator of the Northern Territory who sent a memorandum, in February 1915, to the Minister for External Affairs in Melbourne:

> In addition to a number of half caste and quarter caste children receiving tuition and under supervision at Alice Springs, there is a number in the outlying districts, and is proposed to bring these latter into Alice Springs, making a total somewhere between 25 and 30.
>
> Mrs Standley, schoolteacher, is willing to supervise these children at all times, and undertake complete responsibility for them, which is highly necessary, more especially as the Protector of Aborigines, Constable Stott, cannot of course always be there. I recommend, therefore, your approval to Mrs Standley doing this work, with an extra renumeration of 50 pounds per annum as from the 1st proximo. Her total salary will be 206 pounds per annum.[82]

Approval was forthcoming and Ida Standley resumed the additional duty of matron from 1 April 1915. Permission was also given to build another shed to accommodate 'other half-castes from outside districts'.[83]

In early 1915, to the Chief Inspector of Aborigines, Ida wrote,

> I am very interested in these children. They have made marvellous strides with their schoolwork since you saw them, particularly so as they receive only 1½ hours teaching per diem. I have been taking the adult h.c. for an hour every evening since Xmas; they are doing well also. At present there are 17 h.c. on the school roll and younger ones at the bungalow. I am just wondering how I'll get on in my new position. My head is full of plans and schemes for the little ones. Well, Mr Beckett, I'll just do my best; failures and disappointments are plenty no doubt. Nevertheless I am going to win.[84]

The NT Administrator's Report of 1914–15 tells of a school in Alice Springs that has been provided for 'white, half-caste, and quadroon children'. The white children attend in the morning, and the 'coloured in the afternoon'. The teacher had also been appointed matron in charge of the bungalow in which the children were housed. A small entry by Ida Standley follows.

> On the 1st April I took up my duties as matron of the half-caste girls' bungalow. I have started the sewing class, which tends to be a great success. Up to date the girls have completed 22 articles, dresses, bodices and knickers for themselves and shirts for the boys. On the completion of the girls' bungalow I hope to get everything in full going order. At present doing all I can to improve their condition.[85]

The white men in charge were itching to get their hands on every last 'mixed-blood' child across the vast expanse of the Central Australian desert. They believed there to be double the number again that had already been brought in, twenty-five to thirty in all. It appeared they wouldn't rest until every single last one of those children had been brought to live at the Bungalow.

This perspective can be seen in the following itemised list, presented by Stott to an enquiry in 1917:

> There may be a few half caste children out there.
> In October last M.C. McKay brought in three from the Fink River.
> M.C. Noblet brought in two from Arltunga.
> Instructions have been issued to constables to bring in any such children they may find between the ages of 4 and 11.
> Kelly was instructed to bring in a half caste child out of Raggarts, but on his arrival there no one was present.
> Mr. Kunoth lives with a half caste woman by whom he has had two children, the elder about 10 is at school at Oodnadatta and the younger I consider too young, besides being properly cared and provided for.
> Meyers living with a half caste Afghan has a child born October 10th 1915, this child is also properly cared for.
> The girl already mentioned as being at Raggart's, both the child and the mother are fed and clothed at the station, and this child I propose getting in when opportunity occurs.

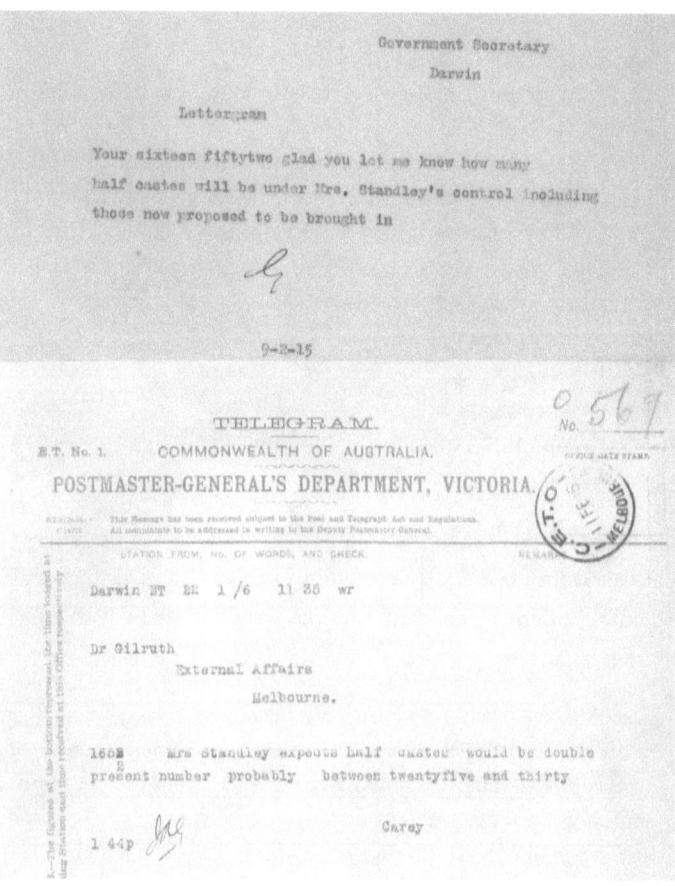

W.H. Liddell has a half caste girl Mary aged about 27. Four children, two in the bungalow whom he pays for, one in the bungalow of whom he is not the father, and one living with her born April 14th 1915. Mother and child are both properly cared for.

James Turner has a half caste lubra about 23 years, one child born 29th March 1917, second child born March 26th 1915 by another father, both living with and provided for by James Turner.

William Riley has a half caste child at the Barrow, born November 28th 1916.

There is a half-caste Edie Sargeant, aged 17, who has a child born Crown Point Cattle Station August 31st 1917.

Hetty Hayes, half caste, aged about 22, one child born

February 9th 1915, mother and child are cared for at Neutral Junction Station, by the mother's father.

Jenny, an aboriginal, has a child born June 23rd 1915, at Bond Springs, both of these have gone bush.

Alice Grant 18, half caste, quadroon child, born April 23rd 1915, mother and child at Mary Vale Station, properly cared for.

Mr. Plowman was going out to Arltunga. He said 'I may be going out on the Devois country. If I see any half castes shall I bring them in?' I said 'Certainly, we shall allow you for their food.' He did not bring any in.

There are two quadroons in Devois country living at Devois station. The reputed father is down south and M.C. Noblet has instructions to bring them in as soon as possible. These are two of the children that Plowman alluded to above.[86]

In June 2015, the Department of Home and Territories received a package from Ida Standley containing a collection of samples of the schoolwork done by children from the Bungalow along with a handwritten letter:

Dear Sir

It affords me great pleasure to forward you some specimens of work done by Half-Caste children at Alice Springs. The results indicated by these specimens are in my opinion very gratifying and when one considers that the children have received but 1½ hours daily for 12 months it speaks well for the possibilities of training them to become useful members of the community. I have forwarded similar specimens to Protector of Aborigines. Darwin. Knowing that you are keenly interested in the N Territory – its problems and possibilities – I feel sure you will be pleased to know that the little half-castes have possibilities of a future. The map of Australia is the work of a half caste Chinese boy named Dempsey Hong who receives tuition with the white children and is head of the school in all round work.

I have the honour to be, Sir,
Your obedient servant
Ida Standley
Teacher[87]

Atlee Hunt Esq C.M.G

Dear Sir,
         It affords me
great pleasure to forward you
some specimens of work done by
Half Caste Children at Alice Springs.
The results indicated by these specimens
are in my opinion very gratifying
and when one considers that the
children have received but 1½ hours
daily for 12 months it speaks well
for the possibility of training them to
become useful members of the community.
I have forwarded similar specimens
to Protector of Aborigines - Darwin.
Knowing that you are keenly interested
in the N. Territory - its problems and
possibilities - I feel sure you will be
pleased to know that the little
Half Castes have possibilities of a
future. The map of Australia

is the work of a halfcaste
Chinese boy named Dempsey Hong
who receives tuition with the White
children and is head of the school
in all round work.

         I have the honour to be, Sir,
               Your obedient Servant,
                    Ida Standley
                         Teacher.

Ida's handwritten letter.[88]

Dempsey Hong's map.[89]

Dempsey Hong was the son of Mr Ah Hong and Arrernte woman Ranjika. I imagine him working painstakingly on his map; taking care to record each place name in exactly the right location, checking and rechecking before committing ink to paper, getting every letter right then having a go at sounding out each word:

    LONGREACH.
    FREMANTLE.
    GT AUSTRALIAN BIGHT.
    TASMANIA.

What an exotic place the world must have seemed beyond Alice Springs. Did his schoolteacher tell him about the sparkling ocean waters and how they crash onto the shores where sea meets land? Did she conjure up for him the rich, green forests where rivers flow deep and constant and the cycle of life turns much more rapidly than in the desert? Did she tell young Dempsey, big brown eyes wide open, about the cities men build with their architecture and public spaces, where people meet to advance their causes and develop their versions of civilisation? Or did she just say, in a teacherly voice, 'That's very good, Dempsey. Now go and finish your maths'?

The envelope also contained several samples of the same piece of writing. It was the sort of text that a teacher composes on the blackboard and the children copy, in their neatest writing, date and heading at the top, leave a margin down the right-hand side. The samples were identical except for the place in the text that each student had reached before it was time to put their pencils down.

Here, in these samples of her pupils' writing, painstakingly copied from the board, was Standley's poof of 'the possibilities of training them' and the children's 'possibilities for a future': the fact that they could follow instructions and obediently copy some meaningless piece of text.

How about young Jack and Redwing Cooper, Donnell Stuart, Tom Williams, Essie Simpson, Topsy Fitz, Katie Williams, Dick Gillen, Mort Conway and Amy Collie in that converted warden's cottage, sitting up at the desks for their one and a half hours of formal education each day, figuring things out and doing their best?

Children's handwriting.[90]

> 234
> Transcription 17.6.15.
> In the holidays Nora came
> to stay with Marjory.
> What fun they had! It was
> just like the time when
> they lived near each other.
> and Nora used to come over
> every day to see Marjory.
> In the morning they went on
> Jack Cooper aged 9 years.

'In the holidays, Nora came to stay with Marjory,' or so went the story that the children so diligently copied. Who were Nora and Marjory, they might have wondered at first? Where was it that Nora came to stay with Marjory? In an overcrowded tin shed perhaps? Or in one of them houses like the whitefellas built?

In one of *those* houses, Mrs Standley might have corrected them. Did they stay in one of *those* houses?

'It was just like the time when they lived near each other and Nora used to come over every day to see Marjory.'

Like when they lived out bush with their families perhaps, before the policeman came and took Nora away.

But then the children of the Bungalow came to understand the way the white fellas worked their fiction. Nora and Marjory weren't real. It was made-up stories, a way of getting kids to learn. And look at things in certain ways.

As one of the girls who grew up in the Bungalow told her daughter much later, she learnt to read and write on a slate with chalk. After the older ones had learnt, they taught the younger ones.[91]

Did Ida move around between the desks, supervising her pupils as they diligently copied, or did she sit up the front and cast a watchful eye over her flock?

She'd brought up four children on her own while establishing other one-teacher schools in remote parts of South Australia. Her mother had died when she was three, her father when she was seventeen. Ida was in her mid-forties by now and would have subsisted on a fair amount of goat meat, bread and jam. I'm thinking she might have liked to do a fair bit of sitting.

Was she strict? Did she insist on silence? The children weren't allowed to speak in any language other than English, that's for sure. How did she get the kids to sit up straight, speak only in English and form their letters neatly?

'She was a very nice lady,' said Clarrie Smith, looking back.

'A woman and a half,' said old Mort Conway.

In January 1916, Ida Standley wrote to Chief Protector in Darwin:

> All children have essentially the same hearts, the same natures, but there must be marked differences between two sets of children, the one conscientiously nurtured from birth and the other drawn from haunts of poverty ignorance & vice. Give these nameless little ones a chance – which means remove them as far as possible from every trace of their old lives. It is truly remarkable what the children have accomplished in the way of sewing…they make and mend for 30 and their reading and writing is most creditable…the children have been most kind and obedient and my happiest hours in Alice Springs have been spent with them.[92]

In 1917, the schoolteacher again sent samples of pupils' work to the Chief Protector who forwarded them to the Minister in Melbourne:

> I am forwarding samples of schoolwork, the Bungalow Visitor's Book (please return) and a doyley worked by a coloured child. Everything connected with the school and Bungalow is going on most satisfactorily. With the exception of colds and two cases of weak eyes, the children have been most healthy. We are a very happy family.[93]

There are no samples of the children's work on file this time, nor the doyley. The entries in the visitor's book consistently sing the praises of Mrs Standley for her effort and achievements with the children:

> I was immensely pleased to see the great progress the Half + three quarter Caste children have made. Educationally their progress is remarkable and speaks volumes for the nurturing zeal and sympathy of their Instructoress, Mrs Standley.
>
> The children's dwelling very neat & clean & they appear very happy & contented & thoroughly appreciate Mrs Standley's sympathetic care for them.
>   J McKay 8/10/15 (page 3)

> Having visited the Bungalow almost daily, for the past four months, I have pleasure in expressing appreciation of the good work being done by the matron Mrs Standley. The children behave well & at all times keep the place in perfect order under Mrs Standley's supervision.
>
> I have seen their schoolwork & needlework and am astonished at the progress made.
>   Jean Finlayson, Nurse & Deaconess, Australian Inland Mission 5/12/15 (page 4)

> Have visited the 'Bungalow' Alice Springs by invitation from Mrs Standley, matron, and consider that the improvement made in half-caste children is a credit to Matron.
>   R A Purvis 15/1/16 (page 7)

> I spent a very pleasant afternoon at the 'Bungalow'. The children seemed happy & to fully appreciate the kind & loving care of the matron, Mrs Stanley.
>   Beatrice Fitzpatrick 17/1/1915 (page 9)

Spent a very pleasant hour with Mrs Standley & her little children at the Bungalow. Stuart Town. Both children & home beautifully neat & clean. Much praise & credit is due to her for her loving care of them.

F.B Ross 14/2/16 (page 15)

Having lived at Alice Springs for two or three years and seeing the little coloured children living with the natives in their camps before the initiation of the 'Bungalow' I must say that the children during only 18 months tuition & supervision under Mrs Standley have made wonderful success. One could scarcely credit that so marked an improvement could be made in so short a time.

V A Schrader 23/8/16 (page 23)

Of the forty or so entries in the book, there is just one that gives credit to the children themselves, from a federal Senator, in 1921.

I have visited the Bungalow and have also seen the children at school and consider Mrs Stanley is doing fine work under a very severe handicap. The progress made by the little half caste children at school is a credit to pupils & teacher. My sincere hope is that the site of the Bungalow will soon be shifted to more congenial surroundings and that Mrs Stanley will continue her work in an atmosphere that will help rather than hinder.

H.S. Foll, Federal Senator 14/6/21 (page 37)

For the 1916–17 Administrator's Report, Ida wrote,

At the Bungalow there are eight boys and twenty-two girls, comprising half, quarter and octoroon caste. Their ages ranging from three to fifteen years. The health of the children is exceptionally good. They are happy and contented. The school roll totals sixty – thirty-four white children and twenty-six coloured. The advanced coloured attend morning school with the white children, and the remainder of the coloured attend afternoon school. The annual examination report is good.[94]

To which Sergeant Stott added,

During the year 1916–17 the behavior and health (with the exception of an epidemic of eye trouble early in the year) of the natives throughout the district has been good.

The vegetable garden at the Bungalow has been successful. During the period January to June the value of the vegetables consumed amounted to 27 pounds. There is a noticeable reduction in the consumption of flour. The goats purchased during the year are thriving.[95]

Of Topsy there is no mention in anyone's report nor the visitors' book. In fact, Topsy rarely rates a mention in the archives at all, despite the pivotal role she played. Fortunately, she did make it into the photos and the oral history recordings of her children. We have family stories too, passed on down the line. From Christine Donnellan, Topsy's granddaughter:

> When she was with a white man she was all right. Once he died they were more or less forced into town. She was more or less forced to help raise all the other kids as well. She breast fed lots of kids and a couple of them can still remember that. They were brought in as babies. They was taken off their mothers… She had no choice … I think she just accepted that's what she had to do… Who would have helped her? She would have helped herself I suppose. She had all those other kids.[96]

And from the oral history transcript of Topsy's daughter Ada who grew up in the Bungalow:

> Yeah, well, by jeez she worked hard for us… [She] cooked for us, worked for us, do the sewing for us, dress us, look after us when we were sick. Everybody's kids. Brought one child in when the mother died about a fortnight old and fed her with her own breast, as well as her own little son. Anyone'd think she had twins.
>
> Gallateer trousers, she used to make…its black, [with] a little white stripe… There was trousers for the boys made out of that, and the shirts. And we used to wear the red turkey twill…
>
> Government supplied her with [a] sewing machine Singer sewing machine.
>
> When you go to old Milton Liddle's, he'll tell you all about [her]. He always said that (she raised him like a son).[97]

The Photos

This chapter features the names and images of people who have died. It contains images of First Nations people experiencing the crass inhumanity of colonisation.

The photos shed light on the era in question. They are stored in the archives, all meticulously catalogued and labelled. We pore over them, hoping for greater insights. But they are not neutral representations of the way things were. They were taken through a colonial lens by people who had an interest in representing things in certain ways. Imagine how different the photos might be if Topsy Smith had been pressing the shutter. Or the children of the Bungalow.

The subjects of these photos are the parents, grandparents, aunties, uncles and so on of people who are alive today. The photos can be distressing and they belong, ultimately, to the families who are the descendants of the subjects.

*

The Arrernte camp was about a mile from the centre of town, where the service station and hospital on Gap Road are today. In those days, it seemed well outside town boundaries. Photo taken between 1921 and 1926.[98]

Another view of the Arrernte Camp, 1921–1926.[99]

Women at the Arrernte camp, 1921–26.[100]

Above and below: Children at the Bungalow 1924. The man in the background, seemingly entering the Bungalow, is perhaps anthropologist Baldwin Spencer.[101] [102]

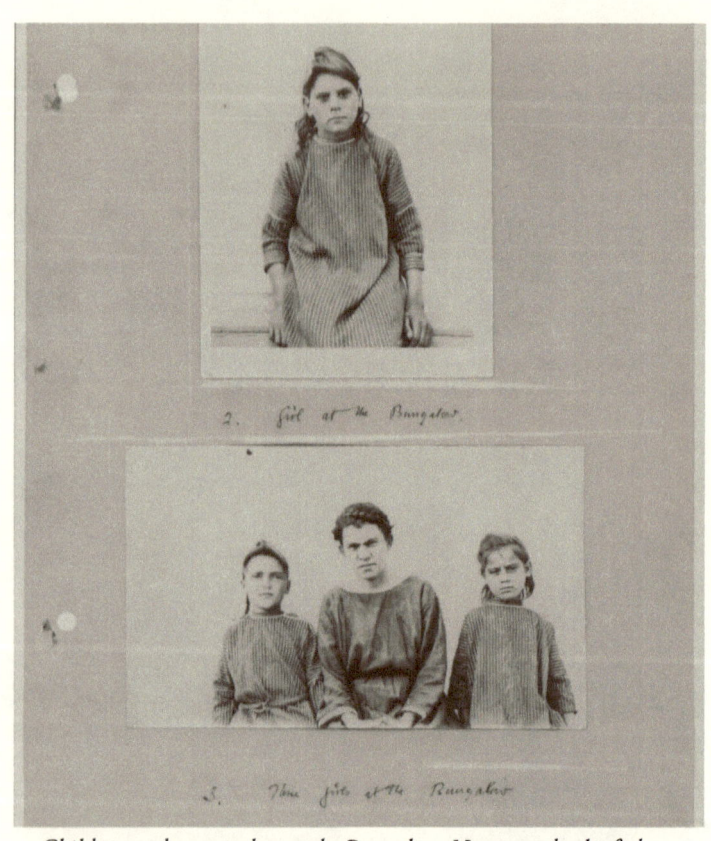

Children and one mother at the Bungalow. Names on back of photos from top and left: Jessie Reid; Ettie Turner; Edie Espie; Agnes Draper.[103]

Named on back of photo from top and left: April(?) Draper, Jessie Reid and Violet Hayes.[104]

*The girl in the top photo is not named.
She is said to be in service with Stott at the school.
The boy from the Bungalow is named as Norman Bray.*[105]

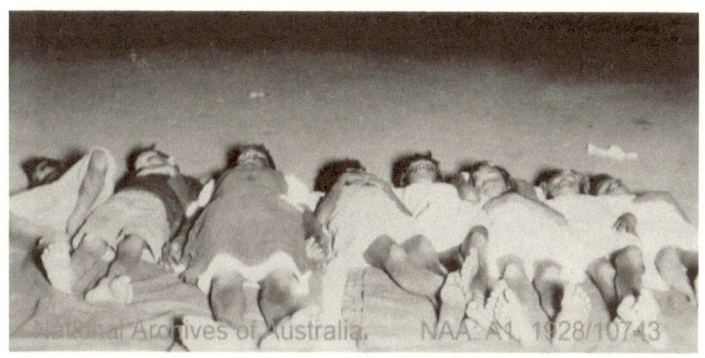

For the entire duration of the Bungalow in Alice Springs, the children slept on the ground outside with little in the way of bedding. Photograph taken at 10 p.m., 15 January 1928.[106]

Another flashlight view of sleeping arrangements at the Bungalow.[107]

At the Bungalow, 1928.[108]

At the Bungalow.[109]

Sergeant Stott on Trial

When an enquiry was held into Sergeant Stott's conduct in December 1917, the people of the district rallied in his defence. Sergeant Stott! He was the conductor of enquiries, the go-to man, the officer-in-charge.

Stott had thirty-four years of service as a Northern Territory police officer tucked under his belt by then. The last six of those had been in Alice Springs. Judge, jury and jailor, sub-protector of Aborigines, keeper of the Stuart town gaol for an extra ten pounds per year, clerk and bailiff of the local court for an extra fifteen, officiating registrar of marriages, first aid officer, administrator of summary justice, works manager, distributor of rations to the natives: there was little in the management of the town that Stott didn't take care of.[110]

Mounted Constable Kelly arrived to take up duties under Stott on 20 March 1917. He stayed until 1 August; under sufferance, it seems. On day two, at Stott's suggestion that he would be more comfortable once he'd brought his wife up, Kelly replied, 'I would not bring my wife into this country.'

It's hard to know if Kelly's discomfort eased during the months he managed to stay. Did he marvel at the exquisite wilderness he strode across, on camel and horseback, during his official patrols, hundreds of kilometres into the western district to see how they were going on the stations and the mission? Did he wonder at his unique position at the vanguard of Centralian frontier history? Did he have even an inkling that, in a century's time, we would stick our beaks into police journal entries made both by and about him and pour over his official correspondence; such as the letter he sent to Inspector Walters of Darwin dated 3 September 1917?

In that letter, Kelly told Walters,

I tried hard Sir, to stay at least 12 months because of the liability of refunding fares, but when I could get no prospect of transfer, I could only resign.[111]

Poor old Kelly; it seems that the Alice was not his pannikin of bush tea!

A summary of the charges made by Kelly against Sergeant Stott in his letter is as follows:

1. That Sergeant Stott is a bully and indulges in bullying the men under him.

2. That Sergeant Stott was under the influence of drink on the occasion when Kelly returned the papers to Plowman and habitually drinks.

3. That Sergeant Stott uses his men not for police work but as private servants.

4. That Sergeant Stott did not allow Kelly the use of the police horses.

5. That Sergeant Stott uses the police paddock for running his private stock to the detriment of the police horses.

6. That Sergeant Stott keeps prisoners in jail for the full term of their sentence for the sake of the 15/- a week allowed for their keep.

7. That Sergeant Stott does not allow the police buggy to be used in cases of emergency as was intended though he uses it for his own private use and on one such occasion claimed travelling allowance as on patrol.

8. That Sergeant Stott does not provide the blacks with rations allowed by the aboriginal Department but gives them to his private boys;

9. That Sergeant Stott ill-treats and bullies the sick blacks.

10. That Sergeant Stott ill-treats the half-castes in the Bungalow who work for him.

11. That Sergeant Stott never should have been given any authority either over whites or blacks.

12. That Sergeant Stott accepts bribes and does not do his duty by those who do not give him such bribes.[112]

Kelly's complaints led to an official enquiry that spanned several days in the lead-up to Christmas 1917, when the average daily temperature reached 36.7 degrees and not a drop of rain fell for the month.

Judge Bevan came from Darwin to conduct the hearings. He interviewed, as he wrote, 'nearly the whole of the residents of the district as they had all come in from the outlying country for the holiday'. He also received written statements from a few who couldn't be there and caught up with a few others in Oodnadatta and Melbourne.

It was a small and tight-knit community. People fell out and people had favourites, the way we do, but at the end of the day people stood by their own kind. As the Roving Reverend Plowman told the enquiry,

> I'm not surprised to hear the people in the district considered Stott a good man for the district. I know their psychology. They will shield a man in preference to putting him away.[113]

And from Henry Walkington, Justice of the Peace, who wrote in from Arltunga in relation to the trial:

> I have perused and find the charges without foundation... M.C. Kelly is a person unknown to me and appears to have lacked in not only police duty but the ordinary following of bush life.[114]

According to Stott, the allegations were malicious, unfounded, false statements.

The 'whole of the residents of the district', according to Bevan, were, of course, by and large, the white folk. Aboriginal people greatly outnumbered settlers in the Red Centre in the early 1900s but they didn't officially count. Nevertheless, a few Aboriginal folk were called to the stand. The witnesses included

James Baker, storekeeper, Alice Springs

Louis Alex Bloomfield, pastoralist, Blood Creek Station
Leonard Percival Brown, publican
Vivian Rose Brown, publican
William Coulthard, pastoralist, Tempe Downs Station
Dora, Domestic servant of the Stotts
Archibald Giles, pastoralist, Goss Range Station
Robert Henry Harris, pastoralist, Hamilton Downs
Johnnie, worker at Bond Springs station
Edward Henry Kunoth, pastoral manager and former policeman
Robert Harold Lake, pastoralist from Arltunga
Keith Frances McDonald, linesman on the Overland Telegraph line
John Mackay, Mounted Constable from Alice Well
Aaron Meyers, pastoralist, Red Bank Station
Samuel Nicker, pastoralist of Ryan's Well
Charles Noblet, Mounted Constable from Arltunga
Robert Plowman, travelling missionary from the Presbyterian Church
Edie Powell, Bungalow resident and domestic servant of the Stotts
Frederick Alfred Price, postmaster from the Alice Springs Telegraph Station
Fred Raggart[115] from Glen Helen Station
Jimmy Raka, Bungalow gardener
Bernard William Sherman, Mounted Constable, Alice Springs
Ida Standley, schoolteacher and matron of the Bungalow
Sergeant Stott
Carl Strehlow, Lutheran Missionary, Hermannsburg
Tracker Sam, Alice Springs police
Tracker Tom, Alice Springs police
Henry Walkington, Justice of the Peace
Kitty Williams, domestic servant for the Stotts
George Wilkinson, storekeeper Alice Springs

When the town was first laid out in 1888, lots 48 and 49, at the intersection of Hartley and Parsons Streets, had been set aside for governmental use. There, between 1907 and 1909, the new gaol and police compound were built.[116]

The police quarters consisted of a four-room stone cottage with passage, kitchen and bathroom. The walls were made of stone and the ceiling and roof of corrugated iron. Presumably that would have heated the place up spectacularly during the long days of summer in which the temperatures hover around forty degrees Celsius and laconicism becomes a survival strategy.

Building materials were sourced locally, except for the iron, standard roofing material of the day, that was brought strapped to camels. A back veranda, eight-feet wide, was enclosed with iron and divided into a kitchen and bathroom. The other three sides of the house were framed by a seven-foot wide veranda. A stone office, courtroom and gaol stood close to the house. In the yard, was a well of fresh water.

Presumably, the enquiry was held in the courtroom. Did witnesses place their right hand on the Bible? Was a Bible even present? God nary rates a mention in any of the documents that detail the proceedings. Were the sessions open to the public, offering some variety in a town where entertainment included biannual race meetings, singalongs at the hotel and watching the weather roll in? Stott was present at times, cross-examining the witnesses. Other than that, were the sessions *in camera*, with evidence being shared between Judge Bevan and each of the witnesses?

Accommodating Kelly

For Kelly's month in town, he boarded with Stott because, according to his version of events,

> Immediately upon arrival at Alice Sergeant Stott said that if I batched with him I would have to have meals at his place, and pay for them, compulsory, or I could board with him entirely, which I did for peace. I was told I must do either of these if I wished to keep my job.[117]

In response, Stott said that was 'almost too ridiculous for comment'. The sergeant's version of events, that contradicted Kelly's in many ways, was spelt out in his letter to the enquiry:

> March 23 last at 1 p.m. Constable Kelly arrived at Alice Springs for Oodnadatta per mail Camels, reported himself for duty, Kelly arrived almost in a state of collapse, he attributed his condition to Camel riding, Myself and wife left sorry for him, Arthur Neal ex Mailman, now at Undoolya Stn can confirm Kellys condition when he arrived at Alice Springs.
>
> Invited Kelly to have dinner with us, during the whole afternoon Kelly slept in a lounge under verandah.
>
> During same evening in conversation informed Kelly, that his place of residence was Heavitree Gap Police Station, but that on account of his indisposed condition, he could board with us for a few days until he felt stronger, that we had no spare room, in the meantime would have to share with two of my sons ages 10 and 12 years, otherwise could board at Hotel, Kelly said what do they charge at Hotel, informed him thought 30/- or 35/- per week (Hotel is situated about 200 yards from police station) Kelly replied if convenient prefer boarding with you. At this time our youngest child aged 3 years was blind suffering from eye trouble. About one week later child's eye became worse. Mrs. Stott's time was fully occupied nursing child, we were then making arrangements to send wife with child to Adelaide for Medical aid.
>
> Mrs. Stott wished to know whether Kelly intended going to Heavitree Gap Stn, that on account of sick child, she had no time to supervise cooking etc., Without Kelly, lubras could do our cooking for the time. I immediately spoke to Kelly, put Mrs. Stott's position before him Kelly left went to Heavitree Gap returned in the course of an hour. I said to Kelly what do you think of your quarters, once you get your wife up, you will be comfortable. Kelly replied, would not bring my wife into this country. Do you want me to go and live at the Gap, have never done any cooking. I said you can see how we are situated, a sick child, no spare accommodation, besides we have to depend on lubras to do cooking. Kelly replied I am quite satisfied to share room with boys, that Dohy (meaning the principal lubra in the kitchen) seemed a good capable girl, that he would not make much difference being in the house.

After further conversation with my wife, agreed to board Kelly, viz., Board and washing 20/- per week, whilst absent on patrol 1/- per diem for rations. Kelly said am quite satisfied.[118]

On Chains, Patrols and Rations

On 19 April, Kelly went on a patrol of the Western district along with Tracker Tom. Tom was an employee of the Alice Springs police, for which he received, as he told the enquiry, 'plenty tucker and clothes, and some money every month'. It was a nine-day round trip of 236 miles through some of the most majestic countryside on earth.

Such patrolling was standard police duty. The role was to visit key settlements, in this case the mission at Hermannsburg, as well as pastoral stations. As Stott later told the enquiry, of this patrol,

> Had any report been made to Kelly by Settlers of western district his duty whilst on patrol was to investigate any complaints made if possible secure arrest of offenders.[119]

In preparing for this expedition, Stott instructed Kelly to take two pairs of handcuffs as well as a neckchain 'so that he would be prepared to any case of emergency that may occur during patrol'.

Any case of emergency, particularly of the kind that warranted cuffs and chains, would most likely involve the original people of the area. Chances are it would also involve cross-cultural variations in interpretation of ownership of food and water resources. From the perspective of the original people, they were of the land, and operated according to strict rules that governed who had access to what. On the other hand, the perspective of the white men was that the land was theirs for the taking and the cattle they had bothered to drove all that way and were making such an indelible mark on the countryside, were exclusively theirs. The sooner the locals got with the program or buggered off the better.

> Those involved in killing thought that they faced a choice between the survival of their enterprise or the survival of the Aborigines.[120]

Doris Blackwell was a child in 1899 when her father accepted a posting as the postmaster of the telegraph station at Alice Springs. She travelled with her family by train, as was the way, from Adelaide to Oodnadatta, then the rest with horse and buggy. Many years later, in her memoir, Doris recollects, with a child's wisdom and honesty, a scene she witnessed in Oodnadatta:

> Chained to the post by their wrists were six or seven natives, who sat on the ground with their feet towards us. I have never forgotten the horror of seeing human beings thus chained, but worse still was the sight of their bleeding and swollen feet. They stare dumbly at us, perhaps aware that there was nothing we could do to alleviate their suffering. We were told that they had been caught spearing cattle on one of the big station properties in the Centre and were on their way to Port Augusta gaol to serve long prison sentences. A police trooper with two aboriginal trackers, all mounted, had brought the poor creatures from Alice Springs. The prisoners, chained together by their wrists, and at night by their ankles as well, had walked every step of more than three hundred miles to the railhead. In the years that followed I saw many natives in chains, but I was no less revolted on subsequent occasions that I was at Oodnadatta with this first glimpse of man's bestiality to man. The chaining of human beings, even to my young mind, seemed depraved and sadistic. Yet is was so commonplace that I cannot recall ever having seen aboriginal prisoners who were not in chains. Once or twice I saw men who had walked so far in lawful custody that they had no skin left on the soles of their feet.[121]

Doris's memories are reinforced by correspondence from the mounted constable and Protector of Aborigines at Illamurta police camp, south-west of Alice Springs, in January 1912 to the Minister for External Affairs in Melbourne:

> In July 1906 seven aborigines were arrested by me and sentenced to 6 months Pt Augusta gaol for cattle killing and in 1906 2 was arrested by me and sent to Pt Augusta for 6 months for cattle killing. Prior to this in the year 1899, 16 was sentenced to 6 months each and sent to Pt Augusta gaol. In 1902 4 aborigines was taken to Pt Augusta for cattle killing.

The within mentioned offenders has to be taken to Alice Springs to be tried, from thence to Oodnadatta a distance 330 miles. From there to Pt Augusta per train about 400 miles. Thus incurring a great expense to the government.[122]

By 1917, the extreme brutality of earlier days had, to some large extent, abated. The bullets and incarceration of earlier times had given way to the distribution of rations; a new form of social control that brought with it the added advantage of a casual labour force.[123]

The sorts of supplies given out as rations to the Indigenous people in the Illamurta district in 1912 can be seen in the list sent from the mounted constable to the Minister for External Affairs:

In Stott's first six years in Alice Springs, he charged and convicted eighteen individuals, in nine separate incidents, for cattle killing.[124] This was a huge reduction from earlier times, as Judge Bevan was told frequently at his enquiry, with statements such as from William Coulthard:

> The cattle killing by natives is now nothing like as frequent as it used to be.[125]

and Carl Strehlow:

> I have made no complaints to you since my return in 1912 of cattle killing as there have been no instances that we know of in that time. In former years the natives out west were a nuisance but they were dealt with by the police and of late years have been of little or no trouble.[126]

Mounted Constable Kelly and Tracker Tom rode back into town on 28 April 1917 at four p.m. and reported that all was quiet out west.

The Search for Henry Moyle

Mavis Stott, aged three, was suffering from an eye disease that required urgent attention in Adelaide. Her sight was in the balance. Sergeant Stott was preparing to take Mavis and her mum in the horse and buggy to Oodnadatta, when a report came in that Henry Moyle was missing. It was believed he had either gone insane or was suffering from delirium tremors in a camp near Burt Well.

Moyle was an 'excellent bushman' and big drinker who had recently passed through Alice, heading north. The other thing we know from the public record about Moyle is that he was 'a big man and ugly when drunk'. It's an unfortunate way to go down in history.

Stott directed Kelly to go with Tracker Tom and two camels and head out to search for Moyle. Stott would remain in Alice Springs to care for the one prisoner in gaol and keep the station open. He arranged for Huddlestone (no further details) to take Mrs Stott and her daughter to Oodnadatta.

Stott's instructions to Kelly were

If Moyle found insane arrest, if all right see that Moyle goes on, if suicided or dead examine body and bury. If left camp and gone with horses follow tracks for at least 10 miles, if tracks found to be making a straight North along Telegraph line Track and passed Burt Well need not follow, or if tracks making straight out in Easterly direction towards James Turner's camp Bald Hill) follow tracks for at least 10 miles, if tracks not deviating needless follow further.[127]

One of Kelly's complaints was about having to take the camels. He maintained that horses were faster and would have led to Moyle's rescue. Although not mentioned in his initial report about this journey, Kelly squeezed into the police journal later, in different ink, that the camels were lame and not good for riding.

In response, Stott explained that the camels had been at the station and ready to go. He immediately 'picked two of the best riding survey camels, to facilitate speedy travelling'. Tracker Tom put two (horse) pack saddlebags with food in front of his camel saddle. Kelly put a water canteen in front of his saddle. Had Kelly waited for the horses to be caught and brought up from the police paddock, they would not have got away until next morning, said Stott. As it was, he was on the road within an hour of the report coming in.

That there was anything lame about the camels used in the search was refuted by a number of witnesses. There were suggestions, though, that there was something lame about Kelly's approach to the search.

Tracker Tom, along with Johnnie from Bond Springs station, found Moyle. Johnnie told the enquiry, 'follow him up a little bit more and we been see him there. Him been lie down dead.' Johnnie went on to explain how he and Tom prepared the grave and laid the man to rest. 'Kelly no more been there… Tom and me been cover 'em up Moyle, nobody been tell us, we been do it ourselves.'

Private Use of the Police Paddock

The police paddock sprawled out across the flat land, bordered by the MacDonnell Ranges to the north and the Undoolya Range to the south. These days that same area hosts the sewage ponds, the BMX track, the showgrounds and the RSPCA animal shelter. It was two miles from the police station in town, five miles wide at the eastern end, three at the western end and five miles north to south. In 1917, it supported twenty-three police horses and two foals as well as Stott's own forty head of cattle and two horses. Stott had been keeping his own cattle in the police paddock since 1912 which, as he explained to Judge Bevan,

> I keep for domestic use as there is no butcher here, and all residents are dependent on their own stock for meat. I have only sold 9 head since I came here. I have at present about 40 head of cattle, and of these I shall require 8 for killers during next year, and these 8 are the only killers in the mob... In addition to the cattle I have two private horses in the police paddock. My goats approximately 500, and 50 sheep, are not kept in the police paddock and never have been kept there but are depastured on Hayes and Son's Block 1, with their knowledge and permission... At present there are five prisoners in the gaol in for six months, and my rate of killing will be during that period one goat a day or one bullock a fortnight. At present I am killing goats as the weather is too hot to kill a bullock.[128]

Kelly claimed it was unreasonable for Stott to keep his personal stock in the police paddock, to the detriment of the police stock. Stott testified that all animals were healthy. He had shown the arrangement to the administrator the last time he was in town and the administrator had made no comment.

'Keeping Black Boys, Keeping Goats'

As well as keeping their own stock for milk and meat, many of the settlers referred to 'keeping black boys'. George Wilkinson also kept goats which he killed for 'his black boys'. Wilkinson said it cost at least ten shillings per week to keep each boy and could be as high as fifteen. That would include tobacco and clothes.

Robert Harris came into Alice Springs every fortnight or three weeks, from the station at Hamilton Downs. As a rule, he got all the boys he wanted to help him on the station but at times he was 'stuck for a boy'. He didn't go into their camps, he said, but as far as the working boys were concerned, they lived quite decently. He said it was sometimes difficult to get a boy who understood the work.

Keith MacDonald considered the condition of the Aborigines to be very good. He could get them to work, never had one refuse and had always found them orderly and not given to petty thefts.

Sergeant Stott Good Fellow Boss All right[129]

In about 1915, Edie Powell was brought in from the bush to the Bungalow with her 'quadroon infant'. In Stott's opinion, she was a wilful young woman who needed to be disciplined at times. As he described it, he had,

> On various occasion given her a smack with my open hand on ear for her defiant misdeeds. As protector of aboriginals I may state that during the past two years Edie has given myself and Mrs. Standley considerable trouble on account of her immoral and defiant behaviour. About 3 years ago Edie with her quadroon infant was taken into the bungalow at Alice Springs. From enquires made, found Edie Powell was in the habit of waiting until all inmates in bungalow went to sleep, left her child asleep, went out and slept with men camped at Alice Springs... January 1916 a man named Briscoe was fined 5 pounds for inducing Edie to leave the bungalow. Soon after the prosecution of Briscoe Matron Standley and myself had a conversation about Edie. We both considered it advisable to expel Edie from the bungalow and to retain her child in the bungalow. I took Edie into my employment.[130]

One day when Ida Standley was outside the hotel, where she was living at the time, Edie Powell approached her and complained about having been kicked by Stott. Vivian Browne, Ida's daughter, was also present. (Vivian had been in Alice Springs since at least 1916. She married Leonard Percival Browne when he came to town in December 1916 and together they ran the Stuart Arms Hotel until 1921.) Edie was crying and lifted her dress to show the injury. Ida could see nothing, although Vivian saw a bruise.

'Oh dear, oh dear,' Ida remembered having said to Edie. 'Go back and be a good girl.'

Edie went away as advised and when Ida saw her a few days later she asked, 'Well, Edie, are you all right?'

Edie replied that she was and continued to work for Stott. The implication was that things can't have been that bad for Edie to go on working there. At the same time, her choices were extremely limited.

In her testimony, Edie explained,

> Sergeant Stott hit me with his hand on the face, and he kicked me twice. He hurt me. There was a bruise. I worked for Mr. Stott after he hit me. The night I went out with Briscoe the next day Sergeant Stott hit me and kicked me. I told Mrs. Standley and she said 'Why?' I said 'Because I go out with Briscoe.' She said 'oh, well, you shouldn't go out with Briscoe'... Mr Stott said 'If you don't come back to work for me, I'll send you to Darwin'. I didn't want to go to Darwin, and that's why I went back to Sergeant Stott. These were the only two times Stott treated me badly. He was a good boss except the two times he hit me.[131]

Several witnesses spoke of Stott's administration of health care and first aid. As Tracker Sam told it, 'plenty of blacks come up, get medicine, any time'.

Bill Liddell and his partner Mary were passing through Alice Springs. Mary (an Arrernte woman known as a 'half-caste') was with her youngest, aged three, in Wallis & Co.'s kitchen when the child pulled a billycan of boiling tea off the table and scalded her arm. Mary took the child to Stott where, in the presence of Constable Kelly, Matron Standley and Mrs Stott, the sergeant treated the child's arm with lime water and olive oil and dressed it. Next, as Stott explained to the enquiry, he told Mary off for 'talking to other lubras and neglecting her child'. That evening, Stott and Standley paid a visit to Liddell's camp to check up on the child, who was okay. The next morning at the Bungalow, Standley put a fresh dressing on the child's arm and gave Mary a bottle of lime water and some more oil. That afternoon, Liddell and Mary left Alice Springs en route to Hamilton Downs.

Tracker Tom vouched for the medical treatment Stott provided to the 'black fellows'. In addressing Stott, at the trial, Tom provided several examples:

> I been work for you soon as you come along this country. I get plenty tucker and clothes, and some money every month. I like work along police all right. I never been see you drunk.
>
> I remember that boy Mick when McNamara bring him up. Him been sore along leg. Him been come up, plenty time long Station, get medicine every day... I been see you give him paper. Him been take him along store and been get flour...
>
> I know half-caste Mary Liddell's lubra. I remember that time she been bring up little girl with burnt arm. You been tie 'em on rag...
>
> I know Donald. Him been break 'em leg, long well. You been tie 'em up along waddy. Him been sit down here, him been stop here long while. Him been get all right, walk about.
>
> I savvy Saddane's boy break 'em arm him bin come here. You been tie 'em up arm. I know plenty black fellow come up sometimes, get 'em medicine.[132]

Frederick Price told the enquiry he was a constant visitor to Stott's house and had always seen the half-castes treated with the greatest of kindness. On the whole, he said,

> The natives around the Alice were not ill-disciplined, the native camps around the Overland Telegraph Station were good and the camps at the Alice appeared to be all right[133]

Henry Wilkinson saw the 'natives' in and around the Alice as

> ...an orderly crowd. Most of the able-bodied natives apparently are employed. There are occasional instances of petty breaches of the law but on the whole the natives are a well behaved, well fed and well clothed crowd.[134]

Fred Raggart said he had never heard Sergeant Stott bullying his men nor ever heard any complaints from them. In his opinion, there had been an improvement in the conduct of the natives around the township.

Rations

On Saturday mornings, as Fred Raggart told it, the 'blacks' gathered around, waiting for 'the bell or whistle for the distribution of rations'. On the distribution of rations, Stott told the enquiry,

> On an average seventy to one hundred old and infirm aboriginals receive from 2½ to 3 lbs flour, ½ a stick of tobacco every Saturday morning. Jim Raka and his lubra, bungalow vegetable gardeners, receive 1 lb tea, 3 lbs sugar, 15 lbs flour, 4 sticks tobacco weekly. An aboriginal named George, nearly blind and his lubra, camp at the Gap Police Station. When no surface water in paddock, George and lubra keep troughs full at well for use of 23 police horses, 5 cow camels, 1 bull and 3 calves, property of Lands Dept…George and lubra receive weekly 16 lbs flour, ½ lb tea, 2 lbs sugar, government rations…I further beg to point out during May and June of this year I had 7 aboriginals and their lubras engaged repairing McDonald Range track, supplied them with aboriginal rations, clothing etc.[135]

Whitefellas gave out rations, blackfellas received them, thus bringing the two groups into close proximity. At the same time, little communication or mutual understanding was involved. Those giving the rations had their notions of what the rations were for and how they were to be received. The recipients had their own notions and went about their business as they saw fit, often to the frustration of the suppliers of the rations. Such intercultural variances in interpretation continue to confound.

An example of this intercultural variance in interpretation comes from Jim Baker's observation that

> You can never get a boy to do anything. They are too independent

to do any work. The old blacks who receive food from the station share it with the boys. They have been too well treated.[136]

What kind of a society was this in which grandfathers shared what they had with the young fellas?

Baker went on to lament that

This season is a good season for Aboriginal food. They get their stomachs full and are not inclined for work.[137]

The Alcohol Question

When Stott was at home by himself, he generally consumed two or three 'noblers' a day. With company he might have two or three more during the evening. Unless he had company, he said, he never touched it after dinner. It would be ridiculous to describe him as a bottle a day man, or a drunk as Kelly had done.

Many witnesses vouched for Stott's drinking behaviour. He imbibed in moderation, never went to the hotel and no one could ever recall having seen him drunk.

In Summing Up

Stott wasn't without his adversaries. Robert Plowman fell out with Stott over the removal of the Smith children from Arltunga, although later conceded it was for the best. In Plowman's estimation, however, Stott was

A bully, he is overbearing to most people. He is not courteous. He is tactless. My boy told me that he used to hit him.[138]

That's not bad coming from the roving reverend who told the enquiry that 'the way to treat the blacks is to thrash them if they need it'.[139]

Jim Baker, in reflecting on the way Stott had spoken to him during a recent falling out, reflected that 'he must think he was talking to blacks of the NT'.[140]

Staines considered natives in and around the Alice to be very ill-disciplined and their living conditions unsavoury. He believed that Kelly had been kept too much in Alice Springs and the outlying areas hadn't been patrolled as much as they should. Nevertheless, he considered Stott a friend and was 'indisposed to believe any ill of him'.

Aaron Meyers said Stott was 'too lenient with the blacks and half castes if anything. And that the general opinion in the district as to this report was that it was altogether wrong.' The vast majority of witnesses spoke firmly in Stott's defence. The general opinion of the district, according to Louis Bloomfield, was that Sergeant Stott was a good man, capable of his business. Bloomfield had never heard anyone speak otherwise.

Harry Walkington believed that the general public feeling regarding the charges was that they were a 'concocted lot of falsehoods'.[141]

Robert Harris had been the jail warden until April 1914 and resigned when all the prisoners were released. As far as he was concerned, 'there couldn't have been a better man in authority over whites and blacks', and the general opinion was that the charges were 'a tissue of lies'.[142]

Kunoth said that Stott was always ready to welcome people to his house for social reunions, sickness or otherwise and the people in the country come to him for anything and everything.

The Verdict

In his summing up, Justice Bevan declared,

> After hearing the evidence of the various witnesses and inspecting the files, documents and records I am of opinion that the charges as a whole are without foundation, and that Sergeant Stott is completely exonerated.[143]

Telegrams, congratulations and apologies ensued. And Kelly had to pay back the relocation allowance to which he would only have been entitled had he stayed at least twelve months.

Road gang probably working on Stuart Highway through hills north of Alice Springs.[144]

Removal

Eileen Briscoe

When Eileen was about nine years of age, in 1927, she was taken from her mother Kanaki at New Crown Station. About ten girls were removed at that time. They were taken by camel, over three hundred kilometres, through mountainous terrain, along dry sandy riverbeds, through rocky gullies and canyons and into Alice Springs. It took about six days. During the trip, two of the older girls escaped and progress was halted for about forty-eight hours. Eileen's uncle was a police tracker in the party and his wife Nada was the cook. Trackers were brought along specifically to capture any children who tried to escape. At the Bungalow, Eileen was given the surname Briscoe. It was supposedly the name of her father.[145]

Emily Liddle (née Perkins)

Emily Liddle was nine, in 1929, when police picked her up from New Well Station. Emily remembered them saying, 'These kids will have to go…to school. They're getting a bit too old, they wouldn't learn.'

Said Emily, looking back,

> We come by camel. When we left the station to come to Jay Creek, the old people that we had working on the station – the old goat shepherd and old Charlotte and old Ruby, and, oh, I think there was old Fanny there too, few of them that was in the camp – they just cried and cried [laughs].
>
> It upset us too. We was crying too then, and they were singing out:
>
> Goodbye! Goodbye! And I suppose we'll never see you again.

[Laughs] Because we'd been with them for so long, more or less grew up with them, really.[146]

Milton Liddle

Milton's father, Bill Liddle, was a white station worker, on Maryvale Station, just out of Alice Springs. Milton's mother, Mary Earwaaker, born in 1883, had an Arrernte mother and white father. Milton, born in 1913, was the second-born of Bill and Mary's four children. As he explained in 1981,

> A police officer went down there and told my father that he had to send all his kids into Alice Springs school, where there was an institution run by the Government for the purpose of part Aboriginal children, and so Dad bought us in there in 1916 – he bought us into school and left us in there, and we went to school there until we was the age of fourteen years.[147]

Maggie Plenty

Maggie spent the first five years of her life in the vicinity of the Plenty River, two hundred and fifty kilometres north of Alice Springs, with her young mum Ladie Lady and the mob. Maggie's people used to hide their kids out in the rocky hills. There was a ledge with space underneath. They could fit the kids in there and put shrubs in front when the white men came. One day when Maggie was about five years young, the system failed and Maggie was taken, away from Ladie Lady, away from the Plenty River and its fertile floodplains, away from the extended family who nurtured her.

Ladie Lady followed on foot as far as Arltunga. It was quite a walk. The policeman there stopped her and wouldn't let her go any further. Maggie didn't know that until much later in life. As a child, she always waited for her mum to come and visit her at the Bungalow, like some of the other mums did, but Ladie Lady never came.[148]

Solid Rock[149]

Solid rock
The mountain range
Strides across the desert floor
To the first people
Stone-age survivors
It's Yipirinya – sleeping caterpillar

Burnt orange rock against cobalt sky
Orange against blue
Settling in your heart
Over aeons

John Citizen records a man pissing through a shopping trolley
Coles carpark, broad daylight
And posts it on Facebook
No prizes for guessing the colour and creed
Of the pisser or the pissee

The ensuing conversation
Idiot opinions
Flapping in the breeze
of an ignorant online forum

The ranges give birth
to dry riverbeds
That snake across the land

Nestled in a valley
On the banks of the river
Someone spelt out God save the Queen
In bricks and mortar
Then watched
To see what happens

When Bush Survival meets Airs and Graces

They're sniffing Rexona
On Billygoat Hill
Akeyulerre – a sacred site
Bored black kids
High
On the hill

In my painting two *wurlkumanu* (old women)
On red and white striped couch
Drinking VB and fagging on
The desert they know and love
Knocking at the window
Two white-haired hags
Who've lived the good life in this place
I know those two old white-haired women
Me and my mate down the track

It doesn't rain much in these parts
But when it does
It pours
And the underground burrowing frogs come out

In my other painting
Women dig for honey ants
Sitting cross-legged
On broad red earth
Coolamons, nulla-nullas
Fat dirty babies crying for more
Then gurgling with joy when they get it
The whole scene is told through the iconography of the First People
And my memories

If you want to be struck
By beauty on a gargantuan scale,
Blue and orange juxtaposition
By ancient stone-age meets dot dot digital,
Quiet wisdom
And earth-shattering ignorance…
Try Alice Springs

In Their Place[150]

Unless immediate steps [are] taken to send them away, he warned 'eventually…we will have white women living as savages. Can anything be more appalling to our much-vaunted civilisation of the 20th century?'[151] (John McKay 1909, Postmaster and Special Magistrate at the Alice Springs Telegraph Station 1908 to 1916)

Vaunted or haunted? It depends which way you look at it.

In 1909, McKay proposed that 'half-caste' girls in the town camp, up to the age of seven, should be taken out and sent to Adelaide, to a 'good institution where they could be trained for domestic service'. He said they were 'very docile and teachable'. In this way, McKay pointed out, the children might be 'protected' and at the same 'the great demand for domestic servants could be alleviated'.[152]

Up to the age of seven, McKay said. At that stage. Perhaps at first, he thought those older than seven were beyond repair. Whatever he thought, it took a few more years before the much-vaunteds started sending the Bungalow children away, and by then they had decided on the older ones.

In 1916, when John and Ida McKay packed up their Central Australian experience, loaded it onto camels and headed back to Adelaide, they took with them Topsy Smith's eldest daughter Maud, and Topsy Fitz, two of the older girls growing up in the Bungalow. They were the first girls to leave Alice Springs under such an arrangement. The McKays had signed three-year contracts for the services of those girls with Stott, who was taking over from McKay as Regional Protector of Aborigines. This made Stott, under the terms of the Aborigines Act of 1910, the legal guardian of every Aboriginal and every half-caste child in the district.

Down in Adelaide, this got the ball rolling.

I want one of them, McKays' peers seemed to say.

Stott started sending more girls who had reached the age of thirteen or fourteen, to meet the demands of southern settlers.

In those days, Alice to Adelaide involved a slow and lengthy journey down the Track, from the Centre to Oodnadatta, then three days on the train to the city. Stott seems to have organised lifts for the girls with whoever happened to be going that way, in an era that firmly predated Working With Children checks. In 1925, having had several years to reflect upon a system she helped establish, Ida McKay reported she had been told of one girl who had recently arrived in Adelaide, Julia C, who had been sent from Alice Springs to Oodnadatta with three men in a car. The journey took five days, which was an unnecessarily long time. Julia's older sister had been sent four or five years earlier by camel in the charge of 'a white man' and that journey took some weeks. 'This girl's conduct does not appear to be satisfactory,' McKay pondered. 'Can you wonder at it?'[153]

By 1927, Ida McKay was opposed to the removal of Central Australian young women to Adelaide altogether. By then, in her experience,

> All her life a half-caste girl bears that brand of a despised race. The finer she is, and the more fitted for life among white people, the more she will feel it. Octoroon girls, who are practically white and highly thought of by the people who know them, cannot walk along the street without being hailed as 'Nigger'!' by larrikins. People often say that whatever you do for half-castes they go back to the life of the camp. Do people realise why? It is to get away from insults like these.[154]

At that same time, Mrs McKay observed that

> Native people, by the way, have the utmost contempt for white people. They think that as a race we are dishonest. Many white people will promise a native anything with no idea of keeping the promise.[155]

Once in Adelaide, there are accounts of the girls being...

Overworked

I have been here since 1916... I have not had a weeks holiday it has been nothing but work from one week to another (Topsy Fitz, 1927, aged 25).[156]

Abused

She hits me with saucepans and anything she gets hold of...the little boy always hits us three girls...and calls us black and Beast and blames us for every things if he does wrong. And she never lets us go out a tall... We all wish we wasent hear. I rather go back than stay down hear they all call us blacks in this house and we sleep on the floor (Mavis M, aged 14, 1928).[157]

Isolated

One 16-year-old was not allowed out alone, even to go to church. Her complaint that she was not permitted to see her 'Half-caste' girls friends was dismissed on the grounds that they were 'rather undesirable' for her to mix with.[158]

In his investigation into 'the Half Castes and Aboriginals of the Southern Division of the Northern Territory' in 1923, Baldwin Spencer noted that

> At the present day a certain number of the girls are sent down to Adelaide to domestic service in private houses. Though these, thanks to the Protector, Sergeant Stott, are carefully selected, the advisability of this system is open to grave doubt. The girls are isolated, they have no friends on their own footing and, with their peculiar natures, may be very easily led astray and ruined.[159]

In 1922, seven girls were living as indentured labour in Adelaide. In November 1924, there were ten. By 1925, another eight had been sent.[160] As Stott told a government meeting in Melbourne in January 1925, he had 'no difficulty in placing eight or twelve each year', and was, at that time, 'considering over a dozen applications for girls'. Stott also told the meeting that 'the children…had done very well and would not have been placed without the institution', and that largely the requests came 'from people who have seen the half castes in southern homes and approach the Commissioner of Police in Adelaide with a view to getting one'.[161]

Under the terms of agreements, made between Stott and the employers, the workers were paid five shillings a week, three of which was sent to Stott and banked on their behalf. To access their accounts, the workers needed permission from Stott or the Chief Protector of Aborigines in Darwin. The employer was to provide food, clothes, bedclothes, medical attention and proper accommodation. The agreement could be cancelled by the government should the employer be found to be an unfit person or to have failed to comply with the Act. The employer could cancel the agreement by giving the worker two weeks' notice.

Who was looking over the employers' shoulders, to find them unfit or otherwise? To ensure that they were complying with the terms of the agreement? To look after the interests of the children?

Stott had a contact in Adelaide, Mr Dudley Kelsey, whom he had known for forty years. Kelsey, born in Darwin, had worked in the Postal Department for many years. In a letter to the Chief Protector in Darwin in November 1924, Stott explained that Mr Kelsey had had

> a half caste girl named Maude Hantkin in his employ for the past four and a half years. He takes great interest in the welfare of these girls. On several occasions whenever a complaint has been made, by either Employer, or Employee, have appealed to Mr. Kelsey to investigate trouble. Whenever he found employer at fault, on my approval he Mr. Kelsey has replaced Girls in new homes.
>
> Girls now look on Mr. Kelsey as their friend, whenever they are dissatisfied, they appeal to Mr. Kelsey who voluntarily investigates and advises me result.[162]

Stott enclosed his most recent correspondence from Kelsey and recommended that he be engaged, in an honorary capacity, to 'look after these unfortunate Girls interests and see whether they are being properly cared for etc'.[163] The correspondence from Kelsey follows:

Dear Mr Stott

Re: Tiny

On receipt of your first wire, I interviewed Mr. Bauer and then looked round for a new home for the girl. Wishing to have her close by me so that I could see what was wrong with her, I held off placing her until I could get some one near us. I have now got a place nearly opposite our home with Mr. and Mrs. Gill. They are nice people, and will take an interest in Tiny (if only she behaves herself). So far she is proving all right, but at the start she tried to play up, and I told her that if I took her away from there, she would have to go to the Reformatory for bad girls and that the police would call and take her away in the police van, and told her what a hard place it was. This has had a good effect on her, and she has been much brighter since. Maudie said it scared the life out of her. She seems a nice little girl and I feel pretty sure that if she behaves herself, she will have a very good home with the Gills, and will grow to like them...

AMY COLLEY (with Mrs. Statton) This girl called on me last Sunday and wants me to write you 'that she wants to leave her present place', From what she says, she is not properly treated there and kept down too much. I merely mention this to you for your advice, and if you think it necessary, I could go and see Mrs. Statton and find out what the trouble is; or as you direct. I like to see the Girls contentedly fixed. Katie Kill, I hear, is pretty cheeky to Mrs. Just, but I fancy that is owing to their own fault allowing her to do so. Mrs. Sims is very pleased with Tessa and Tessa likes her home. Maudie is the Mother of them all, and gets onto them like a big dog. We have had Tiney sleeping in Maudie's room since she came from Bauers so that we can direct her, and Maudie talks to her pretty straight...

Yours faithfully,
D.E. Kelsey.[164]

In December 1924, Kelsey was appointed by the Chief Protector of Aborigines in the Northern Territory as his nominee, 'to safeguard the interests of Halfcastes that have been sent to South Australia from Alice Springs'. Kelsey was asked to communicate with Stott from time to time and Stott would keep the Chief Protector informed.

In accepting his new honorary position, Kelsey told the Chief Protector in Darwin,

> The need for an authorised person to watch and safeguard the interests of the Halfcastes that have been sent to this State from Central Australia, has long been felt.
>
> The average Employer of the Aboriginal, knows nothing of the nature of these people, and thereby often loses control over them, followed by discontent and trouble. I have had one or two cases of this kind lately, and after placing the Girls with suitable Employers, they become contented and happy.
>
> You can rest assured that (after my many years association with the Aboriginal) I will do my utmost for the welfare of these people.[165]

In all the excitement, Kelsey also wrote to the Minister for Home and Territories announcing his appointment and seeking clarification on points related to the execution of his duties. This was, perhaps, a tactical error. The federal government declared, in May 1925, that Northern Territory officials (such as Stott and the Chief Protector in Darwin) had no business to be making appointments outside of the Territory. Aboriginal people from the Territory who were now living in South Australia came under the jurisdiction of the South Australian Aborigines Act of 1910 and would therefore be overseen by the Chief Protector of Aborigines for South Australia.

Kelsey's appointment was discontinued and the nomination of a suitable person to oversee the wellbeing of these vulnerable children and young women, isolated and so far from home, was left in the hands of South Australian officials. They kicked around and deliberated, for the next eighteen months or so, on issues such as whether the South Australian government should be reimbursed at five or ten pounds per worker per year for the cost of the visits; whether Stott had overstepped the mark by writing directly to the Secretary for Home and Territories instead of going through the Chief Protector in Darwin and, if an 'Official Visitor' was to be appointed, whether it mightn't be more efficient for her to just attend to the girls in the metropolitan area and get the police to look in on those in rural areas.

After all, those country cops were bound to be ideal advocates for these girls from Central Australia who occupied a rung fairly well down the South Australian social ladder.

One of the points of deliberation between the Centre, the South and the Commonwealth was who was responsible for any of the girls who fell pregnant. Some of them did fall pregnant and you probably won't be surprised to know that the fathers generally went unknown. In 1927, there were seven such girls who had returned to the Bungalow in Alice Springs with their babies. In 1927, the Prime Minister sent the following request to the Premier of South Australia:

> Dear Sir
>
> I desire to inform you that my colleague, the Minister for Home and Territories, has been advised that from time to time half-caste girls from Central Australia, who have been sent to service in South Australia under agreement with South Australian employers, return, when in trouble, to the Half-caste home at Alice Springs, and that there are at present a number of such girls at the home with children whose fathers are residents of South Australia.
>
> It has been suggested that the responsibility for the care of the children of these girls is one which might reasonably be assumed by your Government and that arrangements should be made for them to be admitted into some Institution in your State instead of being returned to Central Australia.
>
> There are also at the Home at Alice Springs a number of quadroons and octaroons under five years of age who could hardly be distinguished from ordinary white children. My colleague is assured that, if these babies were removed, at their present early age, from their present environment to homes in South Australia, they would not know in later life that they had aboriginal blood and

would probably become absorbed into the white population and become useful citizens.[166]

The South Australian Premier was having none of this. Bearing in mind that these documents reveal far more about the person doing the talking than those being talked about, the Premier's reply, even for the standards of the day, is particularly repugnant. The gist of his response was that there was no suitable home in Adelaide for the reception of young 'quadroon and octaroon' children although he didn't call them young 'quadroon and octaroon children'. He called them 'quadroons and octaroons' as if they were something you could bake. Not as if they were people at all. He said accommodating the like would be 'greatly to the disadvantage of South Australia, as it would be increasing an undesirable element in the population'. Experience had shown the South Australians that mixed marriages were often not a success, particularly because people with Aboriginal blood tended to 'mate with the lowest class of whites and, in many cases the girls become prostitutes'.[167]

Marriage breakdown? Prostitution? Lowest class? These assertions of the Premier read just like the predictable baseless prejudice and stereotyping that have been trotted out by his kind since the advent of colonialisation that, if repeated often enough, take on a life of their own.

In January 1927, Mrs Alberta Owen was appointed 'Protector of Aborigines for the Central Aborigines District (Adelaide), to act as Official Visitor and Inspector of half-caste children from the Northern Territory in situations in Adelaide and neighbourhood'. Each girl was to receive one visit per year.

Katie Hill received her official visit from Mrs Owen sometime between January and April 1927.

Let's play fly on the wall at that event…

'Hello, Katie, I am Mrs Owen.'

'Hello, Mrs Owen, I am very pleased to meet you,' Katie replied, the way Mrs Standley had taught her to do all those years back. Mrs Standley. The Bungalow. It seemed like such a long time ago and so very far away. Katie wiped her hands down the front of her apron: to dry them even though they were dry and to straighten her clothing. She had been so looking forward to this visit. Then she held out her hand for a polite touching of the fingers.

'Pleased to meet you too, dear,' Mrs Owen laughed. 'Please take a seat.'

Katie sat as indicated on one of the chairs she cleaned and plumped daily.

Mrs Owen settled back into another. Her eyes settled on Katie, who was looking down and to the side. 'This is a lovely room isn't it, Katie?'

'The sitting room, yes, ma'am. It's my favourite.'

'A lovely room in a fine house. Are you happy here, Katie?'

Katie nodded.

'Is everything going all right? Is there anything you would like to talk to me about?'

Katie summoned up her courage. It was now or not for another year or more. She tried eye contact the way she knew you were meant to. 'I would like to ask for my freedom,' she announced. It was the way she'd been practising in her bedroom, in the bathroom, inside her head and out loud at any chance, since she had first been told of Mrs Owen's visit. She had felt so strong and positive about it but now the words trickled out and fell away.

'I see,' replied Mrs Owen. 'I am afraid that is beyond my authority. You will have to take that up with Sergeant Stott but…very busy man…best interests at heart…ungrateful.'

Katie shut down and steeled herself, the way she had taught herself to do.

'But everything's all right here? The work? Your living conditions?'

Katie nodded, standing. 'Thank you for coming, Mrs Owen,' she said plainly, and excused herself from the room.

Mrs Owen made some notes in her official report book, which she then slid back into her bag.

> KH. A rather pleasant girl, polite and well-mannered. The Justs are quite pleased with her, although find her sullen at times. Can find no fault with her living and working conditions. Made a meek request for her freedom. Informed her she would have to go through Stott.

No, you're right. We don't know if that's how it went. Perhaps they went outside to smell the roses. Perhaps they had a longer and more meaningful discussion than indicated. Perhaps Mrs Owen did give Katie some ideas about how to approach Stott with her request and where she stood legally. What we do know, from documentation of the time, is that Mrs Owen's visits, one per year to each worker, were brief; during her first visits, three of the older girls, including Katie H, asked for their freedom but Mrs Owen had absolutely no authority to act; and the reports she wrote about each visit were 'perfunctory and uniformly positive'.[168]

On 13 April 1927, the Chief Protector of Aboriginals in Adelaide sent the following in a memo to Sergeant Stott:

> Dear Sir
>
> You will be interested to hear that the lady I appointed as visitor to inspect girls from Alice Springs in Adelaide and neighbourhood has completed her visits and with general satisfactory results.
>
> Two of the girls, Katie Hill with Mr William Just and Topsy Fitz with Mr. W.E. Sims are asking that they should now be at liberty as they are over 18 years of age and this is the age limit according to your act. Evidently someone has given them this information. What procedure have you followed in the past in such cases and what answer shall I give to these girls?[169]

This request would have come as no surprise to Stott. For two months, he had sat on letters from Topsy Fitz (aged over twenty-one) and Eileen Cooper (aged over eighteen) in which they asked for their rights and their freedom. Someone had told them about their rights. Perhaps it was Mrs Owen. The letters certainly had some characteristics in common. They read as follows:

> February 22nd, 1927
>
> Dear Mr Stott
>
> Just a few lines to let me have my bank book as I am old enough to be on my own. As you know I have been working for Mr W E Sims for 3 years this month. I feel now I would rather

work for higher wages & keep myself in clothes & things. I am just fed up with working for almost nothing…I don't think that it is a fair thing to keep us girls working hard like this for paltry 3s. a week when we are old enough to earn more. We have to work such long hours. It is quite all right when we are young & first came down here and we know nothing all. I don't ever want to go back up to Alice Springs to live because that life would not suit me after been down here all these years. I have been down here since 1916. I don't think myself a child any longer & I don't think that it is fair to treat me like one all the time. I have been down here I have not had a weeks holiday. It has been nothing but work from one week to another. I don't want you to think that I am ungrateful for writing to you like this, because I am very grateful indeed to you for sending me down here & giving me a chance to be decent & learn to be a useful woman instead of living up there & be useless & good for nothing & ignorant. Mr & Mrs Sims & all the boys are very kind to me but for all that I don't want to work for such a little bit. All that I do in this place is worth more than that. I have to wash, iron, clean the house & cook & do everything that is done on the place. I don't mind work Mr Stott & I do all that I am asked to do willingly. I hope that you will consider this & let me know as soon as possible.

I am anxious to know. Please kindly remember me to Mrs Stott.

I remain yours sincerely
Topsy Fitz.[170]

8/2/27

Dear Mr Stott

I thought that I'll write and ask you if I could get my freedom from being under the Government. It is seven years since I left school & I must be 21 years of age now. I'm quite capable to look after myself. Ive lived a different life to some of these other girls & done my best in every way. And I'm a member of St Andrews Presbyterian church & I'm also a member of the Young Women's Bible Class. And I go to church every Sunday. And of course Mrs & Mr Nicolson could tell you too. And if you like a testimonial from my Minister Mr Shannon I will send it on when you want it also one from the Sunday School teacher. And another is this that I know how to be careful with my money. Mrs Russock has taught me to be careful. And I want to get on in this world by looking after my own affairs. And another thing I must say is this. I am not dissatisfied or unhappy, but I feel that I ought to have freedom. Of course I've got a good home here at Mr & Mrs Russocks they are very good & kind to me & likes to see me happy & mix up with other nice girls from the Bible Class. And I love going to it. I see in the paper that you are having a lot of rain up there at Alice Springs. I suppose every thing will be nice & green soon. Hoping to hear from you soon as possible.

I remain
Yours Truly
Eileen Cooper[171]

Topsy Fitz, Katie Hill and Eileen Cooper were all now asking, clearly and politely, to be liberated from the provisions of the Aboriginal legislation. As Aboriginal people, living in South Australia, it was the South Australian Aborigines Act of 1910 that applied to them. According to that Act, these young women were entitled to their bank books and their freedom. In a lengthy memo from the Home and Territories Department, in which the finer points of the law relating to this case were thrashed out, it was recommended the three 'girls' in question 'be given their liberty'.[172] This was presumably not because it was the right and decent thing to do but because

> if they develop on rebellious lines, it would be in practice be impossible to control them at their present age.

The Chief Protector in South Australia broke the good news to each of them. Just so they didn't get too far ahead of themselves, he also added that he would be keeping their bank books in his office and if they wanted to operate their accounts, they would have to come and see him.

The thing was, if Stott's opinion in 1926 was anything to go by,

> Half-caste girls are practically minus sense of care with money,

would be likely to squander their savings, hence would be likely to become poorly clad.[173]

However, according to Stott,

> This does not in any manner apply to the Male Half-caste the majority of them are quite capable to fight life's battle at the age of 21 years.[174]

It's a pity he didn't apply that logic in his dealings with Mort Conway. Conway was one of the earliest Bungalow kids. Since the age of fourteen, he had been hired out to the cattle baron Sidney Kidman. By 1923, at the age of twenty-two, Conway was working at Mundowna Station in South Australia.

It was from there that he made several attempts to gain control of his own passbook and be released from Stott's guardianship. Kidman's general manager had reported to Commonwealth government officials that Conway was a good worker but inclined to be a 'flash spendthrift'. It's hard to imagine how, with such limited access to money and a savings of over two hundred and twenty-six pounds.[175] After several months of waiting, Conway wrote again to Stott:

> You know that I am in a civilised State. I like my rights as well as anyone else, so if you don't give me a satisfactory answer before the end of this year I am leaving. The way you people have treated me is ridiculous.[176]

With Commonwealth prompting, Stott conceded, but not without one final swipe:

> Ever since you left the Bungalow, have always impressed on you the advantage you may gain in years to come to be careful and save your earnings, during the past 18 months my action does not seem to have been appreciated by you. Have therefore decided to post your Bank book direct to you.[177]

If only Mort had flattered Stott a bit, the way Topsy and Eileen had done. Or maybe, at the end of his tether, he had given up being polite.

Stott continued his ranting with the Department of Home and Territories:

> My experience when Half Castes reach the age of Maturity they usually become very selfish, minus any sense of gratitude or gratefulness... [They] seem to become wasteful commence drawing on their Banking Account, don't seem to give the same satisfaction to Employer, hence some of them now find it difficult to procure employment.[178]

Mort Conway went on to work for Sidney Kidman for many more years, becoming one of his legendary drovers. He then lived in Alice Springs and held a variety of positions, including taxi driver, butcher and custodian of the Mparntwe (Alice Springs) region. There is no further information on his 'flashy spendthrift ways'.

In early 1925, Stott told the conference in Melbourne that the hiring out of girls as domestic servants did not 'solve the problem'. He said that while the problem of the boys was nothing, the future of the girls had to be considered. He wanted to encourage the boys to marry the girls. To that end, he advocated that blocks in town be made available for 'half castes' who should be 'encouraged in their holdings'. The hiring out nevertheless continued until 1929. By then, there were said to be no more suitable girls available for service. By 1939, none of the twenty-four who had been working under agreement in South Australia in 1926 was still under the control of South Australian authorities. Most had turned twenty-one, secured their release and made their own way. Some negotiated much better wages. Some chose to stay with their original employers. Some married. Some, like Topsy's daughter Jean, had babies and returned to Alice Springs.

No blocks in town were ever made available.

Stott's inventory of children from Central Australia who had been hired out in South Australia. 28 October 1926.[179]

> 51 Hughes St
> North Unley
> 3/2/27
>
> Dear Mr Stott
> I thought that I'll write and ask you if I could get my freedom from being under the Goverment. It is seven years since I left School, & I must be 21 years of age now. I'm quite capable to look after myself. I've lived a different life to some of these other girls & done my best in every way. And I'm a member of St Andrews Presbyterian church & I'm also a member of the Young Womens Bible Class. And I go to church every Sunday. And of course Mrs & Mr Nicolson could tell you too. And if you like a testimonial from my Minister Mr Shannon I will send it on when you want it also one from the Sunday School teacher And another is this that I know how to be carlful with my money

Above and page 137: Letter from Eileen Cooper.[180]

2

Mrs Russack has taught me to be careful. And I want to get on in this world by looking after my own affairs. And another thing I must say is this I'm not dissatisfied or unhappy, but I feel that I ought to have freedom. Of course If I've got a good home here at Mr & Mrs Russack they a very good & kind to me. & likes to see me happy & mix up with other nice girls from the Bible Class. And I love going to it. I see in the paper that you are having a lot of rain up there at Alice Springs. I suppose every thing will be nice & green soon. Hoping to hear from you soon as possible

I remain
Yours Truly
Eileen Cooper.

> February 22nd 134 Park Terrace
> 1927 Maryville
> west
>
> Dear Mr Stott,
> Just a few lines to ask you to let me have my bank book as I am old enough to be on my own. As you know I have been working for for Mr W. E. Sim for 3 years this month. I feel now that I would rather work for higher wages & keep myself in clothes & things. I am just fed up with working for almost nothing. I think that I have been in the city long enough to know everything. I don't think that it is a fair thing to keep us girls working hard like this for paltry 3/- a week when we are old enough to earn more. We have to work such long hours

Above and pages 139–140: Letter from John Fry.[181]

3. It is quite alright when we are young & first come down here & we know nothing at all I dont ever want to go back up to Alice Springs to live because that life would not suit me after been down here all these years. I have been down here since 1946. I dont think of myself a child any longer & I dont think that it is fair to treat me like one all the time I have been down here I have not had a weeks holiday it has been nothing but work from one week to another. I dont want you to think that I am ungrateful for writing to you like this.

(2)

because am avery grateful indeed to you for sending me down here & giving me a chance to be decent & learn to be a useful woman instead of living up there & be useless & good for nothing & ignorrent. Mr & Mrs Sims & all the boys are very kind to me, but for all that I don't want to work for such a little bit. all that I do in this place is worth more then that. I have to wash iron clean the house & cook & do evrything that is done on the place. I dont mind working Mr Stott & I do all that I am asked to do willingly. I hope that you will consider this & let me know as soon as possible

I am anxxcous to know, please Kindly remember me to Mrs Stott
I remain yours Sincerly
Topsy Fitz

Sarah Breaden
'a refined and splendid kind of girl'

I come across a digital file titled 'Sarah Breaden (Half Caste) Education 1925–1928' on the website of the National Archives. It's an unexpected discovery and piques my interest. Perhaps it is relevant to my study, another piece in the puzzle. I click it open and come face to face with page after photocopied page of the intimate details of someone else's affairs, beginning with the pages of her bank book.

I tell my sister about it during one of our Friday evening catch-ups. 'Her bank book!' she exclaims, showing immediate recognition of the inherent violation. 'How come they copied the details of her bank book?'

My sister is a bookkeeper; she takes care with people's finances. Her indignation is spot on. What she's overlooking is the transgression of Australia's history; the intervention into Sarah Breaden's life owing to the circumstances of her birthright. When I point that out to my sister, she gets it. We all do, don't we?

It feels invasive, this act of peering uninvited into someone else's financial affairs. But that is what they did back then to Sarah and all her coequals: children born of Aboriginal mothers and white fathers in Central Australia in the early decades of the twentieth century.

On the inside cover of the bank book, in the simple type print of bluish-purple hue that was standard for the day, we read,

Address
Sarah Breaden
c/o Robert Stott
Alice Springs

On 10 March 1922, the first deposit of three pounds, five shillings was made; handwritten on the left with a big round ink stamp on the right declaring Alice Springs. In May another three pounds, five was deposited. In July, tenpence interest was added. Thereafter, every two or three months, a further three pounds five; then three pounds five and six was added, in Alice Springs, which had increased, by the last entry in December 1925, to three pounds six.[182]

Sarah Breaden's bank book.[183]

Remember the old passbook? You handed it to the teller along with the deposit slip and the cash or cheque to be banked.

'Thank you, Miss Breaden. How are you today?' the store proprietor who was also responsible for this outpost bank branch might have enquired as she opened the book, checked the amount tendered against the deposit slip and prepared to proceed with the transaction.

'Fine thanks, Mrs Jones,' Sarah might have replied, because in those days in that town everybody knew everyone. *'It's warming up outside.'*

'How's your father?'

'Well, thanks. He's just gone back to Henbury after a spell in town. How's young Arthur?'

'He's right. Growing up wild and free. We'll be sending him away to boarding school soon.'

As pleasantries were exchanged, the teller would have completed the transaction, thumped Sarah's book with a stamp and passed it back. Such are my memories of passbook transactions.

But we mustn't jump too quickly to conclusions. Just because the stamps from 1922 to 1925 say Alice Springs doesn't mean that's where Sarah was. Just because the bank book belonged to Sarah Breaden doesn't mean she presented it with her capable hands to the teller and managed her own affairs, not in those years at least. In fact, the idea of a person of such dual heritage presenting at the bank and managing their own financial affairs was ridiculous.

In Sarah Breaden's file, photocopied pages of the bank book are followed by letters, telegrams and handwritten memoranda, a hundred and five pages in all, of correspondence between the people who had the most direct control over Sarah's life between 1922 and 1928. They include Sergeant Robert Stott, the Protector of Aborigines for Central Australia; various secretaries for the federal Minister for the Department of Home & Territories; the Government Resident of Alice Springs; Mrs Jean Crittenden of 'Mons', 808 Nicholson Street, Fitzroy, Melbourne; and Mr W.J. Aldus, college tutor and 'Specialist in the Individual Tuition of Backward Children and Adults'.

Many of the official letters and memos in the file bear the heading 'Sarah Breaden – halfcaste'. Stott's letters directly to Mrs Crittenden make no such categorisation and nor do Jean Crittenden's polite, handwritten communications of advocacy to any of those men.

Sarah Breaden, I learn from the documents, was born at Henbury Station, Central Australia in 1907.[184] This was a cattle and horse breeding station, about a hundred miles south of Alice Springs on Pertame or Southern Arrernte country.[185] Sarah's mother was a local First Nations woman and her father a white station worker, Allan Breaden. Sarah, who I assumed would have lived at the Bungalow at some stage as a child, was sent, 'under an arrangement', to live with Mrs Crittenden in October 1921. Mrs Crittenden had five children of her own, of which the eldest in 1921 was thirteen years, around the same age as Sarah. The agreement was made and entered into on 25 August 1921 'between Robert Stott, Protector of Aboriginals, of Alice Springs in the Northern Territory and Jean Crittenden Married Woman 808 Nicholson Street, Fitzroy, Melbourne'.[186]

Jean Crittenden agreed to 'remove Sarah Breaden, Quadroon, aged about 17 years Beyond the Northern Territory, To Wit 808 Nicholson Street, North Fitzroy, Melbourne' and employ her 'as domestic help' for a period of two years in compliance with the terms of the following contract:

Remuneration and Conditions

1st The said Sarah Breaden to receive Food, Clothes, Bedclothes and Proper accommodation and whatever Medical attention she may require

2nd The said Sarah Breaden to receive Wages Five shillings per week commencing from Date Sarah Breaden's arrival in Melbourne.

3rd. Wages to be paid quarterly through The Protector of Aboriginals at Alice Springs into Sarah Breaden's account, Commonwealth Savings Bank at Alice Springs.

4th. No withdrawals of money from Bank by Sarah Breaden without the consent of The Chief Protector of Aboriginals Darwin or The Protector of Aboriginals at Alice Springs.

5th. Sarah Breaden to be under the entire control and supervision of the Chief Protector of Aboriginals, Darwin, or his nominee.

6th. This agreement may be cancelled at any time by a Protector of Aboriginals of the Northern Territory of Australia, by notice in writing if he deems Jean Crittenden to be an unfit person to have the said Sarah Breaden under agreement Or that the said Jean Crittenden has failed to comply with Ordinance No 9 of 1918, or Regulations thereunder.

7th. This agreement is granted under and subject to compliance on the Part of the said Jean Crittenden with the said Ordinance and Regulations in Force thereunder, and may, subject to the Regulations be renewed by the Protector of Aboriginals at Alice Springs, from time to time by endorsement thereon for a further period of two years.

8th. The said Jean Crittenden reserves the right at any time to terminate agreement by giving the said Protector of Aboriginals at Alice Springs two weeks notice in writing, and in compliance with conditions of Recognisance.

9th. The said Jean Crittenden to furnish Protector of Aboriginals at Alice Springs a Half yearly report with reference to Sarah Breadens behaviour and usefulness.[187]

Sarah was by no means the only young woman with an Aboriginal mother and white father who was sent away from Central Australia under such an arrangement. She does, however, seem to be the only one who ended up in Melbourne rather than Adelaide.

In Melbourne, until April 1924, Sarah went to free night school. When it closed down, Mrs Crittenden wrote to Sergeant Stott, proposing that Sarah's earnings of five shillings per week be put towards the furthering of her education. Of Sarah's education Mrs Crittenden wrote,

> As you know it has been sadly neglected and it is now Sarah misses it as she has some very nice girl friends from the Sunday School and elsewhere, but it is a big drawback to her being so backward in writing, English and arithmetic… Sarah is very anxious to learn, I think the little education will do her more good than money.[188]

In reply, Stott thanked Mrs Crittenden for the two photos of Sarah. 'She seems to have grown into a fine girl thanks to your able and careful training'. Alas, those photos didn't make it to the file. As to the proposal of retaining five shillings a week for education, Stott was in favour but not, as he said, in a position to authorise it. He suggested that Crittenden contact the Secretary of Home & Territories in Melbourne who he was confident would 'give matter his kind and favourable approval'.[189]

At which Mrs Crittenden donned her gloves and hat and presented at the Home and Territories Department in Melbourne. She reported that Sarah was a 'refined and splendid kind of girl' who it would be difficult to distinguish from 'an ordinary Australian child' but for her lack of education. Mrs Crittenden said she treated Sarah the same as she treated her own.

One does wonder, however, how much scrubbing, polishing and stirring Mrs Crittenden's own children did, in exchange for board, lodgings and five shillings a week that was managed elsewhere. Also, if having been denied any decent sort of education in their earliest years, were Mrs Crittenden's children then expected to use their weekly earnings to pay for their own?

Sarah commenced lessons with Mr W.J. Aldus of 80 Collins Street, Melbourne, on 14 August 1925. She initially attended for one hour a week and received a report card at the end of each visit. The reports itemised how Sarah's reading, spelling, writing and arithmetic were for that day and what she was to prepare for the next lesson. 'Good', 'excellent' and 'improving' are words used often on Sarah's report cards. Each report card also contained work to be prepared for the next session.

Work to be prepared by Sarah for 2 October 1925 included two pages of writing on Captain Cook. Unfortunately, those two pages of homework didn't make it to the file. Perhaps they went something like:

> *Captain Cook was an explorer and sea captain from Great Britain who lived between 1728 and 1779. He sailed the seas and made maps of new lands. During one of his journeys on the Pacific Ocean brave Captain Cook discovered Australia, despite my people's best efforts!*

Of course she wouldn't have written that last bit, but I couldn't resist. Oh, Sarah, what did you make of it all? In the 1970s, when I went to school, the myth of Captain Cook having 'discovered' Australia was still being taught as fact.

Sarah continued with her tutoring until December 1926. In a letter then, to Sergeant Stott, Mrs Crittenden wrote,

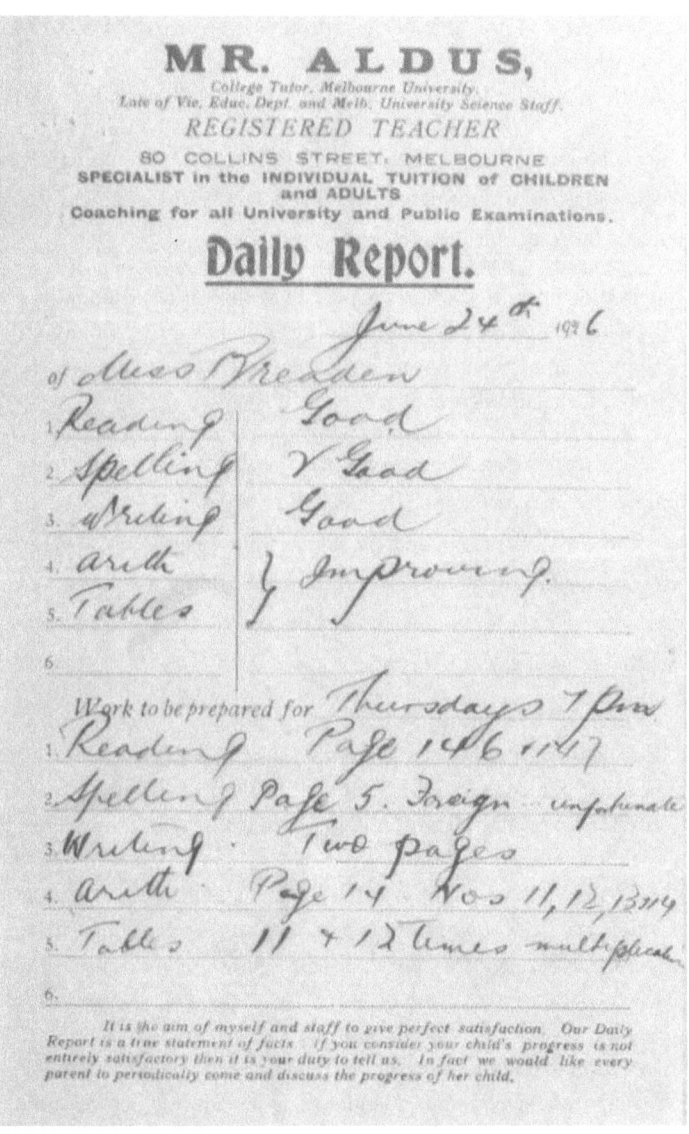

One of Sarah's report cards, from 24 June 1926.[190]

Sarah is doing very well and has received great benefit from the schooling she has received. She can both read and write very well now and her figures are also good. I think she has had enough schooling now to carry her on through life...her teacher is extremely pleased with the progress she has made...we are all going to the seaside for five weeks, leaving on 20th December.[191]

At about that time, the Department of Home and Territories began to question the 'arrangement' involving Sarah. The department sent a letter to Stott, enquiring into Sarah's age because

> it would appear that when she reaches the age of twenty-one, this Department or the Northern Territory Administration would not be justified in exercising any further control over her employment or her savings bank account.[192]

Stott replied that he believed Sarah Breaden was between nineteen and twenty years of age and if 'so desired' he could 'procure Sarahs exact age from Allan Breaden Sarahs reputed father a man over 70 years of age, at present residing on Lower Henbury Station Finke River'.[193] He then offered his opinion more broadly on a subject of which he had positioned himself as quite the expert:

> I fear it will be a serious matter for a great many of these unfortunate half-castes, quadroons and octaroons girls at present hired out under agreement and nearing the age of 21 years, when the Northern Territory administration ceases to have further control over their well fair and savings.
>
> There are several girls of Sarah Breaden's calibre who would be quite capable of looking after themselves and their savings, freed from the NT admin control, in my opinion would command much better wages, and in some instances may be fortunate enough to get comfortable married in their own walk of life. Unfortunately, this class of girls are greatly in the minority. The majority of them would squander their savings minus protector's control, most of them would be easily decoyed into the lower world, hence to the lowest degradation of immorality.
>
> In my opinion the halfcaste female is more lustful than her full blooded sister. At the age of 21 years, should control cease, the majority of these girls are doomed to fail.
>
> This does not in any manner apply to the male halfcaste the

majority of them are quite capable to fight life's battle at the age of 21 years.

In conclusion I respectfully suggest that provisions be made for the control of Halfcaste females, irrespective of age, unless the NT Administration are satisfied that a female is capable of being exempt from further control.[194]

In a memorandum of 30 March 1928 from the Home and Territories Department, eighteen months after the initial query about Sarah's age was raised, it was noted that

> The girl is engaged to be married to a very respectable young man…shows no indications of aboriginal blood, has had an excellent training and is…quite capable of looking after herself… It is recommended that she be released from control and given charge of her bank account.[195]

Sarah's bank book was mailed to her and she was released from state's oppressive control, as represented by her file coming to an abrupt end. Good for Sarah. Not so for us curious onlookers down the track. What happened next? Did she marry the respectable young man? Stay in Melbourne or return to Central Australia? Have children? How was she shaped by the experiences of her early years and how did they determine the course of the rest of her life? And now that Sarah was, presumably, afforded the right to privacy of any regular citizen, how was I to find out?

*

In the 'Family history search' section on the Victorian government website of Births, Deaths and Marriages, options include

Name of the person on the historical/marine index		
Family name		⑦
Given name(s)		⑦

I enter the details I have for Sarah and the site offers me a wedding, of Sarah Helen Breaden to Robert Robertson in 1929.

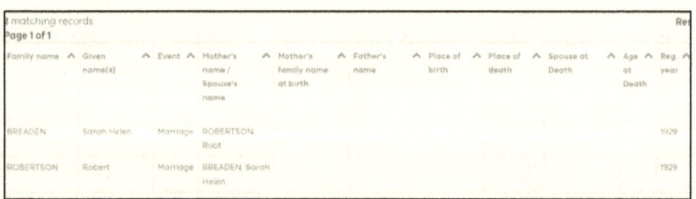

Is this our Sarah? To find out more, I take the chance and purchase the wedding certificate. From this I learn that Sarah Breaden who was born at Henbury Station and now of 808 Nicholson Street, North Fitzroy, married Robert Robertson, produce merchant of 14 John Street, East Brunswick, in November 1929. Sarah's father is Allan Breaden, station manager; her mother – Leisha White. Robert's father is Adam Robertson, labourer. The wedding took place in the Presbyterian Church, Carlton.

I plug in some new terms, searching for what other major life events might be on record: Sarah Breaden's death – nothing. Sarah Robertson's death – nothing. Robert Robertson's death?

Several results are offered for the decades I have entered. I discount

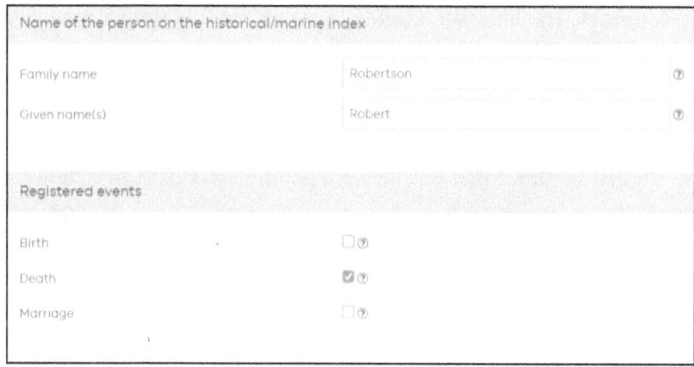

the Robert Robertsons with a middle name. Surely if our Robert had a middle name, it would have shown up on his marriage certificate. I keep scouring and here it is:

Robert Robertson. Mother Marion. Father Adam. Place of birth, Rutherglen. Place of Death, Gembrook. This is the Robert who married Sarah. I place the order and download the certificate.

Robert Robertson, forestry worker, aged fifty-eight, died in Gembrook on 21 February 1961 and was cremated in Springvale. This certificate was witnessed by T. Atkinson, son-in-law, of Gembrook. Robert was married to Sarah Helen Breaden and had one child, Evelyn Marion, aged twenty-five at the time of his death. Presumably, the son-in-law who witnessed this certificate was Evelyn Marion's husband.

*

An internet search for 'Sarah Breaden' takes me to the webpage of a woman named Kayannie, who refers to Sarah Breaden, in a blog, as her great-grandfather's half-sister.

I find Kayannie on Facebook and send a message, explaining my interest. I then go to the local library where lists that I am dreading, of Victoria's historical electoral roles, are stored on microfiche. If I can locate Robert and Sarah Robertson, I might be able to track more of their movements. The librarian has just shown me to the reader, the tapes and the convoluted instructions for its use when my phone rings. It's Kayannie.

'Oh, Aunty Ev, I can give you her number,' she says.

In that instant, Sarah Breaden and her mob go from being subjects on elusive historic documents into living, breathing people with phone numbers!

*

'Sure, come on up,' Evelyn tells me, 'but make it early because the Bombers are on at three.'

I get that. There are Bombers supporters in my family too.

Evelyn greets me at the front door of her big, comfortable home amongst the gum trees. Standing there in the foyer, she is flanked by the familiar dancing colours, the swirls and patterns, the iconography, of distinctly Central Australian art. There are wooden artefacts too: music sticks, little carved animals with patterns burnt into them. Evelyn, of the green and leafy outskirts of Melbourne, shows all the warmth and generosity that is credited to country folk. She fills in so many gaps over one leisurely lunch, showing and telling and helping me build a big picture that wouldn't have been possible had I scoured dusty records for the rest of my days.

Sarah lived with the Crittendens right up to when she got married. She moved in with her husband then. Their one child, Evelyn, came along six years later. When Evelyn was a kid, she used think they lived in Easter Brunswick, she tells me, laughing. She picked that up from the Greeks and Italians they lived amongst. They moved to the country and managed a farm. Sarah was a great cook. Evelyn remembers her mum's sponges and scones. We discuss how she might have learnt such baking from Mrs Crittenden. Sarah killed the chooks and skinned them, was a skilled horse rider and great shot with a rifle: skills she presumably learnt as a child, on Henbury Station.

We ponder why Sarah went to Melbourne when all the other girls

Name of the person on the historical/marine index		
Family name	Robertson	⑦
Given name(s)	Robert	⑦

Registered events		
Birth	☐ ⑦	
Death	☑ ⑦	
Marriage	☐ ⑦	

the Robert Robertsons with a middle name. Surely if our Robert had a middle name, it would have shown up on his marriage certificate. I keep scouring and here it is:

Robert Robertson. Mother Marion. Father Adam. Place of birth, Rutherglen. Place of Death, Gembrook. This is the Robert who married Sarah. I place the order and download the certificate.

Robert Robertson, forestry worker, aged fifty-eight, died in Gembrook on 21 February 1961 and was cremated in Springvale. This certificate was witnessed by T. Atkinson, son-in-law, of Gembrook. Robert was married to Sarah Helen Breaden and had one child, Evelyn Marion, aged twenty-five at the time of his death. Presumably, the son-in-law who witnessed this certificate was Evelyn Marion's husband.

*

An internet search for 'Sarah Breaden' takes me to the webpage of a woman named Kayannie, who refers to Sarah Breaden, in a blog, as her great-grandfather's half-sister.

I find Kayannie on Facebook and send a message, explaining my interest. I then go to the local library where lists that I am dreading, of Victoria's historical electoral roles, are stored on microfiche. If I can locate Robert and Sarah Robertson, I might be able to track more of their movements. The librarian has just shown me to the reader, the tapes and the convoluted instructions for its use when my phone rings. It's Kayannie.

'Oh, Aunty Ev, I can give you her number,' she says.

In that instant, Sarah Breaden and her mob go from being subjects on elusive historic documents into living, breathing people with phone numbers!

*

'Sure, come on up,' Evelyn tells me, 'but make it early because the Bombers are on at three.'

I get that. There are Bombers supporters in my family too.

Evelyn greets me at the front door of her big, comfortable home amongst the gum trees. Standing there in the foyer, she is flanked by the familiar dancing colours, the swirls and patterns, the iconography, of distinctly Central Australian art. There are wooden artefacts too: music sticks, little carved animals with patterns burnt into them. Evelyn, of the green and leafy outskirts of Melbourne, shows all the warmth and generosity that is credited to country folk. She fills in so many gaps over one leisurely lunch, showing and telling and helping me build a big picture that wouldn't have been possible had I scoured dusty records for the rest of my days.

Sarah lived with the Crittendens right up to when she got married. She moved in with her husband then. Their one child, Evelyn, came along six years later. When Evelyn was a kid, she used think they lived in Easter Brunswick, she tells me, laughing. She picked that up from the Greeks and Italians they lived amongst. They moved to the country and managed a farm. Sarah was a great cook. Evelyn remembers her mum's sponges and scones. We discuss how she might have learnt such baking from Mrs Crittenden. Sarah killed the chooks and skinned them, was a skilled horse rider and great shot with a rifle: skills she presumably learnt as a child, on Henbury Station.

We ponder why Sarah went to Melbourne when all the other girls we know of who were sent as servants from Central Australia, went to Adelaide. Evelyn tells me that Sarah's father sent her to live with a Mrs Sharp at Oodnadatta. There she slept on the back veranda and looked after Mrs Sharp's kids. When Bob Buck, bushman and nephew of Allan Breaden, saw Sarah carrying Mrs Sharp's kid, he relayed that back to his uncle. Allan wasn't happy. He believed that Sarah wasn't being looked after properly and was called on to do too much work at the expense of her education. He then arranged for her to go and live with the Crittendens in Melbourne.

I realised that Sarah never lived in the Bungalow after all. She must have been one of very few children born of an Aboriginal mother and white father, in the vast Central Australian region at that time, who managed to avoid that particular fate. She might have gone to school briefly in Oodnadatta.

Allan wanted Sarah to go to school and certainly at that time an education would provide her with more options than she would have been afforded by remaining at Henbury. Perhaps Allan reasoned that in Central Australia Sarah would never rise above the status of 'half-caste' and always be treated as such. With her appearance as a white person, if she went away and received an education, Sarah could assimilate into mainstream society.

The nearest school was in the rough, frontier town of Alice Springs where school was held in a makeshift one-roomed stone hut beside the prison where the white children and the Bungalow kids were taught separately. The Bungalow kids lived in squalid conditions and abused by drunken white men at night.

By contrast, Oodnadatta was a bustling, cosmopolitan centre at the head of the railway line where children of various heritages were educated together and Sarah could live in a house with a family.

Sarah once took Evelyn as a child to visit the Crittendens. She recalls that they were 'proper', and she had to behave. It was probably around 1940, the time that Allan Breaden died. Perhaps that is why they went. Sarah and Allan had kept in touch over the years, through letters.

Sarah went back to Henbury Station in the 1970s, with Evelyn, and uncovered some truths about her family. Her mother hadn't died when Sarah was a baby. She had given birth to five more children and suddenly Sarah was wrapped up in a huge Central Australian family; an

Sarah on her wedding day.[196]

Aboriginal web of belonging. Sarah visited Central Australia twice more and after she died in 1995 at the age of ninety-two, Evelyn took her ashes to Henbury Station. Memorials were erected there later for Sarah and her sister Susan.

Evelyn hands me a photo of Sarah on her wedding day. I gasp at the intimacy of it, the reality. I can just about reach out and stroke her soft cheeks. The photo disrupts and replaces the image of Sarah's face I had created in my mind. Evelyn allows me to take a photo of the photo.

In that framed and treasured picture, the young bride is adorned with lace, flowers and pretty jewels. I could say she looks hopeful and composed but that is, of course, projection.

'She was special,' Evelyn tells me, 'lovely, and never spoke ill of anyone.'

A wedding invitation had been mailed to Allan Breaden at Henbury Station. He replied, after the event, that he'd been out droving and was delayed, owing to floods. By the time he got back to the station and received the invitation, he had missed the wedding. Sarah didn't invite her mother because she believed her to be dead.

Evelyn and Trevor had four sons, all grown up now with families of their own. They are proud of their grandma and what she achieved, and they love the Aboriginal side of their story.

We ponder why Sarah had an apparently more positive experience than so many of her peers who were also removed from their families and sent away as indentured labour. Sarah's father took responsibility for her which was uncommon for white men in Central Australia who fathered children with Aboriginal women at that time. Some of the rare exceptions were at Henbury Station, where at least two white station workers around that time partnered with Aboriginal women and took responsibility for their 'wives' as well as the subsequent offspring. Presumably, Sarah spent time with her father as a child while believing that her mother was dead.

'I don't think she was part of the stolen generation,' Evelyn tells me.

I guess what Evelyn means is that her mother's experience didn't seem to be too hurtful and when we think Stolen Generations we think of deep wounds.

'She was taken from her mother who she was later told was dead,' I suggest, 'and when she was sent to Melbourne she was told not to tell anyone she was Aboriginal.'

Evelyn nods.

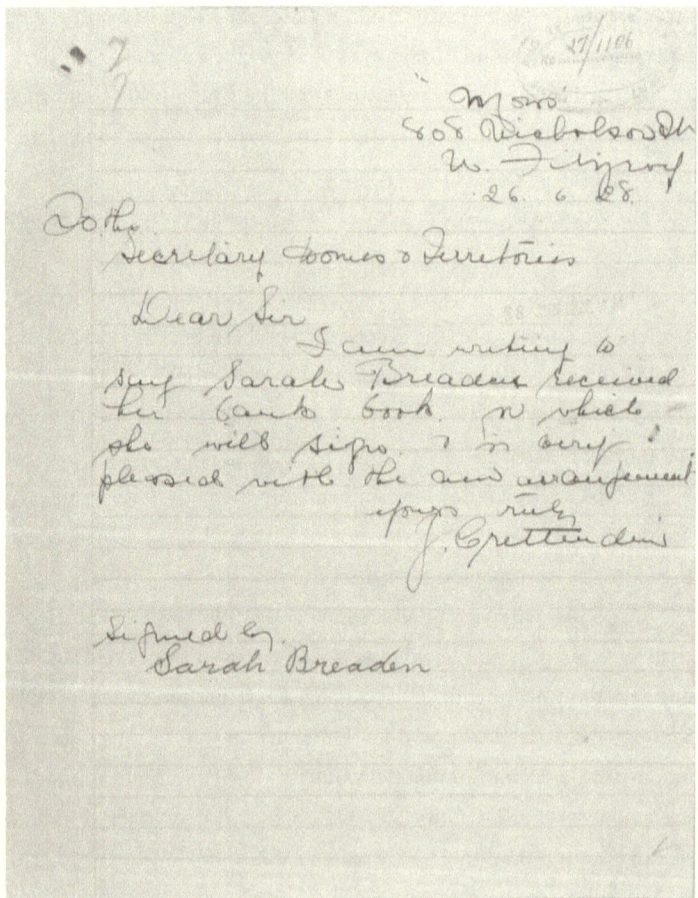

Letter from Jean Crittenden, co-signed by Sarah, to verify receipt of her bank book, 1928.[197]

The Sacrifices

In the introduction to *Bringing Them Home*, the report of the National Inquiry into the Separation of Aboriginal and Torres Strait Islander Children from Their Families (1997), it is noted that while the bulk of the evidence presented to the inquiry detailed damaging and negative effects of child removal, the terms of reference were not confined to these. The inquiry received some submissions from witnesses that acknowledged the love and care provided by their non-Indigenous adoptive families. Such witnesses also noted appreciation for a higher standard of education than would have been received had they remained with their families and communities. Nevertheless, all witnesses who made these points in their evidence to the enquiry also expressed their wish that they had not had to make the sacrifices that they did.[198]

Iron and Squalor 1

If anyone saw the irony in building an institution for vulnerable children adjacent to the watering hole where the wild men of the Centre came to get hammered, it wasn't apparent, not initially anyway.

When Ida Standley, officer-in-charge of child welfare, got to town in 1914, did she take one look out at the Bungalow, sniffing distance from the Stuart Arms Hotel, throw her arms up and declare, 'This will never do. The children's home twenty yards from the public house. Something must be done!'?

Evidently not, although as reported in 1924,

> When first appointed, Mrs Stanley pointed out that, owing to the position of the Bungalow and the fact that it was unfenced, and further that there was no accommodation for herself, she could not be responsible for the moral welfare of the children except during such time in the day when there were under her personal supervision.[199]

Not so much concerned with the well-being of the children as her own liability, Mrs Standley didn't want to be held responsible for system failings.

In his letter of complaint back in 1917, about the way Sergeant Stott conducted himself, Constable Kelly had written,

> With regard to the Half caste bungalow at Alice…it needs an 8' impregnable barb wire fence… At present niggers can get into the girls quarters and the girls can get out at night if they want to. Not the matron's fault. She endeavours to strictly mother these children who all dearly love her. There are several of these girls now fast developing into womanhood. There is no prospect for them in the district, that is decent. There are two, but not decent. First, the

black camps, second cook useful housekeeper unwed wife or convenience to a white man, both undesirable prospects…[200]

It was not Indigenous people who were posing danger to the children of the Bungalow but rather drunken white men from the pub. Blaming others and an apparent inability to take responsibility for their own misdeeds – a monotonously regular aspect of the colonial condition.

Note also the complete absence of Topsy Smith from the discussion. She was the one at the Bungalow day in and day out, doing her best to care for the children. This seems to have escaped Kelly's attention.

At the enquiry into those allegations, various witnesses had made comments about the Bungalow. Ida Standley's daughter Vivian Browne noted that

> I think the bungalow is in a very bad place. It is too near the hotel, I don't think it should be here at all. I think the children should be taken away so as to be right away from the influence of the natives.[201]

Henry Wilkinson, storekeeper, said,

> I do not think the bungalow is in the right position. It is all right for the boys, but as the girls grow up I think it is the wrong place for them. It is too near the influence of the black camp, and I suppose it is too near the influence of whites also.[202]

Frederick Price, postmaster, was of the opinion that

> The situation of the bungalow is bad, it is too close to the hotel, too open, too easy of access. The children can get in or out just as they wish; too far from the matron to be under her direct supervision; she lives 300 yards away from the bungalow. There should be a white person to sleep on the premises for strict supervision, also a night warder. I think it would be better if the bungalow were removed from the district altogether.[203]

The roving Reverend Plowman said,

> I think the bungalow is in a bad position; it is right at the backdoor of the hotel. Otherwise as far as I can see of the children it seems to me to be conducted very well.[204]

And as Stott told the enquiry,

> The situation as it was originally chosen as I was in charge of it had to be near. Now, with an independent person in charge, I consider it should be removed.[205]

What any Indigenous people had to say about it has, of course, not gone down in the annals.

In his final report Judge Bevan wrote,

> The generally expressed opinion is that the bungalow is in an unsuitable position. I am of opinion that it is. It is too near the hotel and consequently in the direct track of all persons passing through Alice Springs. With the half-caste girls growing up as they are, this is a difficulty. Further it is a very undesirable thing that the matron in charge should live away from the bungalow itself. It is quite impossible for her to keep any sort of control unless she be on the spot.[206]

The location and general conditions of the Bungalow remained for many years to come, as described by adventurer Francis Birtles in late 1924:

> A blot on Alice Springs and a blot on our civilisation.[207]

During fact-finding missions in 1921, two federal government ministers recorded their impressions in the Bungalow visitors' book. They were Senator Foll, whose visitor book entry, presented earlier (page 75), offered a rare example of credit being given to the children; and Syd Jackson from the House of Representatives, who wrote,

> It has been a revelation to me to see what is being done towards the education of the half castes in the Territory but regret to see the conditions under which this is being carried out. Their teacher is to be complimented on the result of her labours. I shall do my

best to bring about an alteration particularly regarding the site. A necessary work in the interests of those whose position in life precludes them from most of the comforts that we enjoy & it is our duty to see that they have the opportunity to become good citizens. (Syd Jackson, 14/7/21, page 38)

In 1922, Northern Territory Administrator Urquhart made his own foray from Darwin into Central Australia. After checking his personal effects into the Stuart Arms Hotel, he headed over to introduce himself to the women and children of the Bungalow:

Good afternoon. I am the Administrator of the Northern Territory. Urquhart is my name. How are all of you most remarkable people, a product of both the oldest living culture on earth and colonisers of a completely opposing ilk. Of what assistance may I be?

Hello, sir.

Pleased to meet you.

Hello, sir.

Thank you for coming.

I would like to go home to my mum.

And me.

And me.

And me.

Me too.

I would prefer to not be scrubbed each morning with phenyl that stings and stinks and renders me raw.

No matter how hard you scrub, it won't make us any whiter.

Hello, sir. Fine, thank you. I go off at night and have sex with drunken white men who give me things in return. Some of them nice. Some of them smelly and itchy and red. How are you?

No, that never happened. How the meeting did go isn't recorded. I imagine Urquhart crunching over gravel, taking long strides in solid boots. I imagine him upright and shoulder to shoulder with other men of the Territory, all considering themselves to be of maximum import: Stott, for example, and businessmen of the town, and senior public servants – peering down their collective noses at the 'half-castes' and 'aborigines' and anguishing over the 'problem'.

We don't know exactly how Urquhart conducted himself, but we do have his thoughts on the matter, as per his official report. Urquhart didn't go into detail about conditions at the Bungalow, but he did recommend that 'something should be done promptly'.[208] He recommended the establishment of a 'centrally situated, well equipped and above all efficiently staffed (Urquhart's underlining) training institute'. Its purpose would be to attempt to raise the 'half caste to the status of their white parents with the view to their eventual absorption in the white population'.[209] According to Urquhart,

> The training should include the formation of character by means of reasonable discipline and by the force of example on the part of the staff…
>
> The material part of the training apart from ordinary elementary education should be – (a) for males in station and farm work… (b) for females, domestic duties generally.[210]

Urquhart thought the most suitable interim location was the police paddock. That was down through Ntaripe (also known these days as the Gap), a mighty chasm in the range, just a couple of miles south of the heart of the town.

Ntaripe, view looking north, towards the town of Alice Springs, 1928.[211]

Beyond Ntaripe and onto where the police paddock used to be, these days you will find these days such outlying utilities of contemporary urban life as the rubbish dump, sewage ponds, showgrounds, BMX track and RSPCA animal shelter. In Urquhart's time, there was, according to him, 'a stone building in fair order, but requiring some repairs, which would be suitable as a residence for a married superintendent and Matron teacher'. There was also a well. Using the iron from the present Bungalow, some more that was stored at the police station, as well as one and a half tons of new iron, by Urquhart's reckoning, 'decent and sufficient quarters could be built for the half castes near the stone residence'.[212]

Back home in the tropical north, the Administrator got the ball rolling. He had plans drawn up and lobbied for funding for his newly envisaged institution. Meanwhile, the federal government was more circumspect. A year later, in his Annual Report of the Administrator of the Northern Territory, Urquhart noted that he had made recommendations in July 1922 which would, he believed, 'if adopted, have been very beneficial'. Instead, as he understood it, 'further expert advice' had been sought and action deferred pending receipt of it.[213]

The further expert advice sought was from the by now Sir Baldwin Spencer. In April 1923, armed with his trademark notebook and camera and sporting his pet moustache, Sir Baldwin took leave from his role as Director of the National Museum in Melbourne and strode in once again, this time to investigate and report on the Aboriginal mission stations of Central Australia.

If there's a time above all others to be in Central Australia, it's April, when the rocks glow from months of summer baking yet the extreme heat of summer has abated. Temperatures in April tend to hover in the mid-twenties and nights are deliciously cool. Spencer stayed three months, until the short, sharp winter had set in. His ensuing *Report on the Half Castes and Aboriginals of the Southern Division of the Northern Territory with special reference to the Bungalow at Stuart and the Hermannsburg Mission Station* was comprehensive and his recommendations were largely in line with Urquhart's.

Spencer spent some time with the children of the Bungalow and reported that they 'could read and write very well while the singing was quite pleasant to listen to'. He also noted that

> One morning on the playground I took the opportunity, by means of a South Australian School Reader, of testing independently their reading powers, and found, not only that they were quite good, but that they were keenly emulous as to who could read it best.[214]

On the location and general conditions of the Bungalow Spencer noted,

> Only 65 feet to the east of it is the back fence of the block on which stands the Stuart Arms Hotel. A gate opens through this fence directly onto the Bungalow ground, and, at the side of this gate, are the sanitary conveniences of the hotel…
>
> It will be evident that its close proximity to the Hotel is a very serious matter from the point of view of both the Bungalow and Hotel which, in hot weather suffers from the lack of adequate sanitary premises in the former, and it is also fortunate that the Police Station, under the charge of Sergeant Stott, Protector of Aboriginals, is nearby…
>
> Apart from the total inadequacy of the buildings both in regards to size and equipment, the position is eminently unsuitable.[215]

Spencer echoed Urquhart's call for a new 'half caste station,' which he saw as best located 'at some distance from the central overland route or any projected railway or stock route. It should cover approximately 1,000 square miles of country capable of carrying stock'.[216] The fundamental purpose of the station, according to Spencer, was to provide for the housing of the half castes and 'their training in industrial and domestic work'.[217]

I could go on here, provide details of those dusty resorts of Urquhart and Spencer's imaginings, as they did in their reports. Dormitories. Training sections. Playgrounds. Specifications. Building materials. Locations. Suitable Christian couples in charge. Guiding the children up for a life of useful servitude. But what's the point? It never happened. Perhaps the dreams of others matter more here than those of the Director of the National Museum and the Administrator of the Northern Territory who could, after all, retreat to their urbane lives.

Of what do you dream, dear children, as you lie on the ground at night, tangled up with your Bungalow brothers and sisters?

Of what do you dream, Topsy Smith; for yourself, your own children, and all the others in your care?

Family reunification?

Your husband and children, out at Arltunga, in the life you built together?

Honey ants, fat goanna and sitting down on the land?

In June 1924, the Minister for Works and Railways met with the Minister for Home and Territories, who had ultimate governmental responsibility for the Bungalow. At that meeting, it was decided to

> Make arrangements with the Salvation Army or other religious body in Adelaide which may have suitable institution for them, to receive and train all half caste girls over the age of seven or eight years, and for the institution after educating and training them to place them in employment, supervising them until reaching adult age or marrying.
>
> Half caste boys to be educated at Alice Springs and after education placed with suitable employers in the District.
>
> Remove existing buildings and reerect on more suitable site, making such additions and alterations as are necessary. In particular to provide a schoolroom more suitable than the present one for the climate.[218]

They fiddled and farted for years to come. No one could find a more suitable site that met the requirements for water, timber for building, sufficient distance from stock routes and the telegraph line, proximity to main routes, access to police protection and distance from the 'natives'.

In the meantime, the tin can home continued, the inmates making do the best they could. To the inmates, I suppose, it was simply how it was, their home, their lot in life. Together, they would have found love and comfort. Daydreamed. Made up games. They had each other and the adults who cared for them: Topsy, Mrs Standley, Stott's wife, Stott himself. They had a secret, whispered language and were able to steal out to the periphery to meet with the curious dark people who shared with them the precious offerings of the culture of their births.

Being a Kid

Oh, it was all right like, you know, being a kid, I suppose we were free to run around like here and there. But our schooling was very poor, also. We used to play the wag a lot but, there you are, we were punished for that quite a bit.[219]

That's how Clarence saw it, looking back through the years. Clarence lived at the Bungalow from birth until the age of twelve, when he was sent off to work for the Hayes family at Undoolya Station. He stayed there until he was twenty-one.[220]

For Clarence and his mob, school only went for an hour and half each afternoon. He reflected on what they learnt at school:

Well, very little, you know. Spelling and so forth. Only got up to about grade three. Well, you wouldn't expect anything more anyhow – an hour-and-a-half a day at school.[221]

Milton Liddle who lived at the Bungalow from the age of three had similar memories:

We only had an hour and a half for schooling a day, because there was too many kids. The white kids went to school in the morning, that was all the Hayes, and Nickers, and all them mob, and part-coloured Aboriginal kids went to school in the afternoon, which was only hour and a half a day, and you got very little education of course. In that time, too many kids. Mrs Standley was teaching from kindergarten upwards you may as well say.[222]

From the Alice Springs section of the Northern Territory Administrator's Report 1916–17:

At the Bungalow there are eight boys and twenty-two girls, comprising half, quarter and octoroon caste. Their ages ranging from three to fifteen years. The health of the children is exceptionally good. They are happy and contented. The school roll totals sixty – thirty-four white children and twenty-six coloured. The advanced coloured attend morning school with the white children, and the remained of the coloured attend afternoon school. The annual examination report is good.

IDA STANDLEY
Teacher (1916–17)

For the first two months, school was held in the prison cell, after the prisoners had gone off to their hard labour assignments for the day.[223] When the conversion of the old warden's room was complete, which was still in the police complex and right beside the jail, school moved in there.[224]

Clarence remembered a time in 1926 when visiting dignitaries came to town. The schoolroom was turned into a dining room or sleeping quarters and school was called off. As he recalled it,

> There was a party of cars – parliamentary party come through here… I think the governor of South Australia come up here…a Sir Thomas Bridge I think his name was.
> And they took up the whole school… They stayed here for about three days… I know we had to go to the police station. They had big hot water containers. They stood about eight to ten gallons of water in each container and they were placed in this big fireplace, and we had to light the fire about half-past five, six o'clock in the mornings so they'd have hot water…
> And we had to keep this hot water system going for them – a big fireplace and wood and that, we had to cart across from the big heap that the prisoners had chopped.
> There [was] no school for about a fortnight… They had to prepare it and that, a week or so before. We reckoned that was really good, you know – we were on holidays [laughter].[225]

Clarrie's memories coincide with official correspondence between the Department of Home and Territories and Stott. According to that, the school was closed from 24 to 30 June 1926 for the school premises to be converted into a dining room. A party of twenty-three, including several federal members and their wives were in attendance in Alice Springs for the opening of the Australian Inland Mission Hospital. Such a school closure was also 'done on the occasion of the visit to Alice Springs of Lord Stradbroke and party'.[226]

Of the prisoners, Ada and her sister Jean remembered,

> They had black fellows chained up there…
>   Chains around – they'd bleed and…
>   Around the neck; it was awful…
>   Legs'd be all swollen and…they used to have a rag around it.
>   Might be 3 weeks or might be 6 months.
>   Some died there too.[227]

Clarence recalled,

> When we were kids we used to see quite a bit of that. The police'd be bringing in say, half a dozen to a dozen prisoners on chains. They'd be coming in from The Gap up to the police station; you couldn't help seeing them, poor devils. They were all in chains from head to foot…
> Chains around their neck and I don't know whether it went around their waist or not now. But it went down to their ankles on both legs; whether it was on their arms or not I just couldn't describe…but they were in heavy chains.[228]

They might have walked a couple of hundred miles, Clarence thought, from stations out bush where they'd been done for killing cattle. They'd do fifteen miles a day or so and 'they'd be pretty tired by the end of the day I think, with them big chains on their bodies'.[229]

That old gaol has two cells, a smaller one at the front for the white prisoners and a larger one to the rear for, yep, the bulk of the prisoners. Aboriginal. (Since the introduction of prisons to Central Australia, in the late nineteenth century, Aboriginal people have always made up the bulk of their population. This is not because Aboriginal people are inherently criminal but because the system has been stacked so convincingly against them.) Metal rings, spaced at intervals, are concreted into the floor of the larger cell.

Clarence doesn't know if the prisoners were chained to those rings. 'I couldn't say,' he said, laughing. 'I never got that far.'[230]

The National Trust says there is no evidence of the rings ever having been used. There is no evidence they weren't used either. These days, you can visit the gaol as a sightseer. Sometimes, concerts are held there too. All that concrete and stone is said to work for the acoustics.

I wonder what the acoustics were like in the schoolroom; of the prisoners living, dying and rattling their chains from within the prison walls.

The prisoners were generally sentenced to hard labour. One of the jobs both Ada and Clarence remembered them doing was going out to the bat caves for manure for the vegetable gardens:

> Bat manure for the police station – he [Stott] wouldn't have bullocks manure or…horse manure, he used to believe in the bat manure…
>
> These white men with rifles…take them down there, all chained up in the cart, get a load of manure…15 miles out and 15 miles in. They'd pull the cart instead of…donkeys or something like that.[231]

Sometimes when the Bungalow kids went out onto the outskirts of town, they had dealings with people from the bush. Clarence remembers,

> Well, they were very nice to us, the old people… We used to talk to these old people and they used to advise us not to be frightened of any Aboriginal whatsoever; that we were safe and we belonged to them; they wanted us to just live quietly and be one of them; not to be frightened of them 'cause they'll never ever hurt us. So that gave us a lot of confidence amongst the Aboriginal people…
>
> They lived everywhere really. There was a big camp there behind that little hill opposite the hospital there where the Shell service station is. Probably three or four hundred Aboriginals lived there…

When they had a death in the camp, they shift away from it, so there was never really a permanent camp. There'd be a big camp along Charles Creek there but soon as there was a death in the camp they'd all make a new camp somewhere else.[232]

The camp was made up of wurlies built up four to five feet high, with brushes, like branches, off trees. As for clothes, the men might just have a pair of trousers that they'd cut the legs off to make shorts. The women wore 'old dresses or whatever they could pick up to cover themselves up', said Clarence.[233]

> And their way of living, no-one starved in their camps. Any food that came into the camp was shared amongst the whole community, even it was only a loaf of bread.
> If there are twenty, thirty people in the camp, it was shared right through the camp, even if it was only a mouthful each, everyone had to have that little bit.[234]

As far as Clarence knew, a few of those people had jobs, the men perhaps chopping wood and the women doing housework, but there were only four or five houses, a couple of shops, the Stuart Arms and the police station 'so there was no such thing as employment in the town'.[235]

People also got weekly rations from the government. Clarence remembers,

> When we were kids we used to run over and watch them being rationed out with flour and a bit of tea and sugar and rice, I think they got – just a couple of handfuls of rice or something each person. Probably about two to three kilos of flour; probably rice and then tea and sugar – a couple of handfuls of sugar; probably a handful of tea or something like that. That was their weekly ration.[236]

The people also hunted, for kangaroos, rabbits and other game. They had dogs for hunting and probably spears as well.

Milton remembered being hungry and how

> Some of the old women used to come in and get their rations and

so on, and then they'd feed us... They'd go down to the Todd there, where that high school is now, and then pull up there, and cook Johnnie cakes for us...

And then they'd go around gathering also bush tucker...they'd go out and get these honey ants and so on – some of the grandmothers – old grandmothers would bring it to us, and then we'd share it – and then eat caterpillars... They used to bring them in jam tins...or rusty fruit tins... They'd cook them out bush and bring them in...and they'd be dry sort of chips sort of things – you'd crunch them up – just like the twisties you'd buy in packets – they were sort of like that. And they'd come in with big bags of... what you see on the gum tree leaves... It used to be very thick here one time.[237]

Along with what the bush people brought, Milton remembers,

When we couldn't get anything to eat there, we'd go out hunting all over the hills, or at Anzac Hill. There was miles of rabbits, and goannas, and all sorts of things in them days, and berries. We'd go around scrounging everywhere and then we'd go doing odd jobs for sixpence, or sometimes some people used to pay us sixpence a week, and we'd go around Stuart Arms there. There was no telephone in Alice Springs town then, and then we used to take telegrams up to the post office for 60 cents – or 6 bob them days, and there'd be about 15 kids to 6 bob...

You could get a stick lolly for, it might have been about 5/8 of an inch thick and nearly a foot long, for threepence in them days. We done all right out of it. Or go around cleaning yards up or cutting wood or something like that. We'd get sixpence a week for that; watering the garden and cutting the wood in the mornings, you'd get sixpence a week...

There used to be a big scrub of cashew bushes there – old Ben Walkington used to live there, and Mrs Standley, the teacher, and every time we went into Mrs Standley's to water the garden, old Ben Walkington , when the season was on, he used to give us these big bunches of cashew seeds, and we used to just take them back and boil them...Just like eating green peas – they were lovely to eat, them cashew seeds.[238]

The kids had plenty to do outside of school. As Clarence told it,

> We had to clean up around the place... Each kid, or little groups, had their own little jobs to do.[239]

Carting water was one of the jobs Clarence and Ada remembered clearly, decades later:

> We had oh, probably fifteen, sixteen drums, we had to cart water from the police station to the Bungalow...and fill up our storage tank. Probably each day, I think, that went on – each evening or something like that. And the whole community had to hop in and cart water.
>
> Sometime we'd have stick across and one on each end of this stick... Oh, we were only kids about five and six, seven.[240]

And if they didn't do it properly, look out!

> He used to watch us; we got a bit lazy there carting water; they used to belt us with these jockey whips...with the wire ends on... It's come through, cut you to pieces just about, and the marks – collect you here and slash you there.[241]

As for the Bungalow itself, Milton recalls,

> There was no beds, no chairs, no tables – only there was tables inside there, but it was fixed to the floor for wet weather times, and it was covered with sheets of galvanised iron – ordinary tables made out of bush timber... The beds – we used to sleep up during the wet weather, was about two tiers high and about 2 foot 6 in-between sort of thing, and the kids used to crowd up into there when it rained. The boys had one room, and the girls had one room, but when the summertime come, they used to sleep altogether – girls and boys, brothers and sisters, because there was not enough blankets – in winter time even...
>
> In the summertime we just used to camp out on the flat – like a mob of sardines – in one bed. And the kids grew up... like brothers and sisters, all of them; and whoever had a close relative would look after the other kids that come in from the bush. Some kids came in there, couldn't speak a word of English – their basic En-

glish would be yes or no; nothing else, and then these old ladies that used to look after us; they had to turn around and teach them English and also the dialect what we spoke, so they could understand one another. The kids used to speak in their own dialect at the home but speak English at school.[242]

The boys remembered running errands. Sergeant Stott used to pick Clarence to take mail up to the old post office at the Telegraph Station. Sometimes it would be in the evenings, getting a bit dark. 'It was an order and you had to just go up there.' Clarence would get three or four kids to come with him because he was too frightened to go by himself. They practically ran all the way up and back.

Milton remembered,

> The girls used to do all the cooking, the washing, and all that – bed making…and then when the kids got to go to school, the bigger girls, you know the teenage girls would scrub all the boys – feet and legs – with a scrubbing brush – to get them to school.[243]

After the jobs had been done, there were games. Ada recalled,

> We used to run around and play hockey with the old sticks. They used to have races there for us and that, sports, that's all. And bag race, two-legged race we used to just get lollies if we'd win, a handful of lollies.[244]

At Christmas and Easter, the station people used to come and, as Ada recalled, 'put lollies in' and make a sports day. Clarence remembered the sports days too, throughout the 1920s:

> We used to have a wonderful time…we used to get lollies, fruit and that…from travellers that used to come in, or people from the mines and…stations.[245]

Clarence remembered swimming in the river, in 'nice clear water-clean as crystal' that ran for weeks and weeks. He also remembered being in the first boy scout troop in the Northern Territory, around 1925. Denny Smyth, one of the police constables, was the scoutmaster.

They had khaki uniforms with high-pointed scout hats and regular meetings.

> In the evenings, yes, we done a lot of drilling and that…Used to go outings at the weekends whenever the police[man] was off duty. He'd take us out about two or three miles out of town and we'd build a big shed…you know, how to light a fire and so forth…[246]

They also learnt to swim and play cricket and boxing.

As far as Clarence was concerned, the white people were a little bit stand-offish to the coloured people and the Afghans. They didn't really invite them to their communities. The station owners were very strict, like they were lords for the country and, as Clarence saw it,

> we were the underdogs. There was no such thing as you were on the same level or anything like that – oh, no [laughter]. They still have that attitude, too.[247]

Ada recalled the station people coming in for horse races at the racecourse at Christmastime:

> Everybody camped there. We used to walk from the Bungalow. Nobody wouldn't give us a ride. We used to walk there and walk back. We used to chase the buggies and the wagons… We used to hang on at the back sometimes. They had to whip us [and they told us to] get down [or else] we might have an accident. But we used to be still there.[248]

And she never forgot her dealings with 'bandy bandy' Jones:

> Mrs Jones had store where Ansett is now. We used to go over there and buy some lollies…she used to hunt us out and call us 'Jubilee mixtures'…We wanted 'Jubilee mixtures,' see. She said, 'Get out you jubilee mixtures yourselves.' She was terrible to us. And we used to call her 'bandy bandy' because…both her legs were that bent, you know, and so any rate she told old Stott, the policeman, so the policeman come along and give us a terrible hiding – never mind about the 'Jubilee mixtures', stuck up for her because we called her 'bandy bandy' [laughter].[249]

*Sports day, Alice Springs, 1924.
Bungalow and hotel property in the background.*[250]

Boxing lessons with B. Laver.[251]

EC.
27/2982

20th June, 1927

Dear Mr. Needham,

           With reference to the request recently made by you for certain information regarding the Bungalow at Alice Springs, Central Australia, I desire to inform you that the following items of food are at present supplied to the children at the Bungalow :-

           Meat, bread, tea, sugar, jam, syrup, rice, oatmeal, sago, preserved potatoes, dried and split peas.

           The cost per head per week of food is 4/-.

           The Matron(Mrs. I. Standley) receives the following salary and allowances :-

Salary:	£210	
Allowances -		
Aboriginal	75	
Cleaning	5	
Freight on Stores	17	
Total	£307	

Yours faithfully,

(Sgd.) J. McLAREN

Secretary.

The Reverend J. S. Needham,
  C/- A.B.M.A.,
    Leigh Street,
      ADELAIDE.
        S.A.

Letter to Rev. Needham.[252]

Iron and Squalor 2

It is almost incredible that these half-castes should be herded together in shameful discomfort at Alice Springs, there to be exposed to the bestial influences to whose effects their pitiful racial isolation bears continual witness (Mrs J McKay, September 1924).[253]

By 1924, pressure was mounting from people in faraway places for something to be done about the Bungalow. Mrs McKay was a member of the Women's Non-Party Association (WNPA), that had been campaigning since 1909 on issues affecting women and children. Addressing the WNPA in September, Mrs Mackay 'charged the Federal authorities with inhumanity in their treatment of the aborigines and half-castes of the Territory'.[254]

They lobbied federal Senator Benny to ask a question about the Bungalow in the Upper House, which he did on 18 September 1924:

Senator BENNY: Can the Minister for Home and Territories inform the Senate whether the Government is taking steps to inquire into the circumstances and the conditions of the half-caste children at Alice Springs, in the Northern Territory?

Senator PEARCE – Yes. The housing arrangements and the conditions generally are at present most unsatisfactory. I am having explored the possibility of removing these children from their present surroundings, and placing them either in a state Government institution in South Australia, or in the charge of a mission. We have not been able to complete the matter.[255]

A few weeks later, the Bungalow the matter was followed up in the House of Representatives:

1. Is it a fact that the Government has established a camp or home at Alice Springs for half-caste children

2. Were the children taken from their mothers and placed in a galvanized iron shed erected against the back-yard of an hotel

3. If so, what moral effect will this have on the children

4. If such a state of affairs exists, will the Government agree to the appointment of a caretaker for the children.

1. Yes, in the year 1914.

2. (3) and (4). A number of half-caste children in the district who were being neglected were housed in an iron building specially erected for the purpose. The building is located close to an hotel but is under the direct supervision of the Sergeant of Police and is in charge of a resident Matron. Arrangements are being made for the construction of a new building for the half-castes in a more satisfactory position.[256]

Of course, the children weren't removed because they were being neglected. That came later, at the hands of the state. The children were removed because they had some white ancestry and, as such, were considered by the white authorities as both capable of being civilised and a threat to White Australia. The threat started in the immediate domestic settings where certain 'missuses' of the bosses weren't too impressed with looking out the homestead window at children who, despite their dark complexions, bore a remarkable resemblance to those women's own husbands.

As Gordon Briscoe tells it,

From our grandmothers who lived through this brutal past, and from our mothers, who were born of it, we learned that most of the white men, who ventured into the Tywerentye, Western MacDonnell Ranges, and the river regions of Leratupa and Umbarntuwa, came alone, without wives. They came to build and operate the telegraph stations, the pastoral leases, the small stores and the railways stations. Slowly, between the 1890s and 1914, a few white women began migrating from South Australia and other colonies, and many learnt that their white husbands had black children whom they had abandoned to Aboriginal camps. As the half-caste population grew, the small number of white women residing in the service towns dotted along the arterial route from Oodnadatta to what is now Darwin began to panic. They panicked not only because they saw the presence of half-caste children in the same classrooms as disadvantaging their white children, but also because their white husbands had sired these same children.

The increasing presence of half-caste children aroused deep-seated fears and anxieties in the settler women. Their men were equally intent on denying the existence of these offspring. Each morning when their men washed their faces and looked out across the creeks in service towns, they would see their abandoned children in the Aboriginal fringe camps running around before their very eyes, barely existing. Meanwhile, the children themselves were forced to rely on these same belligerent, brutal and racist males, their fathers, for food, occasionally supplemented by bush food, although for the most part government rations were their only form of economic support.[257]

For the children who were living in conditions of hardship or neglect, it was because of the extreme conditions into which their Aboriginal families had been forced.

The WNPA also lobbied a South Australian member of parliament expressing their concerns about the 'appalling conditions of the home for half-caste children, which is situated next to the hotel [in Alice Springs].' They sought his help in a matter they had raised with the federal government, that of the appointment of a woman protector to 'look after the interests of the aborigine and half-caste women and children, and that she should be stationed at Alice Springs'. This position was required, they said, in addition to that of the current Protector of Aborigines.[258]

Another organisation that took a keen interest in goings on in the Red Centre was the Aborigines Friends Association (AFA). They had had been operating in Adelaide since 1858, out of 'concern for the moral, spiritual and physical wellbeing of Australian Aboriginal people' of the Northern Territory and South Australia.[259] The AFA was comprised of Protestant clergymen and laymen and played a role in the establishment and staffing of Aboriginal schools and missions. The

WNPA and AFA had an uneasy and at times oppositional relationship. The AFA, for example, was strongly opposed to the WNPA's push for a female protector.[260]

On 28 October 1924, the AFA wrote to Senator Pearce to inform him that it was 'deeply interested in the solution of the problem of the housing and training of the half-caste children at Alice Springs'. They were of the opinion that it would be unwise to remove these children from federal territory to South Australia and that 'the children should be placed in a home built in a suitable locality off the highway'. A 'suitable superintendent and wife' should be placed in charge, which 'would be a distinct advance on the present system'.[261]

The AFA offered to gather information on the best location for a new home and to 'make some recommendations for the practical oversight, discipline and training of these half-caste children so as to make them useful members of the community'.[262] Consultations between the government and the AFA continued, as progress on a new home was made.

In October 1924, a feature article by special reporter Malcolm Ellis appeared in the *Sydney Daily Telegraph*. Prefaced by a sensational list of headings and subheadings,

Grave Scandal at Alice Springs
HALF-CASTE HORROR
SCENE OF WRETCHEDNESS
GOVERNMENT INDICTED

the article begins,

> One hesitates generally to say anything is a scandal. There is no need for hesitation in saying it about the half-caste children's 'bungalow' at Alice Springs, because that is an institution which must make everyone who sees it burn with indignation. It is more than a scandal. It is a horror.[263]

Ellis goes on to detail the building, living conditions and his own racial prejudices:

The material of the buildings is galvanised iron. The method by which they have been built is this:- Upon a rectangular frame sheets of iron were nailed. A few sheets were left out to allow a door to be inserted on each of the long sides of the building. On each side of the door sheets were left out to make windows. There is no glass in the windows: they have iron shutters, and when the doors and windows are closed no air can possibly enter the buildings. There is no lining to the iron either in the way of ceiling or walls. There is no flooring except mother earth.

In the girls' house (may Heaven pardon me for so describing that kennel) there are three rough bunks in which a sailor would flatly refuse to sleep. There are no sheets, seemingly few blankets; no pictures on the walls; not enough chairs to seat half a dozen people; no verandahs so that the heat or the cold or the rain must beat directly onto the walls of the building.

In rainy weather, which, fortunately, does not come very often either, the place must be sealed, or the floor becomes a puddle.

If rain and heat come together the interior of these buildings must be like the Black Hole of Calcutta. The hottest period on record in Alice Springs was one of eight consecutive days during which the temperature was over 100 degrees every day.

There is no need to fear the cold. When the girls go to bed (and my measurements are generous) they have each exactly a space of nine feet by two to accommodate them from end to end of the building, and even mountain air at 4000 feet cannot over come the self-generated heat of such packing. The boys are just as well off in that respect.

NO BATHING

There is no water supply at this school: the children themselves carry whatever water is needed over 100 yards from the Police Bungalow and across the main road. There is one small lavatory; no bathroom except such as is improvised with a tub.

There is not enough table accommodation to let these humans – many of them, as I say, as white as you or I… sit down and have their meals like civilised human beings: if there were there would be no chairs or forms for most of them to sit on.

The cooking accommodation consists of a short of sentry box affair, with an ordinary stove in it which would send the ordinary housewife on strike if she were asked to cook for a family of ten on it. The cooking hutch is open to the winds that blow; the cook and housekeeper is an old black gin.[264]

An old black gin. Presumably, that's a reference to Topsy who worked her guts out for those kids but received so very little in the way of acknowledgment from the whites. *An old black gin.* A saviour. An angel.

Between October and December, similar articles by Ellis were rolled out in the broadsheets of Australia's capital cities. One made it as far as the *Daily Telegraph* in London.

The Australian government, through their high commissioner in London, himself a former antipodean prime minister, stammered a reply.

> I am officially informed that this statement is grossly exaggerated…
>
> The children are in the care of a competent matron who has three half-caste assistants…
>
> There was only one case where a girl was absent from quarters at night. The man responsible for inducing the girl to absent herself was proceeded against under the Aboriginal Ordinance…and a fine was imposed.[265]

The National Councils of Women of Australia held an interstate conference in the Melbourne Town Hall in October 1924. High on the agenda were the conditions of Aboriginal people in Central Australia in general, as well as those at the Bungalow.

Said Mrs A.K. Goode, South Australian social and political activist,

> Conditions among the aborigines in Central Australia are appalling. Venereal disease has spread in the most terrible manner and demoralisation is general.
>
> When the white man took over Australia the aborigines were frightened from the water holes, the cattle ate their food and starvation drove them to the camps where they are becoming more and more demoralised. Dr Basedon who has spent most of his time in Central Australia has shown me photographs of dreadful cases that were the result of venereal disease.

In 1922 the govt published a report from the Parliamentary Standing Committee on Public Works but nothing has been done. Octaroon children are living amongst the blacks in degenerating circumstances. Many of the natives are shockingly diseased and are allowed to spread their infection unchecked. A training school should be established for half-caste children who tend more towards the black race than the white and a separate training school should be kept for octaroons. Reservations should be established like those in Queensland and severe penalties should be imposed upon white men found within their boundaries.[266]

Mrs Goode appealed to the women of Australia to unite in their efforts to improve the conditions. She also moved that the various state Councils of Women be asked to study and discuss the treatment and care of the Aborigines.

Mrs J.R. Bowman did not like to 'talk of the scandals of our country as it is cabled all over the world, but the conditions of the bungalow, where half-caste children are living', were, she said, 'a scandal':

The house for fifty half-caste children adjoins an hotel. There are about thirty girls whose ages range from about fourteen to eighteen, and who are huddled together in a manner that is not at all good for them. There is only one small lavatory. I understand the Federal Government was going to allow these half-castes to be removed to South Australia and I think the experiment should be made.[267]

While the advocacy was not based on any kind of consultation with the people being advocated for, at least Mrs John Jones had, as she pointed out, lived amongst the 'aborigines' in Central Australia:

She said that educated half-castes were most desirable and useful citizens. The aborigines, she found, were not naturally immoral, but were corrupted by their white neighbours.[268]

From the conference came a resolution:

That the Federal Ministry be asked to give full consideration to the conditions existing among half-castes and aborigines in Central

Australia and contiguous to the east-west railway, with a view to remedying the present unsatisfactory state of affairs.[269]

In response, Senator Pearce told reporters that he would 'very much like to provide a new building on a new site', but could not 'make bricks without straw'. For two years, he said, he had had a sum of money on the estimates but Treasury had not approved it. In defence of conditions at the Bungalow, Pearce explained that the police were nearby and 'the half-caste women' were well cared for. 'The matron in charge is a most estimable woman who pays every possible attention to her duties' and Sergeant Stott and his wife also gave much attention to the children.[270]

Again, no mention of Topsy.

By 28 October 1924, the Treasurer had 'agreed to provide 5000 pounds for the purpose of erecting suitable buildings near Alice Springs, Northern Territory, for housing half-caste children of Central Australia' on the police paddock reserve, about two miles from the township of Alice Springs.

By 1925, even the 'obedient servant' Ida Standley was expressing discontent such as the following, from her annual report for the Administrator:

> The general welfare of this institution leaves much to be desired, and until the children are removed from the precincts of the Hotel to suitable building a mile or so out of the town things will remain as they are at present.
>
> The children are well behaved and the happiest and healthiest family I have ever worked amongst. The matron should reside at the home, as these people require constant supervision.
>
> Numbers are growing. At present there are 57 inmates – 28 males and 29 females. In addition there are eight girls employed outside, six of whom return to the home at night.
>
> The Bungalow has its own flock of goats and vegetable garden for supplies. The approximate cost of food per capita is 4s. per week.[271]

Maggie Plenty[272]

Maggie was born when Halley's Comet was in the sky. That took on a worldly significance much later when, in her senior years, Maggie wanted to apply for the pension, but she had neither a birth certificate nor date of birth. Maggie's brother, Jim Drover, recalled the astronomical event at the time of his sister's birth. A date was decided on, in March 1910, and a certificate was issued.

Jennifer Niebour Pott told me that. She told me all sorts of things about her mother's life and one day on the phone she told me about the letters her mother had written to her when she was in her seventies and returning to Alice Springs for the first time in over fifty years.

Jennifer: Oh, by the way, I have these letters Maggie wrote that you might be interested in.

Me: Interested! I'll be on the next flight.

But there was no need. Jennifer had typed them up and she emailed me copies. It was a research boon as was the discovery of Jennifer herself: a second-generation Bungalow child, daughter of Maggie, happy to share information with me about her mother's extraordinary background, through phone calls and emails. The letters were icing on the cake.

Maggie was born at Urandanji in Western Queensland, on the main stock route between Camoweel and Maree. She spent the first five years of her life in the vicinity of the Plenty River, two hundred and fifty-five kilometres north of Alice Springs, with her young mum Ladie Lady, and the mob.

Maggie's people nourished her and taught her the Arrernte ways of the early twentieth century. They were traditional ways peppered with the influences and demands of nearby Huckitta Station.

Charles Dubois of Huckitta Station sired Maggie. He went on to start the horse racing industry in Alice Springs with his mate James Cummins, whose family remains in racing to this day. In 1926, Dubois won the Melbourne Cup with his horse King Ingoda. He fathered a few kids with Aboriginal women. Cummins did too. What a lark it all was. Stations. Horse race meetings. Sex on tap.

Let's pause for a moment to ponder if they shared the racing bounty with their Aboriginal offspring.

No, that's right. Imagine the difference that could have made.

Maggie was taken away, at the age of five, to the Bungalow. There she was given the second part of her name, Plenty, after the area she came from. It is curious that Maggie wasn't given her father's surname, as per Stott's general practice. Jennifer doesn't know why her mum wasn't called Maggie Dubois. She can only think that maybe it was because Maggie was one of the first to be treated in this way. Presumably it was 1915 when the Central Australian practice of taking children away from their mob was just beginning.

> Mum said her brothers and sisters came after her. They took the name Dubois. There was a problem that brothers would marry sisters, not realising. (Jennifer Neibour-Pott)

I ponder on how Jennifer says they took the name Dubois. It's just a turn of phrase, isn't it? You take your husband's name. Take your mother's name perhaps. Make a decision about how you will be known. I don't think those kids took a name but rather were given one, the way they were given a blanket, a dish of food and a phenyl bath each morning.

Maggie Plenty spent the rest of her childhood at the Bungalow. She learnt to read and write on a slate with chalk. After the older ones had learnt, they taught the younger ones. She learnt to scrub and bake. She learnt sex education first-hand by seeing girls give birth on the dirt floor. She learnt sociology first-hand by living the life of a light brown kid growing up in a tin shed. And she never saw her mother again. As Jennifer tells it,

Mum always said the other mothers would come to visit the kids at the bungalow and bring them food, but her mother never came.

In September 1976, in the lead-up to a trip back to Alice Springs to look for her mother, in a letter to Jennifer Maggie wrote,

> If my mum came back to see me I would have been happy. I used to make believe she used to come but never came true. I guess God payed me my reward with a good husband and two good daughters, two good son-in-laws and most darling twins.

Maggie found out later that Ladie Lady had followed the party that stole Maggie. The young mother tracked her daughter as far as Arltunga but was prevented from going any further.

Once, Topsy Smith showed Maggie honey ants and Ida Standley told her off. Which reminds me of a line that Ida Standley wrote in a letter to the Chief Protector early on:

> What it takes us five years to build up is undone by five minutes back with the blacks.[273]

She was kind and dedicated, Ida Standley, and the children were apparently fond of her. She used to put her hands on Maggie's face and call her 'my little pet'; a practice Maggie carried into her own parenting.[274] As Maggie herself wrote in one of her letters to her daughter,

> Our teacher Mrs Standley was a real mum to us she gave us her love and we really loved her. When we saw her coming…we would run and meet her. She was such a kind person.

She was also of her time, Ida, and thought it best, as so many of them did, that the 'half-caste' children leave the Aboriginal ways, including their families, behind.

When a girl starts her period, it's a coming of age event. Some cultures celebrate with a party. Some have special, female only rituals. In some, the young woman undergoes physical challenges to demonstrate her strength and perseverance.

When Maggie started her period, a white lady accused her of having had sex with a man. Maggie hadn't been with a man and Topsy Smith set her straight. Which white woman, I ask?

> Mum never mentioned her name but the only other person there would have been Mrs Standley's daughter. (Jennifer Neibour-Pott)

Mrs Standley's daughter was Vivian Brown. She was married to Leonard Brown and together they ran the Stuart Arms Hotel. I wonder if Vivian was accused of having had sex with a man when she got her first period.

> Sex! No one taught them about sex. They learnt the hard way. They knew where babies came from because the girls gave birth in the bungalow on the dirt floor.
> Drunks from the Stuart Arms hotel would come and take children from the Bungalow for sex. Mum said she never went and always thought sex was disgusting. (Jennifer Neibour-Pott)

Maggie worked on at least one station in Central Australia before being taken by the Stott family in 1927 to work for them. They were going to take her to Perth, where they were moving, but Robert Stott walked in front of a train and that was the end of that. Maggie was sent to Burra Burra in South Australia, to work for someone else.

Maggie teamed up with Elsie Raggatt and Jess Hayes at the Bungalow, connections that lasted a lifetime. To Jennifer, they are her aunties:

> Elsie Raggatt, her father had Glen Helen station. Mum always said he was 'a horrible horrible man'. As a young child I did not ask why, her face was enough to know not to ask. Later from dad I found out he used to use a stock whip on the blacks.
> Auntie Jess, Jessie Hayes, her dad was Ted Hayes. There is a photo of him somewhere sitting on a horse. Mum always said 'dirty old bugger' Undoolya Station. (Jennifer Neibour-Pott)

Jennifer says they all had different ways of dealing with what happened to them in their childhoods:

Aunty Jess wouldn't talk about her childhood. Mum talked about it all the time. Aunty Jess's mum came to see her in Adelaide when she was working. Aunty Jess wouldn't talk to her.

Jennifer thinks that might have been because when they turned twenty-one, they could sign a form to say they weren't Aboriginal. Then they were given their bank books and set free. Perhaps Aunty Jess thought she would lose her privileges if she acknowledged her mother.

Aunty Elsie used to talk about her father like he was the best father there ever was. Mum said there's no way he was that. That was just some fantasy Aunty Elsie had.

Jennifer remembers her mum as happy-go-lucky, joking and laughing a lot.

She had ways of hiding her pain and if anyone was ever rude to their mother, mum would get stuck into them. I remember when Elvis Presley's mother died mum got really upset. I said, mum, you don't even know her, you don't need to get so upset. But it was really about her own pain, from her mum.

When Maggie returned to Alice Springs, in her seventies, it was with Jess and Elsie. In the lead-up to that trip she wrote,

Whilst I am up there I (will) make…enquiries …just for my satisfaction.
   I said to Jess I guess she would have passed way by now and she said you never know Margaret, look at old Hettie Perkins she is nearly 100 and healthy as you and I. She said those people that live in the bush, she said they live for years.
   As dad said no drugs drinks smokes etc etc. They live till quite old so here goes Jen I may have luck.

In Alice Springs, as Maggie tells it,

Went and saw a dear old lady that knew my mum. With tears in her eyes she said to me my mum passed away three years ago. She was crying…also met Perkins mum [Charles Perkins's mum,

Hetty]. She is so old but I was talking to her and she was so delighted. The news spread like wild fire that us three were holidaying in the Alice. Even the paper rang up to interview us but we said no to that. Auntie Kath is taking us out to meet all the ones we know. We are invited to meals, visits. One lady cried on my shoulders when I told her who I was. She said, oh no, not Margaret Dubois. I said yes and she said you look real pretty.

Maggie married in 1943. She had two daughters, Jennifer and Diane. After Maggie died, they took her ashes back home, to her childhood playground by the Plenty, and a plaque has since been erected.

I speak with Jennifer on the day before the eleventh anniversary of the National Apology to the Stolen Generations. She is preparing to attend a commemorative event the next day.

'It makes me cry every time,' says Jennifer. 'I get so emotional. I wish Mum could have lived to see it. It would have meant the world to her.'

Maggie Plenty with her family before she was taken away.

Paying respects to Maggie.[275]

Back in the Alice

There were reasons I stayed for decades
The colours
Namatjira landscapes
The raw-edged outback life
Living, largely, outdoors

I learnt to write here
To pare it back
To think outside the square
Step outside the square
Rub it out

I saw myself reflected in the people, in the place
Carved a niche
Became myself

There were reasons for my departure
That dragged on like each punishing summer

The big issues
Thrashed out endlessly
A collective banging of heads against walls
The stresses of the cultural interface
Racism, both casual and deeply ingrained
Born back
In an era that lives on

The rage of the rednecks
The pain of the past
Blackfella whitefella blackfella whitefella brickbrother whybother bullshit blah

The small town cringe
Oh hi (banal falsetto)
Hi how are you
Good how are you
Nice to see you
Nice to see you
With fingers crossed behind backs

And my family, my kin
The lush country of my genesis
So far away

How do I feel about being back?
Exactly how I felt before I left

Iron and Squalor 3

Perhaps Sergeant Stott enjoyed his foray into Melbourne in January 1925, a reprieve from the annual marathon that was summer in the Alice. Neo-gothic architecture, parks and gardens, the arts, a sea breeze and gentlemen with whom to discuss matters of significance. Conversely, perhaps the city held no appeal for Stott, and he couldn't wait to get back to his family and small-town fiefdom. Stott had, after all, made it his business to live in some of the farthest-flung places on earth. His excursion to Melbourne may have been duty only, this time to attend a conference at which his expert opinion was required.

Those seated at the table with Stott that day were the Administrator of the Northern Territory, the Secretary of the Department of Home and Territories and some of his main men, and the Acting Director-General of Works. The purpose of the gathering, as noted in the minutes, was to discuss 'the question of a new home for half-castes in the Southern end of the Northern Territory…to provide a more suitable site in place of the existing one, and more suitable accommodation'.[276]

Stott had written to the Department of Home and Territories in December 1924, flagging alternatives to the police paddock. He recommended that the 'home for halfcastes' be built outside the township, at a location with an assured supply of good water and suitable country for agriculture and stock breeding, for example Emily Gap, Milners Camp or Jay Creek.[277]

At the January meeting, several sites were discussed and dismissed for one reason or another. Stott told the assembled conference that at Jay Creek a good supply of water was assured, that the area was suitable for stock raising and that 'the half-castes would not, in that locality, be subject to any danger of interference by white people'.[278] Stott suggested there was also a good supply of timber at Jay Creek for building. On the basis of Stott's assertions, it was unanimously agreed that an area of fifty square miles at Jay Creek be selected as the site of the proposed new home.[279]

Jay Creek is forty-eight kilometres west of Alice Springs. It's the classic riverine landscape of Central Australia: an expansive sandy river bed adorned with river red gums, scattered rocky outcrops and plains that extend out from the watercourse. The horizon appears, in all directions, as mountain ranges nestled against sky.

If you dig into the sand of Central Australian river beds, you reach soakages of water. How far down you go depends on how much rain has fallen, and in which part of the river you are digging. The knowledge of where to dig has sustained the desert people for millennia. In July 1925, when construction began, the water source was a small soakage well that had silted up. By November a well had been sunk to fifty feet and was producing about one thousand eight hundred gallons a day. This was considered sufficient for domestic purposes but not for all the requirements of the home.

Construction was another challenge. It was slow; hampered by drought and what is noted in the records only as 'trouble with tradesmen'. There was a shortage of suitable bush timber for framing despite Stott's earlier assurances. In December, Sergeant Stott fell ill and was temporarily replaced, the contractors were paid off and construction came to a standstill.

Attempts to tap into more artesian water continued into 1926. The government geologist of South Australia arrived and identified potential well sites. Hopes were raised. At each site, contractors dug through alluvial soil using hand-boring equipment until they struck impenetrable rock. Hopes were dashed. It's a pattern that continued until June 1926, when it was finally accepted that the water supply they had been sure they would be able to tap into at Jay Creek was proving elusive and the institution would have to be built elsewhere.

By then, just over three thousand of the original five thousand pounds had been spent. What they had to show for this was a sawmilling plant, a concrete floor and accompanying timber frame, an inadequate water supply and a fine collection of detailed architectural plans. No home. Nowhere near a home. Just a concrete floor, a bit of framing and a fine collection of plans.

The plans are still there, just as they were in 1925 when they were crisply off the press. These days ,they are stored at the National Archives in Darwin. 'We are no longer located in the CBD,' the woman tells me on the phone. 'It's a cost-cutting measure.'

Never mind. It's enlightening what you see on the bus, and out through the windows: the pulse of the place and its underbelly; the way the Territory's capital has developed according to plans, and in spite of them.

In the cool quiet of the reading room, I am excited for my next archival adventure. I flip over the large cardboard cover of

THE OLD ALICE SPRINGS NORTHERN TERRITORY IN-STITUTION FOR HALF CASTE CHILDREN[280]

and come face to face with large brittle sheet after sheet, now patched with yellow where age has set in, of this souvenir of time gone by.

SCHOOL BUILDING
DORMITORIES
PROPOSED QUARTERS
DINING ROOM & KITCHEN

It's all here.

STORE
DETAILS FOR JOINERY

All meticulously thought out and laid-out and drawn to precision, right down to where the matron will sleep, and the folded linen will be stored.

I pore over the drawings, one after the next; the lines, the shapes, the labels, the work director's signature at the bottom of each page, as if I'm going to build the damn thing myself. I snap photos with my phone, this way and that. But still I want more. I use the magnifying glass, hold it over each picture, closer, further away, but it doesn't get me what I want.

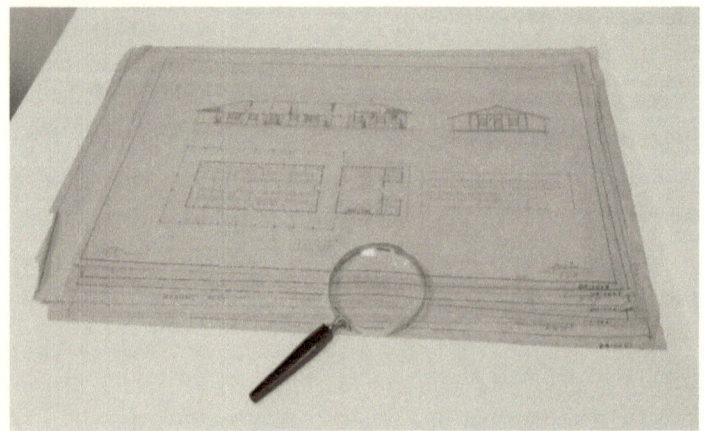

I keep scanning, studying the drawings, peering into them, through them, and at last…

I hear the chatter first, like birds, but it's children, spilling from buildings out onto the verandas and beyond. Chattering. Carousing. Children. I can make out one or two women in the shadows of the buildings, with work to do and reticent little ones hiding in the folds of their skirts. The air is clear and warm and there's birdsong, raked red earth, and beyond that the crackling bush.

It could all still be there today, not the people but the colonial establishment: the deep verandas, the simple quarters, the schoolroom with its chalkboard and little wooden desks. 'The Old Jay Creek Institution' it could be called these days, because we don't say those other words any more. We could go and bear witness to the reverberations of the past. Indigenous tourism is how they would market it. Kangaroo and damper as we look out over the tranquil landscape. Guided by the descendants of that first generation.

They brought the children of 'mixed-heritage' here.
Thought they were doing the right thing.

Trained and educated.

Stolen Generations we call it now.

What's that? Yes, like in Rabbit Proof Fence.

Detailed plans, detailed costings, detailed instructions. An exercise in futility. They never built the 'Institution for Half-Caste children' at Jay Creek. They invested a lot in it but couldn't quite get it together. By mid-1926, the search for water had dried up and the quest for a new location was back on.

Pinta's Creek?

Burt's Plain?

Bonney Creek?

Acacia Well?

They were all either too dry or too bare or too far or too close. Across that whole sweep of the vast Red Centre, not one site was deemed suitable for a home and training institute for young half-castes and their associated fractions. Was that not saying something in itself?

When the Anglican Bishop of Carpentaria turned up in Central Australia in April 1927 to weigh into the 'half-caste question', he confirmed that all sites that had been considered were unsuitable. 'At none could proper police protection be provided. The cost of maintenance at all would be unnecessarily increased, freights are 1/- per ton per mile by camel and 2/- per ton per mile by motortruck.'[281] The bishop represented the Australian Board of Missions in the northern part of Australia. In March the previous year, he had offered on behalf of the Church of England 'to receive all half-caste children of 10 years of age and under in Alice Springs and Darwin into their settlement on Groote Eylandt'.[282] The government declined the offer, 'on account of the enormous distance to be travelled and the heavy expenditure involved'. At that stage, in March 1926, Jay Creek was still their preferred option.

In 1927, the bishop favoured 'the Gap', two miles south of town. There, he said, was a government building, used formerly as a police station and now in use by the stock inspector until his home in town was complete. This area was more commonly known as the Police Paddock. The bishop also thought the Overland Telegraph Station, two miles to the north of the town, might be suitable. They were government-owned buildings, currently in use as post office and telegraph station. With the railway terminus on the way, the bishop considered, a post office would be established within the town area, leaving the buildings at the Telegraph Station vacant. They would be suitable just the way they were – well fenced with abundant water and a good garden.

Continuing, in some sort of crazy stocktake, the bishop found that there were

> Seven adult women not employed in domestic service.
> Four adult women employed in service locally but living in the Home.
> Seven girls over the age of twelve.
> Thirty children, boys and girls, between the ages of eight and twelve.
> Twelve children under the age of eight but over five.
> Nine babies.[283]

The bishop also noted 'at least 50 half-castes and quadroon children in Central Australia, under the age of twelve', who were not in the home. Some of these were the children of legally married parents, but thirty or more had unmarried mothers. He asked that all such children be treated by the government as orphans and sent to the home, unless the fathers would marry their mothers, thus legitimatising the children.[284]

The Postmaster General's Department (PMG) wasn't ready to surrender the Telegraph Station. In response to an enquiry from the Department of Home and Territories, they argued that the removal of the office to Stuart would involve considerable expense which would not be warranted.[285]

Attention turned squarely to a site near the Police Paddock, where a new round of testing for water began.

Tick. Tock. Tick. Tock.

The children continued to grow up in iron and squalor, adjacent to the hotel, where the wild men of the centre came to get hammered. A whole new load of such men, coming with the train line, were well on the way.

In December 1927, the WNPA wrote once again to the Minister for Home and Territories, questioning the long delay in 'building the Home for Half-caste children now at Alice Springs'. They suggested Love's Creek as a viable alternative and objected to the Telegraph Station, which they maintained was too close to the town. It was also surrounded by hilly country in which the girls would be able to continue their associations with 'undesirable people'. The only way to protect them properly, according to the WNPA, was to house them right away from any township or travelling route, where they could 'no longer be tempted or tempt others to immorality. Then under proper supervision they can be trained in useful occupations and so be given a chance to develop into happy, useful beings.'[286]

In April 1928, the Bishop of Willochra in South Australia, having just returned from a visit to Alice Springs, expressed his concerns in a letter to the Prime Minister:

> The conditions under which the half caste children are living at present are deplorable; and a scandalous situation of the utmost gravity may arise there at any time, specially in view of the approach of Railway Construction work.
>
> When suitable buildings are erected by the Government I understand our church is prepared to find a suitable staff to look after the children.
>
> If you would kindly have urgent enquiries made with a view to the erection of buildings without delay I should be very grateful.[287]

And in June, a deputation from the Aboriginal Protection League presented the Prime Minister with the following:

> My chief interest lies in the protection of women and children. I first became interested in the half-castes' home at Alice Springs, and about two years ago I went there to look at matters for myself, and I found that the adverse reports of the conditions there had not been exaggerated. I found as many as 50 half-caste children housed in a little tin shed at the rear of the hotel there. The Federal Government moved in the matter and tried to build a new home. I went with two members of the House of Representatives to the

new site and although I understand that something like 3,000 pounds has been spent on the place, something has been bungled and the children are still in the little hut at Alice Springs.[288]

It would seem that such pressure, along with an urgent need to avert the impending disaster that could be unleashed with the arrival of a flood of young railway construction workers who had been out on the track and shall we say, deprived of certain comforts for a time, led to the sudden and miraculous production, from a well at Jay Creek, of five hundred gallons a day. At the close of the 1928 school year and the beginning of another scorching summer, the three tin sheds behind the Stuart Arms Hotel were dismantled and transported out to the previously abandoned building site at Jay Creek along with the

Eleven adult women,
Seven girls over the age of twelve,
Thirty children between the ages of eight and twelve,
Twelve children aged between five and eight, and
Nine babies

of the bishop's earlier stocktake and an aged and ailing matron who was having heart attacks and desperately needed to retire.

The pre-loved sheets of iron were slapped around the timber frame that had been buckling and bowing in the harsh Central Australian conditions since 1925. A tent beneath a bough shelter was pitched as quarters for the matron.

'It wasn't even fit for a dog to live in, in those days,'[289] said Emily Liddle, who was brought to live at the Bungalow at Jay Creek in 1929. The inmates slept on concrete floors, sharing their blankets to make things a little bit more comfortable. There was 'a little bit of kitchen on the side where the girls used to do the baking' and one out of the two stoves was good enough for baking bread.

That's how it was, for the next four years, at Jay Creek.

*A view of the temporary quarters at the Bungalow,
Alice Springs (Jay Creek), 1929.*[290]

The King

When one of the State Governors made a journey up, the school was paraded for his benefit. He asked the children what country they lived in and they said Australia. He asked them who ruled Australia and they answered, the King. Then he asked who ruled the King. This was a poser. At last one of the brightest cried out – 'Sergeant Stott!'[291] (From a writer who travelled up through Central Australia during Stott's reign)

On 13 October 1927, after a sixteen-year reign in which he held two hundred thousand square miles of Central Australia in the palm of his hand, the by-now Commissioner of Police, Robert Stott, addressed a letter to the secretary of the Home and Territories Department.

> Dear Sir
> I have the honour most respectfully to make application for 8 months leave of absence, also 12 months long service Furlough leave. Have not had any Long Furlough leave, during my 45 year's service…
> At the end of my leave it is my intention to retire from the Police Service.[292]

Stott's leave would take him up to and beyond June 1928, when he would reach the retirement age of seventy.

Robert Stott was born in Aberdeen Scotland to James Stott, a fishery inspector, and his wife Catherine (née Cruickshank). He grew up to join the Lancashire Constabulary before migrating to Australia in 1882 with four of his mates. At the time of landing in South Australia, they had one pound in cash between them.[293] Stott joined the South Australian Police Force on 1 August 1883 then transferred to the Northern Territory of South Australia on 1 February 1883.[294]

In 1899, Stott married Mary Duggan. After her death, in April 1902, Stott married Agnes Heaslip, originally of Cooktown. They had six children, the youngest of whom was born after the family had moved, in 1911, to Alice Springs.

In the words of that same writer quoted above,

> He was elderly, short, burly, and he ruled Alice Springs with a rod of iron. He represented administration in all its branches, except post and telegraph. He was head of the police, mining warden, lands department, stock inspector, protector of aborigines, everything. He was a month's journey from his immediate superiors, the king of the district. He had his own codes, but what he said was law.[295]

By the time the authorities managed to organise a replacement, it was April 1928. Just weeks after leaving Alice Springs, to commence the next chapter of his life, Stott, hard of hearing, stepped in front of a train. He was rushed to Adelaide Hospital unconscious, suffering from severe head injuries including a fractured skull. The iron cop, the recently abdicated King of Central Australia, never gained consciousness and died the following day, 5 May 1928.

Tributes flowed including this, from the President of the Stockowners Association:

> He was a valuable man for the country, and everybody – both black and white – spoke well of him. (*Observer*, 19 May 1928, p. 5)

Now I know that's not strictly true, but it would have been the opinion of many.

In a letter to the Minister for Home Affairs, urging an expression of condolence to Stott's wife, the President of the Senate wrote, in part,

> Robt. Stott had a great reputation in the Northern Territory as a successful, careful and efficient police officer. I venture to think that had he still been at Alice Springs, the recent unfortunate native trouble rising would not have taken place.
>
> I am sure Mrs. Stott and her family would be extremely

gratified if the Government would now send a letter to them expressing appreciation for the work Robt. Stott did for so many years, more especially as a son of his has now joined the police force and will, I am confident, follow in his father's footsteps.

It was the intention of Sgt. Stott to write extensively on the natives and particularly the half-castes in the Northern Territory, but unfortunately he has taken his knowledge with him and it is now lost to us.[296]

What Agnes Stott needed, along with condolences, was financial support. Let's give her the last word on her husband, as she wrote, following her Robert's death, to the Department of Home and Territories,

I have no money, our practice was that I operated in my Husband's account, that account closed quite suddenly...

For 27 years I stood by my husband and have done official work that no one will ever know. We have deprived ourselves and labored, we have gone through deep water and rough weather together...

Our children partly grown away through long years of absence, I have no home, boarding here, my poor husband a good man...[297]

Monies were forthcoming.

Sergeant Robert Stott, 1922. Behind him is Jim Shannon, Alice Springs resident.[298]

This is How Freeman do to Me

This chapter documents sexual abuse against children that took place at the Bungalow at Jay Creek and then after it had moved to the Telegraph Station.

*

A girl, in a dusky corner, pulls out the pencil and paper she has smuggled from the classroom. Her hand shakes as she writes the letter, but she doesn't stop until she's finished.

Alice Springs

Feb 25th 1934

Dear Sir

    I am longing to have someone to help me and I thought I'll write to you. This is how Mr Freeman do to me. When Mrs Freeman went to town one day this is first thing he did to me he sent the rest of the girls down the creek and he took me to his room I don't like it no because I think it over myself that it is wrong to do a thing like that. He should know that himself. On Saturday night he came in and took me out of the room it was on eleven o'clock at night. I am always worry over it. He's just keeping me here for that so that he'll do anything he like to me. Fanny saw myself and him in the bathroom and she came back and told the girls. Everybody laughs at me when they see me go with him. And I want you to help me dear sir I cannot put every thing in the paper I tell you when I see you.[299]

The girl was Dolly Downer[300] and her letter was to Vic Carrodus, Deputy Administrator of the Northern Territory and resident of Alice

Springs. By then, the Bungalow had relocated from Jay Creek to the Telegraph Station. That's another story. The sexual abuse that Freeman started at Jay Creek, he continued at the Telegraph Station.

Some policemen turn up. They talk to Hetti Perkins then she comes over to where Dolly is standing with a group of girls.

'Mr Carrington wants to talk to you and you and you she says,' pointing to Dolly and some of the other girls.

The excitement they have about going for a ride in a white man's car is balanced with trepidation about what is going to happen. It is the day after Dolly sent her letter.

One by one, Dolly and the other girls go into an office in town, where they meet with Mr Carrington and Mr McCann, who they are told is a Justice of the Peace. The girls have to swear on the Bbible they will tell the truth then the men write down everything the girls tell them.

In her statement, Dolly said,

> I have been at the institution since I was a baby and have never been out working. My mother is L... R... an aboriginal at Bonds Springs. One day last winter, I went into house to clean door knob. He (Mr Freeman) got hold of me and put me on the bed in his room. He took all my clothes off and lay down on top of me and interfered with me. I tried to get away but could not do so. After that I often went into school with Mr Freeman and the same thing happened. The other girls often saw me going in with him. I used to let him do it as I was frightened. Sometimes he brought me into his bed-room. I told XXX what he was doing, a long time ago.
>
> On last Saturday night I went to the dormitory with all the other girls about 9 o'clock. I did not get undressed as I fell asleep before I had time. I was asleep and then woke up because Johnny (baby) was crying and I got up to get him a drink of water at the tap. I saw Mr Freeman standing at the back door. He called me outside. He did not say anything but took me by the arm into the school. Mr Freeman unlocked the dormitory door. The school door was open. We went into big school room. Mr Freeman pulled my dress right up and took off my pants. Mr Freeman only had pyjamas on and he took them off half way. He made me lie

down on the floor then he laid on top of me. He then put his thing right inside me. After that I came out and went straight to dormitory. I did not talk to anybody. I saw XX and XX all awake. I did not see Mr Freeman come out of the school. A little while after I went in I heard somebody lock the door.

On Sunday I told XXX that I would tell Mr Carrington and she said if I did not tell him she would tell him herself. On Monday night I wrote a letter to Mr Carrington telling him about it. On Monday night I saw Mr Freeman waiting outside the back door again but I did not go out.

In the file, held by the Northern Territory Archive Service in Darwin, XXX has been blacked out. It was probably Hetty Perkins. By 1934, Topsy Smith had left the Bungalow and Hetty Perkins was performing a similar caretaking role. Names and features that would identify other witnesses who gave sworn testimonies to the Justice of the Peace have also been redacted.

Witness 1

I have been at the institution since I was a little girl. When I was at the Jay I used to go with Mr Freeman about every fortnight when Mrs Freeman used to come in for mail. The first time he called me to house & asked me to go with him & I said 'I won't.' He was holding me & then he put me on his bed and pulled down my pants and got on top of me. Since I have been in here I have been with him a few times in his room – I have not been with him lately. I used to see Mr Freeman & Dolly going into his room when Mrs Freeman was away.

Witness 2

I have been at the institution for…I have heard all the girls talking about Mr Freeman going with girls at Jay –…and…used to go with him about last August he told me to go and clean the hospital while Mrs Freeman was down town. He came into hospital and locked the door. He caught hold of me and I screamed out. The boys heard me screaming. I have seen him going into the school with Dolly in the daytime when Mrs Freeman was away. I told… about him trying to get me.

Witness 3

I have been in the institution at the Jay & here for many years off & on. Last year Mr Freeman asked me to go into his room with him three or four times when Mrs Freeman was away. At first I did not want to go but I was frightened of him. I was 16 years of age last June 1st and I was with him before that time. Each time I went into his room he interfered with me. I told him before I went to the Granites that I would not go with him. I told…that I have been with him.

Witness 4

When we were at the Jay I first heard the boys and girls talking about Mr Freeman going with…since we came in here all the boys and girls have been talking about him going with…and Dolly Downer. One day…said she did not want to go with him anymore and after that everybody know he go with Dolly. One day just before all Darwin boys came, everybody was sent down creek and afterwards Dolly came down crying and told me in front of everybody, 'Mr Freeman take me in room and knock me down.' I said 'you had better let Mrs Freeman know.' I have often seen Mr Freeman and Dolly go into school and one day I saw them lock the door. They used to go into to school in daytime and all the children would talk about it.

On last Saturday night we all went into dormitory about 9 o'clock. I sat up talking to…for a long time. Mr Freeman opened the back door and sang out. '…tell Dolly I want her.' Dolly was near my bed and heard him sing out. Little girl… Was in lavatory & heard him sing out & she sang out 'Mr Freeman is calling you, he wants you Dolly.' Mr Freeman opened the door & Dolly went out. I got up and got drink and I saw them go to into school. Other girls… All saw them go into school. We all kept awake until we saw Dolly come out on her own. The other girls saw him come out afterwards. Dolly came in & went to bed & did not say anything. On Sunday I heard Dolly tell…that she was going to tell Mr Carrington about it.

Mr Freeman, who had been appointed in 1930 as 'Protector of Aborigines' refuted the allegations. He attempted to discredit the main witnesses. He bragged about the great work he had down at the Bungalow under the most trying of conditions.[301]

Father Percy Smith, a Church of England minister living in Alice Springs at the time, told a different story:

> There was an air of gloom and repression about the place and the children were silent and sullen. There was no laughter…The Superintendent, who was also a Protector of Aborigines, was a bully and a drunkard. The children cowered under his rule. They were supposed to have school every day but what a farce! … there were no trained teachers on the staff and the Superintendent only put the children into the classroom when he got the 'tip off' from his scouts in Alice Springs that an official was coming.[302]

Back in 1923, Baldwin Spencer called for 'every official, and above all those who act as Protectors of Aboriginals [to] be married men'.[303] In 1924, the Aborigines Friends Association called for 'a suitable superintendent and wife' to be placed in charge as a 'distinct advance on the present system'.[304] Well, this bastion of Christian suitability, who had run the Forrest River Mission Station near Wyndham in Western Australia for two years; who served his country at the front, during the Great War; who came with glowing references such as

> Knowledge of the natives and half-castes is very wide, temperamentally fitted for the arduous and self-sacrificing life, young enough to put plenty of vigour into the work,[305] hard worker, capable manager, best interests of the natives at heart,[306] conscientious and painstaking.[307]

turned out to be a cruel, incompetent sexual predator.

*

In *Bringing Them Home*, the Report of the National Inquiry into the Separation of Aboriginal and Torres Strait Islander Children from their Families (1995–1997), we are told that almost one in ten boys and just over one in ten girls reported having been sexually abused in a children's institution. The figure relates only to those who offered up that information willingly, as witnesses were not asked directly whether they'd had this experience.[308] The actual rate was probably much higher.

From the report of the Royal Commission into Institutional Responses to Child Sexual Abuse (2013–2017):

> Many survivors who identified as Aboriginal or Torres Strait Islander told us about being abused as children in residential institutions. These included missions, particularly mission dormitories, where there was little or no effective external oversight. These were often violent places where survivors had been humiliated and their identity and culture undermined. Physical, emotional and sexual violence was normalised. Violence by staff towards children, and among children, was condoned or ignored.[309]

Children who had been taken from their families under the guise of 'needing protection' were being raped and impregnated. As we also learnt from the Royal Commission into Institutional Responses to Child Sexual Abuse,

> Police often refused to believe children. They refused to investigate their complaints… Our civil law placed impossible barriers on survivors bringing claims against individual abusers and institutions.[310]

This was not the case in Alice Springs in 1934. Freeman was dismissed from the teaching service and charged with a breach of section 53 (1) of the Aboriginals Ordinance 1918–1933, which stated that

> Any male person, other than an aboriginal or a half-caste, who not being lawfully married to a female aboriginal or half-caste…
> (c) has carnal knowledge of a female aboriginal or half-caste shall be guilty of an offence. Penalty: One hundred pounds or imprisonment for three months.[311]

No further charge existed for the carnal knowledge having been with children or those in his care.

As reported in the *Northern Standard* in Darwin, Freeman was convicted on 3 March 1934 for 'one charge of indecent relations with a young inmate of the home'. D.D. Smith and D. Neck, both justices of the peace, were on the bench. Dr McCann, deputy chief protector. was the prosecutor and Freeman had legal representation.[312]

Five of the girls from the Bungalow gave evidence about the one incident that had occurred on Saturday night, 24 February. That was when Freeman had come to the door of the girls' dormitory in his pyjamas and taken Dolly to the school room. Dolly gave detailed evidence. Freeman denied the charge but called no witnesses on his behalf. After a short adjournment for summing up, Freeman was found guilty and fined £100 or three-months imprisonment. He was given one month to pay the fine. Unable to pay the fine, Freeman was jailed.

*

Dolly Downer was born at a station near Alice Springs. Her mother, an Arrernte woman, lived and worked on the station, along with her Arrernte husband. While the husband was away droving, Dolly was conceived. The station owner was her father.

Dolly grew up, from a young age, at the Bungalow. When she wrote her letter to the administrator, when she gave her testimony to the administrator and JP, when she gave evidence at the trial, Dolly was pregnant. She later gave birth to a son. She loved him and raised him. Old man Freeman had nothing to do with him. Later ,Dolly had another child. Then she met her life partner who was passing through Alice Springs, as many soldiers did, during World War II. They went on to have eight more children. Many of their descendants live in Alice Springs, while some are spread further afield.

'Mum was friendly and happy-go-lucky, and nothing fazed her,' one of Dolly's children tells me. 'Those people who grew up in the Bungalow were like that. They'd been through so much. It couldn't have got any tougher for them. She worked in the hospital and everyone thought the world of her.'

How Emily Made History

Topsy Smith's daughter Emily was eleven years of age when her family left Arltunga and went to Alice Springs. They had buried her father, the cold weather was moving in and they were hungry.

Emily spent the next few years living at the Bungalow and going to school in the afternoon with the Bungalow kids who were big enough. Next she was sent to Adelaide to work for strangers and live with them.

I wonder how Emily found out she was being sent away. Stott made those decisions. Presumably, he then passed them on to Standley, his messenger. Perhaps Standley passed the news on for Topsy to announce or perhaps she broke the news herself.

Big sister Maud was already in Adelaide. She had gone with the McKays in 1916. Thirteen or fourteen was the preferred age as far as Stott was concerned, which is how old Emily was around 1917, so presumably that's when she would have gone.

Maybe Mrs Standley asked them to stay behind at the end of their lessons, or called them over when they were scrubbing the desks down, as they did after class each day.

'*Clara, Katie, Red Wing, Emily.*'

The big girls. They knew it as soon as she called their names; it was what they had been dreading.

'*Yes, Mrs Standley,*' *milling around together in front of her desk.*

'*You will be going to Adelaide tomorrow to take up positions as domestics.*'

They might have grabbed each other's hands, bitten back tears. Perhaps one of them couldn't hold it back and tears started to roll down her cheeks.

'*I want to stay here with my mum,*' *Emily might have said firmly. She knew how sad it made her mum when her kids got sent away. But even as*

Emily protested, she knew it was no use. Walter said he wanted to stay and they made him go. Then Willie. Then Maudie. Now her.

'No, Emily. Mr Stott has decided that this is for the best. You will live with a family and work for them. If you work hard and remember your manners, you will get along just fine. Adelaide is marvellous.' Mrs Standley faltered, then quickly composed herself. 'You will be going by camel, leaving at eight a.m. It is all arranged. Now go along.'

We don't know for sure. Maybe the girls looked forward to an adventure in the big city, although I doubt it. Maybe they were given more than a day's notice. The only solid evidence we have to help us speculate about it was passed on down the family line and told to me by Ada's daughter and Emily's niece, Christine:

> Mum said when they threw her onto the camels, I think Uncle Walter had to take them down, she said all she could remember then, her mother getting flogged by a whip, in the dust, when she was trying to chase the girls. Topsy was chasing the camels to get the girls off. By Stott. He was a very cruel man.[313]

Ada and Jean Smith were six and seven years younger than Emily, so they were only little kids when she got sent. They would have gone later, sometime in the 1920s. That's probably when the incident described by Christine occurred. We don't know how Topsy took the news of Emily being sent away, nor whether she got flogged by a whip in the dust that time or not.

In 1925, Emily was working for Mrs Francis Lewis in Gawler.[314] She then moved to the home of Rubie Cresdee at Henley Beach, where she was in 1926, at the age of nineteen.[315] The next news we have of Emily comes from 1937, when she was living back in Alice Springs and married to George Geesing.

The Bungalow was up at the old Telegraph Station by then, where it had been since late 1932. It was a much larger establishment with better conditions than those in which Emily had grown up. As a later resident Emily Liddle (née Perkins) recalls, they had beds and mattresses, a shower and bathtubs. Moving from Jay Creek to the Telegraph

Station, said Emily Liddle, 'was like coming into a mansion after sleeping on concrete floors'.[316] But it appears to have been more regimented too; less like a tin shed home for a family of sixty and more like an institution where very bad things happened.

Emily and George were no longer living together and Emily was staying with her new partner, Robert Johnson.

On 1 July, Sergeant Koop paid a visit to Johnson's place. There, he saw Emily Geesing and said to Johnson, 'I believe you are living here with a half-caste named Emily Geesing.'

Johnson replied that Emily was not a half-caste but her mother had been. Koop replied that still made Emily a half-caste.[317]

The next day Koop returned with a constable and an order from the Northern Territory Deputy Protector of Aboriginals for Emily's removal to the Bungalow. There she was to be handed over to the care of the superintendent and his wife. As far as Koop was concerned, Emily was a 'half-caste' and living with a man who was not her husband. She was therefore 'aboriginal', and subject to the provisions of the Aboriginal Ordinance.

Section 3 of the Aboriginal Ordinance 1918–1937 defined 'Aboriginal' as

> A female half-caste not legally married to a person who was substantially of European origin or descent and living with her husband.[318]

A 'half caste' was

> Any person who is an offspring of parents one but not both of whom is aboriginal, and includes any person one of whose parents is a half-caste.[319]

Emily was considered to be a 'half-caste' and therefore also an 'aboriginal'. As such, she was subject to the provisions of the Ordinance, including section 16, which stated,

1. The Chief Protector may cause any aboriginal or half-caste to be

kept within the boundaries of any reserve or aboriginal institution or to be removed to and kept within the boundaries of any reserve or aboriginal institution, or to be removed from one reserve or aboriginal institution to another reserve or aboriginal institution, and to be kept therein.

2. Any aboriginal or half-caste who refuses to be removed or kept within the boundaries of any reserve or aboriginal institution when ordered by the Chief Protector, or resists removal, or who refuses to remain within or attempts to depart from any reserve or aboriginal institution to which he has been so removed, or within which he is being kept, shall be guilty of an offence against this Ordinance.[320]

Johnson was charged under section 53 of the Aboriginal Ordinance, which said that,

Any male person (except an aboriginal or half-caste) who
    a. Habitually lives with aboriginals or half-castes or with any aboriginal or half-caste who is not his lawful wife;
    b. Habitually consorts, keeps company or associations with, or who is found between the hours of sunset and sunrise with, or in the company of, any female aboriginal or female half-caste who is not his lawful wife, without the authority in writing of the Director of Native Affairs or other lawful excuse…; or
    c. Cohabits with or has sexual intercourse with any aboriginal or half-caste who is not his lawful wife,
Shall be guilty of an offence.
Penalty: One hundred pounds or imprisonment for six months or both.[321]

Johnson was found guilty. He appealed the conviction on the grounds that Geesing was not a 'half-caste' within the meaning of the Aboriginal Ordinance. The way he saw it, Emily was the daughter of a 'quadroon' not a 'half-caste' and therefore not a 'half-caste' nor 'aboriginal' according to the legal definition.

On 20 August, Judge Wells presided over a hearing in which he examined the definition of 'aboriginal' under Section 3 of the Ordinance. He found in favour of Johnson that an 'octoroon' was not a 'half-caste' and therefore not 'aboriginal'. If any such people could prove their status, before a court of law, they would be free from the confines of the legislation. Emily had not done that, so she was returned, yet again, to the Bungalow.

Three days later, the same judge annulled the marriage of George and Emily on the grounds of misconduct between Emily and Robert. It was the first divorce ever granted in Alice Springs.[322] On 5 September, Emily was one of a group of several mothers and children granted permission to attend the pictures in town. Their leave of absence was for four hours, from seven to eleven p.m. Imagine that sweet taste of freedom!

As Emily Liddle told it, pictures were shown in the big dance hall, across from where the Riverside Hotel now stands. They were black and white silent movies and it didn't cost much to go in. Bungalow inmates with permission to attend were given a lift down in a ute. They all piled into the back, I suppose, the way you were allowed to back then. Snowy Kenna and Bill Burton showed the pictures. They lived under a pepper tree on the flat, over from the dance hall, where the RSL was later built.[323] On this particular Saturday night, when the ute arrived to take the Bungalow mob back home, Emily Geesing was no longer with them. No prizes for guessing where she was! The next day, Emily was picked up at Johnson's and returned once again to the Bungalow. This time, she was charged by her old mate Koop with

> being a half-caste who had been removed to a reserve, to wit, the reserve known as the half-caste Institution at Alice Springs did unlawfully refuse to remain in the said reserve, contrary to the provisions of section 16 of the Aboriginals Ordinance.[324]

On 9 September, Solicitor Pick, acting on behalf of Emily, commenced proceedings for false imprisonment against the police officers responsible for Emily's removal as well as the superintendent of the institution. To win this case, Emily would have to prove, to the white man's satisfaction, that she was an 'octoroon'.

Imagine having to prove you're an 'octoroon'. My computer doesn't recognise the word. In spell checks, it offers options including octagon, macaroon and coatroom. It seems to me that any of them would make just as much sense.

Emily called several witnesses to attest to her 'octaroonity'. They included George Ballingal, a prospector, who had known Benfield, Emily's white great-grandfather, in 1887, way back at Peake Station on the Arabana Lands. Ballingal confirmed that Benfield was the white man who had fathered Emily's grandmother Mary. Mary was light in colour, Ballingal told the court, and from his experience, she had a mixture of 'black and white blood'. It appeared to him that Mary lived with Benfield under his care and protection and not with 'the blacks'.[325]

Mrs Chong, listed as a 'half-caste at law' of Alice Springs, told the court that she knew Mary very well, that Mary was a 'halfcaste' and that she 'always lived with whites and not with blacks'. She also told the court that Mary was the mother of Topsy.

Topsy Smith, 'a half-caste at law' who was brought in from Hatches Creek, told the court that she had been told by her mother Mary that a white man named White was her father. Ballingal confirmed this, saying that the twenty to twenty-five people living at 'Peake' all believed that White was Topsy's father.

The fourth witness, Norman Jones, had been the storekeeper and knew the Smiths from Arltunga. Jones considered that Mary had 'white blood' and at Arltunga it was generally considered that Topsy was the daughter of Mary.

On the basis of the evidence provided by these witnesses, the judge found Emily Geesing to be an 'octoroon'. All charges against her were dropped and she was awarded seventy-five pounds for false imprisonment.[326] Koop, along with the Chief Protector and Deputy Chief Protector of Aborigines for the Northern Territory were hopping mad. By my estimation, not only had they been outsmarted by an 'octoroon' at their own game, but she was a divorcee at that! Koop wanted an appeal, desirous as he said he was of having 'a very contentious matter cleared up in a satisfactory manner'.³²⁷ Satisfactory to whom, Sergeant Koop? I imagine Emily and her mob regarded the finding as rather satisfactory indeed.

*

The Chief Protector disagreed with the judge's interpretation of the definition of 'aborigine'. In his opinion, any individual with 'aboriginal blood', however diluted, came under the definition of 'half-caste'.³²⁸ I like to imagine him on this early September evening, sticky in his colonial tropical Darwin abode, with the concrete shutters open, and a breeze blowing in off the Arafura Sea. Chief Protector Cook is swilling slightly more whisky than usual on the occasion of this foolhardy judicial decision, and boring his wife. Or housekeeper. Or dog. He is outraged, obsessed, frustrated and disgusted by what has transpired in Alice Springs this day and goes on and on, ranting and panting until little flecks of spittle form at the corners of his mouth. Later, he pours his emotions into a rather lengthy letter to the Administrator of the Northern Territory. Key points and phrases of his letter include

> The purpose of the definition is beyond dispute.
>
> It is quite obvious that Geesing is the responsibility of the Chief Protector, she being a person of aboriginal blood not legally married to a person substantially of European origin and living with her husband.
>
> A quadroon (one-quarter aboriginal blood) is 'a person one of whose parents is a half-caste'; he is therefore a half-caste within the definition.
>
> The quadroons' offspring in union with a person of white blood (octoroon – one-eighth aboriginal blood) is a 'person one of whose parents is a half-caste' and is therefore a half-caste also.
>
> Quite clearly the purpose of the words 'any person one of whose parents is a half-caste' are intended to provide for the offspring of such quadroons. It would be manifestly ridiculous for the Chief Protector to attempt the control and management of a half-caste female, admitted to be a quadroon, if he had no jurisdiction whatever over her children.

The ordinance has apparently been framed by people with practical experience in the control of aboriginals and a sound knowledge of what they need.

The purpose of the Aboriginals Ordinance is to confer upon the Chief Protector certain duties which he is required to perform in respect of aboriginals.

The Chief Protector will find in aboriginal camps quadroons who are little more, or nothing more, than white aboriginals and with them their octoroon offspring. It is a function of the Chief Protector to make provision for these people and the Aboriginals Ordinance is supposed to provide the legal machinery for this purpose.

The circumstances of their existence preclude any alternative course than transfer to an aboriginal institution.

A quadroon is a half-caste for purposes of embracing the octoroon within the definition.

A quadroon is admitted by the Judge to be a half-caste subject to the Ordinance.

Hypothetical blood significance.

If it is to be established that we have no legal jurisdiction over them, the complications likely to arise are too numerous and too embarrassing to face without the most strenuous effort to avert them.[329]

If, on the other hand, the judge's definition of 'aboriginal' was to stand, opined the Chief Protector, Emily should have to do a better job of proving her 'octoroon' status:

She must have established, beyond reasonable doubt, that every woman in the maternal line of inheritance was actually married to a person substantially of European origin and living with her husband at the time when the female issue of the next generation was born.[330]

No dirty sex on the side. No extramarital affairs. And 'actually married'.

None of this shacking-up those people did
A mosquito

Mosquitoes
An entire damn family of them
Started up with their infernal buzz around the Chief Protector's head
No matter how furiously he swiped
And tried to smudge them between his plump and sweating palms
He couldn't get that buzzing to go away.

The Deputy Chief Protector also questioned the nature of the evidence Emily Geesing had been required to provide. In his own letter to the Northern Territory Administrator, he asserted,

> Hearsay evidence regarding the identity of her maternal grandmother was given and accepted… Topsy Smith testified that her mother was a half-caste and her father was a white man named Smith. She further stated that she had gone through a marriage ceremony with Smith. All these statements, even the story of the marriage, were given credence by the Special Magistrate.
>
> This matter is of so much importance to the Aboriginal's Department that Judge Wells should not be allowed to have the last word on the subject, but that his interpretation should be tested, at the first opportunity, before a higher tribunal.[331]

Fancy basing your findings solely on the verbal evidence of that motley crew who couldn't produce a document between the lot of them to verify their claims!

*

While the white men in charge went on with their twisted intellectual debates about the actual definition of terms that were meaningless to anyone except for those who had invented them, I suspect the 'octoroons' got down to celebrating. It was a major victory and a milestone in their step towards freedom and respect under the white man's law and it never reached the court of appeal.

Looking back on that time, Clarrie Smith (Emily's younger brother) remembered,

Well, really we wasn't allowed to go the pubs or anything like that… I went around and seen this solicitor that had…defended the case and I said to him: 'How is it for a man to go into the pubs and that now?'

'Yes, you can do what you like now' he said. 'They can't do nothing to you. Your sister's proved that she's not a half-caste, therefore they can't do anything to you now.[332]

Ida and Topsy

Mrs Standley reprimanded Topsy Smith for showing honey ants to Maggie.

'Topsy! Don't be showing honey ants to Maggie. We are trying to discourage any interest in those heinous blackfella ways.'

Heinous? Honey ants? Topsy thought to herself. Honey ants are like bush tucker royalty. You don't know what you're missing, honey.

But to Ida she replied, 'Yes, Mrs Standley', and resolved to keep honey-ants and the like more firmly out of the public gaze.

Topsy used a scrubbing brush on the kids each morning with Ida Standley looking on.

'Never mind his goosebumps and wailing and those patches of raw skin. Have you done behind his ears?'

'Yes, Mrs Standley. No, Mrs Standley.'

Oh, I don't know. My bias shines through.

The long association of Standley and Smith with the Bungalow is 'nothing short of remarkable',[333] writes Tony Austin, who has carefully examined goings-on in the Territory in the early decades of the twentieth century. In my mind, I conjure up

> TOPSY AND IDA, the Thelma and Louise of Frontier Central Australia:
>
> For fifteen long years, against a backdrop of draughts and droughts, government inertia, the dirty drunk men of the Stuart Arms Hotel and complex cultural interrelations, they toiled together to give those children a chance.

But that's just silver screen romance.

It would indeed seem remarkable that Topsy and Ida worked so closely together for those fifteen years, in the most exceptional of circumstances. At the same time and with only a few specific details of their interactions to go by, it seems entirely possible that their relationship, defined to a large extent by their social positioning, was really not very remarkable at all.

That Mrs Standley told Topsy off for showing honey ants to Maggie Plenty, and that Mrs Standley used to stand by while Topsy scrubbed the children each morning, are two of the key details we have about the relationship between Topsy and Ida. Topsy's granddaughter Christine thinks they 'got on quite well. By the sounds of it, Ida Standley was kind.' Christine never heard her nanna or aunties say anything bad about Ida. We can overlay that onto our understandings of the social status of each of those women at that time in Central Australia as well as what we know about them biographically.

Ma Standley as she was commonly known, in front of her cottage, Myrtle Villa.[334]

Ida

Ida was in a position of colonial power and assumed the role of a maternal agent of civilisation. Topsy and the children were obedient under her watch but exercised resistance in their own time and space. Ida was a long way from where she had spent the first forty years of her life. She had been hitched to a man twice her age whose drinking, as she told her charges at the Bungalow, had killed him.

That wasn't strictly true because George Standley didn't die until 1936, seven years after Ida had left Alice Springs. Presumably, Ida presented as a widow, a much more comfortable position for her to be in in those days than a separated woman.

Ida figured out how to earn a living and raise her children on her own. She grew up in Adelaide at a time of great democratic progress and suffrage and was educated at one of the girls' colleges whose aim was the empowerment of women. She appeared to be a capable single mother who raised four children on her own. She was kindly, with a strong sense of duty, and seemed to hold great affection for the children of the Bungalow, and they for her.

Ida lived and worked under the most gruelling of conditions for many years. As the sole teacher in Alice Springs, there was little in the way of down time. In fact, as the matron of the Bungalow as well, she worked seven days a week, fifty-two weeks a year, from early in the morning to the end of each long day. It seems she did manage to squeeze in a dalliance of the intimate kind with Jim Baker, storekeepe, with whom Ida was living in 1915–16. A while ago, Darwin-based historian Barbara James came across an Australian Inland Mission paper that contained a complaint by Sister Jean Finlayson about Ida living with Jim. Barbara passed that information on to Chris Torlach, who told Stuart Traynor, who kindly told me: historians gossip down the line. We don't know how long the relationship between the schoolteacher and the storekeeper lasted, nor what form it took. All we have to go on is that one reference from Sister Finlayson.

Ida took one break, for six months, from September 1922, during which time Stott's wife Agnes and their daughter Mavis filled in.[335] There is a little on file by Ida. She sent a couple of handwritten letters to authorities early on which accompanied samples of her pupils' work. She made a few queries about her wages over the years and in 1927 lobbied the newly appointed Central Australian Government Resident for

Mrs Ida Standley leaving for Oodnadatta, 1923.[336]

a pay increase, which was not forthcoming. She wrote brief annual entries for inclusion in the Northern Territory Administrator's Report. In 1925, Ida requested that she be transferred to Adelaide to a non-teaching position.

By 1928, she was still there, soldiering on. Although she was very unwell and in no fit state to rough it even further, Ida was persuaded to go with the children to Jay Creek. She then set a new requested retirement date of 19 January 1929, on the day of her sixtieth birthday, 'or as soon after that as possible'. Ida produced a medical certificate that verified she was experiencing heart attacks and internal troubles.[337] Nevertheless, she lived in a tent under a bough shelter at Jay Creek, in the most primitive of conditions, until March, when a missionary couple arrived to temporarily take her place.[338] Despite that extraordinary effort, Noblet, who had replaced Stott in 1928 as officer-in-charge and local Protector of Aborigines, saw fit to question Ida's commitment or compliance. Lord knows how his letter was delivered to Ida. Let's say she was taking a few quiet moments at the Residency, the gracious home in the heart of the town that had been built in 1926 for the most senior public servant in the district. It has a lovely enclosed veranda, cooled by a manually operated punkah, where perhaps Ida was taking tea and chatting with Resident Cawood, or his wife, and steeling herself for the return to Jay Creek. Or perhaps she was in Adelaide House, the town's medical centre, receiving advice from one or other of the sisters about how to keep her heart ticking, out there in the tent, beneath a bough shelter. Regardless of which little corner of town Ida was taking respite in when the correspondence arrived, and regardless of whether she said,

Oh, how nice, some personal correspondence from the officer-in-charge.
Or…
Noblet! What does he want now?
…this is what she read:

I respectfully ask you to please to explain to me in writing why you did not apply for my permission to be allowed to leave your post at the Bungalow Institution at Jay Creek as matron in charge as I understand it is a few days ago that you left and came into Alice Springs without my authority in writing. As all your requests to me in such matters from you in the past have had my best attention, I don't wish to be overlooked in my duties as head of this department, please note and return with your explanation and oblige.[339]

There was no how are you going, madam, how is the old ticker? No thanks for the extraordinary service she had provided. No recognition of the commitment or selflessness of her actions over the past fifteen years nor the fact that she had asked to be relieved years earlier, before the heart attacks began, and yet she still remained.

Ida's response was as measured as ever:

Sir,
    In explanation I wish to state that I had verbal permission from the Government Resident to be absent, provided I put someone temporarily in my place. At present Sister Cavanagh is on duty.
    I have the honour to be
    Yours Respectfully
    Ida Standley, Matron[340]

Did Ida have to hold herself steady in order to compose her reply or was she really as respectful and obedient as her words imply? Or too tired for the fight? It was, presumably, the final letter Ida wrote in her official capacity as schoolteacher and matron of the Bungalow. It's the last one on file anyway. On 22 March 1929, Ida Standley retired.

I wonder if they had a little party at Jay Creek. Did the kids cry and hug her tight and feel sorry to see her go? Did she and Topsy embrace? Shake hands? Wish each other well? As was reported in the *South Australian Advertiser* on 11 April 1929,

> In a garden setting, among beautiful natural gum and palm trees, with electric lights, streamers and flowers, a farewell was tendered to Mrs. Ida Standley at Mrs. N. Jones's home on Thursday evening, March. 23. There was a record attendance, and a most enjoyable time was spent.
>
> Mrs. Standley has been resident teacher and matron of the Half-caste Home for 15 years. Mrs. Standley is retiring after 34 years' service in the Education Department. Regret was expressed at Mrs. Standley's departure. She was president of the tennis club and a popular player; also member of the dramatic company.
>
> One of the committee of the A.T.M. Hospital, Mrs. Norman Jones, spoke of Mrs. Standley's love and care of the children in her charge, and the spirit in which she entered into any work for the welfare and amusement of either young and old. Mrs. Norman Jones presented Mrs. Standley with a cheque on behalf of residents and old friends in Central Australia. Mrs. Standley replied. Miss Mary Kramer, on behalf of the white school children, presented a silver tea service, inscribed. Mrs. Standley said she felt the proudest woman on earth that night, and felt leaving the centre very much.
>
> Supper was handed round, provided by lady residents, and dancing followed.

In June 1929, Ida Standley was one of two women to receive distinctions in the birthday honours list. Following the investiture in Melbourne, on 9 November, the *Herald* reported,

> Mrs Ida Standley of South Australia, who was invested with the insignia of a 'Member of the Most Excellent Order of the British Em-

pire' by the Governor-General at yesterday's investiture received this Royal recognition for 15 years' child welfare service in the heart of Australia. In the true pioneering spirit she set about to improve conditions, not only for the white children whose parents had made their home so far away from civilisation, but she also spread a maternal wing about the unwanted half-castes who were in a sorry plight. She established the Federal Government school for white children at Alice Springs, and a bungalow home for the half-caste children.

She retired in April, after acting for 15 years as principal of the school and matron of the home. Mrs Standley was entitled to a month's holiday every three years, while stationed In Central Australia, but at one period she missed taking it and was at Alice Springs continuously – for six years.

Seen after the investiture ceremony, Mrs Standley prompted by a great deal of coaxing, gave a brief impression of her pioneering days. 'When I went to Alice Springs more than fifteen years ago I made the journey from the railhead at Oodnadatta in a four-horse buggy, and it took us 14 days to cover the distance. Since the railway line to Alice Springs was opened a few months ago the Journey can be done in 2 days. Originally I was given board at the police station, and held school in one of the cells. I hadn't more than half a dozen white pupils then. Now 20 to 30 answer the roll call. Fifty children are given a home in the bungalow. Both the white and the coloured children I found always intelligent and quick at their lessons. Life at Alice Springs was a happy one for me, and I really regretted giving up, the work.'

During her brief visit here Mrs Standley was the guest of Miss Jessie Traill, the well-known artist, at her home in Sandringham. Their friendship was formed when Miss Traill spent some time in Central Australia gathering fresh subjects for brush and palette. Mrs Standley has returned to Adelaide.

Perhaps it was during the time of receiving this national honour that Maggie Plenty went to visit her dear old schoolteacher and found her, as she later wrote to her daughter, 'living in a two-room place in Right Street a real junk and her bed was old and horrible'. In Maggie's opinion, Ida was 'in the same plight as we were'.[341]

Later, Ida went to live with her daughter Vivian in Manly, New

South Wales. She died on 29 May 1948, aged seventy-nine, and was buried with Catholic rites at French's Forest.[342] Standley Chasm and the Ida Standley preschool were later named in her honour.

Dear Mrs Standley

I would like to meet with you if we may, for a chat. At the Stuart Arms Hotel perhaps, where you go for singalongs.

I suppose we will have a cup of tea. I was told by Maggie Plenty's daughter Jennifer that you asked the Bungalow kids to promise you they would never drink alcohol because it had killed your husband. Maggie kept that promise her entire life. The irony is that, as far as I can tell, the promise Maggie kept was based on your lie. Your husband was alive, wasn't he, when you told the children of the Bungalow that alcohol had killed him? Old George didn't die until 1936, by which time you were no longer in the Red Centre. It only dawned on me recently that that is what happened. I don't blame you for the little, shall we say, white lie. Perhaps alcohol was killing him. Perhaps it destroyed your marriage. And, amidst the patriarchy of Alice Springs, presenting as a widow would have been part of your survival strategy. I am sorry that you had to do that.

Perhaps we could meet at Coolabah Swamp, where the old eucalypts reach skyward in representation of the dancing caterpillars of the Tjukurrpa.

I have seen photos of the Coolabah Swamp, or Ankerre Ankerre as it's known in Arrernte, in the early days of the town, when you lived there. There were little ponds complete with ducks, nestled amongst native grassland, bushes and the fine old coolabah trees; sixty hectares of it. Species diversity was abundant. These days, suburban development along with a lack of regard for the hydrological importance of the area has messed up the natural water retention capacity of the place and allowed certain species to dominate at the expense of so many of the others. In short, it has turned into a bit of a scrubby wasteland. The ponds and ducks are long gone and these days the area is dominated by straggly salt bush, some coolabahs still doing their best to reach skyward, and introduced noxious weeds, like couch and buffel, that the first settlers erroneously thought to be a ripping good idea.

Never mind, we've all got comfy houses these days and pretty gardens and schools like you just would not believe. We don't walk much any more either. We drive, smack bang through the heart of the Coolabah Swamp and into the town that is full of shops and cafés and people of all skin tones and cultural backgrounds, all mixed up together. We've managed to transcend at least some of the racism and sexism of your time. It's a work in progress. Some people seem to have too much vested in keeping things the way they are. Those prejudices are set in stubbornly deep too; a filthy ingrained stain that is awfully hard to shift.

I would like to have met you at the Coolabah Swamp when it was a beautiful wetland area where you used to go for picnics, across the river and into the wilderness.

I am a schoolteacher too, Mrs Standley. I arrived in Central Australia seventy-five years after you. It's hard to imagine it was only seventy-five years. So much has changed, although some things haven't changed enough.

Can I bring my Indigenous mates and family? I am sure they would like to talk with you too. They love the past and understand its inherent connection to the present and future. I imagine they would like to talk to you too about the people and goings on of your time.

Jennifer also told me that when Maggie went on to become a mother, she used to put her hands on her children's faces and call them 'my little pet' the way you did to her. You loved them, didn't you, Mrs Standley, and they loved you right back. Maggie told Jennifer that when the kids saw you coming, they would run and greet you. I can just imagine it. I have been a teacher of Central Australian bush kids too and experienced their infectious love and joy.

I would like to compare notes, Mrs Standley: we, the privileged schoolteaching white folk.

I know it hasn't always been easy and we don't always feel privileged; the isolation, the loneliness and longing, the sense of duty and uncertainty about whether we are doing the right thing. Did you wonder if you were doing the right thing or is that more of a late twentieth century, postmodern occupation?

Our success and good fortune is built on the demise of the people who were here first with their own rich, unique take on reality. You missed out on that rich take, didn't you? You rejected the honey ants. I went for them and they tasted great.

What's that? You loved and cared for those children and wanted what was best for them. Well, of course you did. You were as kind and maternal as could be. That doesn't mean you weren't a massive socialising force, perhaps the greatest of them all: love and care for the kids and lull them into a false sense of security, all the while imbuing them with the ways of the colonising forces.

Oh, I can't possibly understand what you went through and what life was like for you. I am trying not to judge. What I am trying to do, however, is to figure out how what went on back then, in your time and earlier, has had a direct impact on how we think and look and act today. That's the role of studying histor,y Mrs Standley. We need to look at where we have been to understand where we are now. The colonists have developed various stories about the nation's history. It's myth presented as fact that provides one, narrow, biased and dishonest perspective on the national foundations. The stories of the colonists are so powerful they have led the Australian nation to form an image of itself, based on half-truths and bias. That image is now so firmly entrenched that it's hard to shift. In order to progress as a nation, we need to tell the truth. That is, we need stories of the past that offer other than the standard colonial point of view.

That is why I am keen to talk to you, white woman to white woman, schoolteacher to schoolteacher, with similar experiences only seventy-five years apart. I would like to compare notes, to see what comes up. And I'd love to experience Ankerre Ankerre before it got spoilt.

What do you say?
Sincerely,
  Linda Wells

Topsy

By the white man's definition, Topsy was the daughter of a half-caste and so, officially, a quadroon. She fell in love, her descendants tell us, with a short young man of Welsh descent and together they made a life and family together. She could hunt and gather, tend to livestock, give birth with limited assistance time after time. When her husband died in 1914, Topsy had given birth ten times and was pregnant with her last.

As noted previously (page xx), in preparation for his death, Bill Smith asked Topsy to take the children to Oodnadatta, where they had family and could get an education. Topsy wanted to do that but the white authorities had other ideas and supported her only as far as Alice Springs. Her sons Walter and Jim were sent out to work locally and her eldest daughter Maud, aged twelve, was taken by Stott to work as an unpaid 'nurse-girl' in his home. Topsy and the rest of the children stayed in a tent on a block opposite the police complex until the tin shed was built. Five months later, Topsy gave birth to Clarence beneath a bough shelter in the sandy bed of the Todd River. She continued to raise her own as well as many other people's children. Topsy breastfed babies that weren't her own and wept in the dirt when her daughters were put on a camel and taken away to be servants in Adelaide. She then presumably picked herself up out of the dirt, brushed herself off and got on with what she had to do.

Topsy, also reluctantly, moved with the Bungalow to Jay Creek. By then her children were all serving white people, on stations or at homes in Adelaide. In 1929, not long after Mrs Standley's departure, Topsy's daughter Ada turned up and took her mum away from the Bungalow, to Oodnadatta. I wonder if they had a going away celebration for Topsy. In a garden setting, among beautiful natural gum and palm trees, with electric lights, streamers and flowers!

How amazing it must have been to get out after all those years. To return to the Arabana Lands. To experience the township of Oodnadatta that hadn't existed when she had left there thirty years before. At Oodnadatta, Topsy spent time with her old mum Mary. What stories they must have told. She then returned to Alice Springs, where some of her children had settled. Topsy lived out her days surrounded by her children and grandchildren.

Christine was ten when Nanna Topsy died. She told me,

> She was a pretty placid kind of person. I never heard my grandmother being angry.
>
> She loved having all the kids around her. She liked a lot of bush

tucker, kangaroos and rabbits. Mum used to cook a lot of that stuff in her backyard. My dad used to go out shooting a lot and Topsy always used to come with us. This thing called akingkwe, windbreak, she used to make the windbreak and that's how we used to sleep when we was out bush.³⁴³

Topsy spoke Arabana and Arrernte and her children spoke Arrernte. When they got older, Christine's three aunties predominantly spoke Arrernte, the original language of the Alice Springs region and the language they preferred.

As for her style of dress that we see in the photos,

Topsy wore three skirts at the same time, always had a long-sleeved shirt and she always wore a big belt with a big buckle on.³⁴⁴

Of her nanna, Christine commented,

Old Topsy – they were nomadic people.

A notice in Alice Springs' *Centralian Advocate* of 15 April 1960 tells us that Topsy passed away on 6 April at the Alice Springs Hospital.

Loving mother of Walter, Jimmy, Willie, Emily, Ada, Jean, Clarence, Maud, Ruby, Rose.
31 grandchildren. 20 great grandchildren.

Following notices thank Dr Burry and all the sisters and staff at the hospital for their kind attention 'to our beloved mother' during her long illness. The family also thanked 'all relations and friends for the lovely flowers, cards, telegrams and phone calls'.

Topsy Smith's headstone.[345]

In front of one of the Bungalow sheds. Second left is Topsy Smith. Second right is Ida Standley. Far right is Standley's daughter Vivian.[346]

Algebuckina

Topsy's daughter Ada used to travel on the Ghan with her children, between Alice Springs and Adelaide. As they passed over the Algebuckina Bridge, she would tell them, 'This is where your nanna Topsy was born.'[347]

At Algebuckina, a river system complete with a large, seemingly permanent body of water, supports an outburst of inland life. Perhaps Mary had been born there too, and a whole lot of generations before, at that place of lush fertility in the heart of Arabana country. With the lake, surrounded by stands of coolabah, acacia and associated understorey species, it seems like a perfect birthing site.

There is a steel bridge nearby, constructed in 1892. Other markers of settler culture in the area include the graves of three young men who died building the bridge, a rusting 1948 FJ Holden that was hit by a train halfway across, an interpretive sign about the Old Ghan and a surveyed site from 1858 of the proposed Algebuckina township.

These days people travel to Algebuckina to picnic or camp on their way along the Oodnadatta Track.

I propose another cultural marker for Algebuckina:

> BIRTHPLACE OF TOPSY SMITH
> 1875–1960
> Central Australian Pioneer and
> bridge-builder of a different kind
> Who loved and nurtured her own and
> many other children

Jay Creek

There's a bend in the river at Jay Creek, where the watercourse winds its way around a rocky outcrop. It's a hill of burnt orange that glows in the sunlight, like it's about to burst into song.

Plants, scattered randomly, seem to grow out of the rock. There are native grasses and mulga bushes, then higher up some stately ghost gums, the luminescence of their trunks outlined against the orange. We can marvel at their ability to endure the seemingly hostile landscape – rock substratum and no obvious water. The truth of the matter is that there are pockets of dirt on those hills, enough for seedlings to take root. As for water, it's stored in the rock from past rains and released slowly; nature's own dripper system.

Dry, brittle and gritty are the overriding features, with a vibrancy and lifeforce against the odds. As I write, it hasn't rained here for a hundred and sixty days. Climatologists say that's not a record in these parts, where it's common to go months without rain. Perhaps this is like the long dry spell of 1925–26, through which they worked to lay the foundations of the new institution. And then abandoned when they couldn't find a big enough supply of water. And then returned to when the railway boys were on their way.

Even when it hasn't rained for a while, the life force still radiates. Plants are green. Honeyeaters flit from tree to tree, threading strings of pretty song. Willy-wagtails bounce along. This landscape has evolved to survive the dry.

The original settlement would have been built up away from the river bed, on the flat ground. There are no relics left from that time. There are relics, though, of a more recent era: concrete block houses of the kind that have been knocked up on satellite settlements in the desert since the 1980s. They are charmless and supposedly indestructible, although someone or something has had a good go at this dozen or so tumbledown dwellings with their rooves caving in and their crumbling walls, spread out over an area the size of a small village.

On the besser-block wall of one house, I am pleased by a piece of artwork that someone went to trouble to create; a stencilled outline of people holding hands and looking skyward.

On the wall of another house there is art of a different kind:

> FUCK YOU
> NICK
> BATTY
> YOU BIG SLUT

Is it art? Is it therapy? Post-colonial expression? Or just nonsense?

A powerline runs through the place, humming. We're fifty kilometres from town, in a sun-drenched, broken-down village where nobody lives anymore, set in a great desert wilderness. Why on earth does this singing wire come through here and where does it go?

The Bungalow moved from here to the Telegraph Station, a good sprint north of Alice Springs, in 1932. A few years later the Lutherans from Hermannsburg moved in and set up a ration station.

Doris Stuart, a senior custodian for Mparntwe, remembers, as a kid, walking with her family to Jay Creek from Hamilton Downs.[348] That's fifteen miles through the ranges, for a bit of flour, sugar and tea.

A white tin church stands aloof and alone, across the river from the remains of the village. It could be any old tin shed except for the big white cross at the front, like an angel on a Christmas tree. And its whiteness. The church is whiter than the ghost gum trunks and stands stark against the landscape. Exact rectangular spaces have been left in the walls along each side, for ventilation. The sloping roof is of the standard grey tin and has discoloured patches of watermark and rust. The church has a presence that startles me, like a slap across the face, and is haunting in a way that other leftover buildings are not.

I want to simultaneously throw stones at this building and kneel at one of the pews to ask for guidance.

A while before she came here for rations, Doris's father had been one of the Bungalow children. 'He didn't talk about it,' she tells me plainly.[349]

That's the same story over and over. The kids grew up, made their own lives proud and strong and left the place as far behind as they could. Their children, grandchildren, great-grandchildren and so on know something about what went on and are proud of where their ancestors came from and the quiet dignity with which they carried themselves.

How did they grow up to be okay, the children of the Bungalow; or did they?

They were snatched from their families to grow up in three rudimentary tin sheds without the most basic of comforts; a place of 'squalid horror' as it has been called. The children received one and a half hours of instruction, five afternoons a week, in a crowded storeroom that they had to scrub down each afternoon in preparation for white children's return the next morning. They were constantly hungry, with a staple diet of bread and tea.

But the children of the Bungalow were perhaps loved and nurtured in ways that the children who ended up in the larger, mission-run institutions were not. They had Topsy, one of their own, to love and nurture them. They had Ida Standley, misguided, but loving as well.

At Jay Creek time co-mingles. There's the ancient past held tightly in the landscape and then the white tin church of the frontier. There's the busted down besser-brick and the odd disposable nappy and flattened VB can that suggest an element of passing traffic. Where ancient rock meets disposable nappies; where missionary worship meets a postmodern author; where birds continue to sing the pretty tunes they composed before humans were invented. At Jay Creek, as across Central Australia, the past and present swirl together.

In the riverbed I sit, envisaging it filled with water, and the children splashing and squealing and playing about. I hope they were allowed to play in the river. I picture them too, scampering through the hills in search of food, caring for one another and tasting sweet droplets of freedom against the violent, controlling forces of their lives.

Appendix
The Interconnectedness

I am the river, the river that runs through the town. The desert river. The desert town. Significantly dry. There's nothing wrong with me – nothing, that is, that isn't wrong with the whole town. And all the people in it. I'm a part of the people. The people are a part of me.

I'm messy. Sure. I never was back then. Then, Those Who Knew Me Best held me sacred. They held everything sacred. Every little thing. Every big thing. They wouldn't have dreamed of messing me up, old Lhere Mparntwe. Not back then. No ways.

Curious people advanced. On horseback. Heads held high, no invitations necessary. Invasion is like that. They brought things. New products. New packaging. Flavours and colours and ideas thus far unknown to me. Spilling over from the township They were building. Spilling onto me.

'Out of town after dark,' They ordered, Those Who Knew Me Best. I became a borderline.

Invaders with their foreign seeds. Colonisers. Weeds. Altering the countryside to suit their needs. Altering me.

The people on horseback shot Those Who Knew Me Best. 'Put up or shut up,' They barked before firing their carbines.

Those Who Knew Me Best fought back with spears and the fury of injustice. Both sides were maimed but spears and native Law can't match the firearms of the Forces. Blood spilt onto my sands.

Some people hate. They might go on hating forever. Others traced each other's profiles, moved forward, embracing. They nursed each other's infants, laughed at each other's jokes. Found the common love. Over tea or rum or biscuits or honey ants, they came closer. Sometimes, splashing and squealing and playing about. I hope they were allowed to play in the river. I picture them too, scampering through the hills in search of food, caring for one another and tasting sweet droplets of freedom against the violent, controlling forces of their lives.

Appendix
The Interconnectedness

I am the river, the river that runs through the town. The desert river. The desert town. Significantly dry. There's nothing wrong with me – nothing, that is, that isn't wrong with the whole town. And all the people in it. I'm a part of the people. The people are a part of me.

I'm messy. Sure. I never was back then. Then, Those Who Knew Me Best held me sacred. They held everything sacred. Every little thing. Every big thing. They wouldn't have dreamed of messing me up, old Lhere Mparntwe. Not back then. No ways.

Curious people advanced. On horseback. Heads held high, no invitations necessary. Invasion is like that. They brought things. New products. New packaging. Flavours and colours and ideas thus far unknown to me. Spilling over from the township They were building. Spilling onto me.

'Out of town after dark,' They ordered, Those Who Knew Me Best. I became a borderline.

Invaders with their foreign seeds. Colonisers. Weeds. Altering the countryside to suit their needs. Altering me.

The people on horseback shot Those Who Knew Me Best. 'Put up or shut up,' They barked before firing their carbines.

Those Who Knew Me Best fought back with spears and the fury of injustice. Both sides were maimed but spears and native Law can't match the firearms of the Forces. Blood spilt onto my sands.

Some people hate. They might go on hating forever. Others traced each other's profiles, moved forward, embracing. They nursed each other's infants, laughed at each other's jokes. Found the common love. Over tea or rum or biscuits or honey ants, they came closer. Sometimes, with gay abandon, they threw away the packaging and sometimes it landed on my sand.

I am the river. What you do to each other you do to me. What you do to me you do to each other. What you do you do to everything. Every little thing. Every big thing. Such is the interconnectedness.

Citizenship came for all. I was no longer the divide. The boundaries spread. The grog flowed more freely then to fill the empty gaps in people's souls. To drown the heartache. Some spilt onto me. Angkwele Those Who Know Me Best called it, meaning sweet, but I don't know why. As sweet perhaps, as a Molotov cocktail, as sweet as cyanide.

Another new idea. To dam me a little north of the town. Dam the old dry river. Damn the old dry river. To protect their lifestyles? To extend their lifestyles? They seem to be like that. They've never seemed comfortable with things the way things are. Those Who Know said no and fought for me. They were fighting for themselves and fighting for each other. They were fighting for the whole damn lot. They won that time and for the time being. Laughter and songs of celebration flowed and spilt on to me. I laughed too and lapped it up and just kept on rolling along.

I do roll along. I am honestly, unashamedly, magnificent. My creamy white sand forms, indefinitely, into new patterns. Walk on the sand. Feel it scrunch and squeal beneath your feet. Roll on the sand every which way you like. Rejoice in the madness. Only then can you get up and brush it off and head back. Anything goes, anything that can be restored. How much can be restored? We wonder.

I am the home of the great River Red Gums. They are stately and gracious and divine. They make the honey for the insects, hold the nests for the birds. They are the keepers of the secrets of time passing. They are a home and I am their home. My jewels, most naturally, are stones and rocks and branches you might use to make your fires. Use your discretion. You're welcome. Anything that can be restored.

I am the river. I am full of broken glass, broken dreams, packaging, human refuse, children playing, campfires and decomposing bodies. I'm full of weeds too, numerous and increasing exponentially.

There's nothing wrong with me. Nothing that won't be righted when all the people remember that I and everything else in their world is sacred. Every little thing. Every big thing. When heaven returns to earth.

Until then, if you want a pristine river, go downstream. There's a direct connection between the distance you are from the township They built and my state of disrepair. Keep going. When you can't hear the laughter, you can't hear the dialogue and you can't hear the pain. Keep going. There'll be no more sweet substances to share. No more roly-poly warmth. No attempts to understand. Keep going. Away from the whinny of the horses to where the flies that they breed aren't sticking to your face. End up all alone, standing naked in the desert. The only sounds you'll hear will be the wind whistling through the desert oaks. The leaves whispering in the River Reds. The sound of your own heart beating. That far downstream you'll find I am pristine. Such is the interconnectedness. Keep going.

Notes

1. 'Until we give back to the black man just a bit of the land that was his and give it back without provisos, without strings to snatch it back, without anything but complete generosity of spirit in concession for the evil we have done him – until we do that, we shall remain what we have always been so far, a people without integrity; not a nation, but a community of thieves.' From *Poor Fellow My Country* by Xavier Herbert.
2. Australian Institute of Aboriginal and Torres Strait Islander Studies.
3. C. Donnellan, interview, Alice Springs, April 2019.
4. Forrest, 2007, p.14.
5. Where I have used historical terms that are now understood to be offensive, I have signified their origin and my distance from them with the use of quotation marks.
6. I have presented direct quotes from archival material exactly as they appear in the original with no corrections or comments.
7. NAA, A1: 1911/18824, p. 8.
8. NAA, A1: 1930/1542, p. 4.
9. White, 1960, p. 69.
10. This poem is a mosaic of lines from works of prose and poetry by authors including Bailey, 2006; Davidson, 1980; Daly, 2006; Hill, 1963; Hill, 2002; Hogan, 2012; Hyland, 2006; Inkamala, 2006; Moss, 2010; O'Keefe, 2019; Shute, 1950; Thompson, 2019; Trenorden, 2019; Wells, 2016; and Williams, 1999.
11. Quotations in this section from police journals held by the Northern Territory Archives Service Alice Springs F255, Police Journals Officer-in-charge 1886–1956.
12. Photos of police journals by Linda Wells.
13. In my work, I capitalise the word Indigenous when it refers specifically to the original inhabitants of Australia, in accordance with the Australian Federal Government Parliamentary Counsel, Drafting Direction No 2.1.
14. Stuart, 1858. Expedition 1.
15. Stuart, 1858. Expedition 1.
16. Stuart, 1861. Expedition 5.
17. Stuart, 1861. Expedition 4.
18. Stuart, 1861. Expedition 5.

19. Stuart, 1860. Expedition 4.
20. Hardman, 2011, p. 482.
21. Veronica Dobson, conversation, Alice Springs, April 2019.
22. Kimber, 1986, pp. iv–v.
23. Ibid.
24. Stuart, 1860. Expedition 4.
25. Photo of statue of J.M. Stuart, by Linda Wells.
26. Details on the natural environment, peoples and contact history of the Arabana Lands from Paterson, 2008.
27. Harris, 1998, p. 348.
28. Centre for Indigenous Family History Studies 2015, Series F68 Item A19.
29. All quotes on this page from Paterson, 2008, p. 138.
30. Kimber, 1996, p. 20.
31. C. Donnellan, interview, Alice Springs, April 2019.
32. Details of the Track from Bucknall, 1990; Young & Dalton, 1998.
33. NAA: A66, p. 1.
34. Details of Arltunga from Kimber, 1986, unless otherwise stated.
35. Ibid.
36. C. Donnellan, interview, Alice Springs, April 2019.
37. Forrest, 2007, p. 14.
38. Haskins, 2009. p. 165.
39. NAA: A3, NT1920/204, pp. 50–51.
40. Poetry composed of lines and phrases from government documents pertaining to Central Australia between 1910 and 1930, held in the National Archives of Australia.
41. Oodnadatta historic details from State Library of South Australia research note no. 492; Simpson, 1990; Gibson & Shaw, 1987; Shaw & Gibson, 1988; Gibson, 1988; Dallwitz & Fazio, 1992.
42. Traynor, 2016, p. 238; NAA: A518, F241/6/11, p. 181.
43. 'Women Pioneer Matron', News (Adelaide SA), 2 May 1929, p. 9.
44. Details of the Hancock and Standley families from Genealogy SA, https://www.genealogysa.org.au/ and confirmed by multiple other sources, unless otherwise stated.
45. Pocius, 'Lithuanians in South Australia'.
46. Wauchope & Hynes, 2008.
47. Details of Ida Standley's teaching career at Boothby and Buchfelde from Spriggs & Wauchope, 1979, pp. 3–4.
48. Education Gazette of South Australia, 1914.
49. NAA: A518, F241/6/11, p. 366.
50. Ibid.
51. NAA: A518, F241/6/11, p. 213.
52. NAA: A518, F241/6/11, p. 242.
53. NAA: A518, F241/6/11, p. 240.
54. Reynolds, 2005, p. 57.
55. Reynolds, 2005, pp. 3–8.
56. Reynolds, 2005, pp. 7–8.

57. Ibid.
58. NAA: A518, F241/6/11, p. 240, p. 222.
59. NAA: A518, F241/6/11, p. 208.
60. NAA: A518, F241/6/11, p. 197.
61. NAA: A518, F241/6/11, p. 201.
62. Holmes, 1990.
63. PRG 1365/1/147, Jack Laver Collection, State Library South Australia.
64. Wade, 1981, p. 11.
65. Wade 1981, p. 6.
66. Kimber, 1986, p. 32.
67. Ibid.
68. Smith, 1988, side A, tape 1.
69. Smith, 1988, side B, tape 1.
70. Holmes, 1990.
71. Blackwell & Lockwood 1965, p. 50.
72. Smith 1988, side A, tape 1.
73. Smith 1988, side B, tape 1.
74. NAA: A1, 1930/1542, p. 4.
75. NAA: A1, 1927/2982, p. 293.
76. NAA: A1, 1927/2982, p. 330.
77. NAA: A518, F241/6/11, p. 58.
78. NAA: A518, F241/6/11, pp. 402–403.
79. Wade 1981, p. 6.
80. NAA: A518, F241/6/11, pp. 390–392.
81. Ibid.
82. NAA: A518, F241/6/11, pp. 386.
83. NAA: A1, 1927/2982, p. 214.
84. NAA: A518, F241/6/11, p. 292.
85. Northern Territory Administration, 1915, p. 25.
86. NAA: A3, NT1920/204, p. 65.
87. NAA: A1, 1927/2982, pp. 285–6.
88. Ibid.
89. NAA: A1, 1927/2982, p. 280.
90. Samples of writing from NAA: A1, 1927/2982, pp. 270–279.
91. J. Neibour Pott, interview, November 2018.
92. Austin, 1993, p. 62.
93. NAA: A518, F241/6/11, p. 353.
94. Northern Territory Administration, 1917, p. 53.
95. Ibid.
96. C. Donnellan, interview, Alice Springs, April 2019.
97. Wade, 1981–2, p. 10.
98. PRG 1365/1/291, Jack Laver Collection, State Library South Australia.
99. PRG 1365/1/281, Jack Laver Collection, State Library South Australia.
100. PRG 1365/1/298, Jack Laver Collection, State Library South Australia.
101. PRG 1365/1/252, Jack Laver Collection, State Library South Australia.
102. PRG 1365/1/248, Jack Laver Collection, State Library South Australia.
103. NAA: A1, 1930/1542, p. 34. Photos probably taken by Baldwin Spencer during his visit to the Bungalow in 1923.
104. NAA: A1, 1930/1542, p. 36.

105. NAA: A1, 1930/1542, p. 38.
106. NAA: A1, 1928/10743.
107. Ibid.
108. NAA: 1928/10743, p. 1.
109. PRG 1365/1, Jack Laver Collection, State Library South Australia.
110. Details for this chapter come from NAA file A3, NT1920/204 unless otherwise stated.
111. NAA: A3, NT1920/204, p. 21.
112. NAA: A3, NT1920/204, pp. 21, 27.
113. NAA: A3, NT1920/204, p. 17.
114. NAA: A3, NT1920/204, p. 91.
115. The surname was frequently spelt this way in earlier documents. Later, the spelling was changed to Raggatt.
116. Holmes, 1990, Lot nos. 48 & 49.
117. NAA: A3, NT1920/204, p. 151.
118. Ibid.
119. NAA: A3, NT1920/204, p. 73.
120. Rowse, 1998, p. 18.
121. Blackwell & Lockwood, 1965, pp. 26–27.
122. NAA: A1, 1912/9236, pp. 60–62.
123. Rowse, 1998, p. 17.
124. NAA: A3, NT1920/204, p. 52.
125. NAA: A3, NT1920/204, p. 68.
126. NAA: A3, NT1920/204, p. 42.
127. NAA: A3, NT1920/204, p. 74.
128. NAA: A3, NT1920/204, p. 52.
129. NAA: A3, NT1920/204, p.54.
130. Ibid.
131. NAA: A3, NT1920/204, p. 69.
132. NAA: A3, NT1920/204, p. 46.
133. NAA: A3, NT1920/204, p. 30.
134. Ibid.
135. NAA: A3, NT1920/204, p. 78.
136. NAA: A3, NT1920/204, p. 63.
137. Ibid.
138. NAA: A3, NT1920/204, p. 70.
139. Ibid.
140. NAA: A3, NT1920/204, p. 78.
141. NAA: A3, NT1920/204, p. 159.
142. NAA: A3, NT1920/204, p. 61.
143. NAA: A3, NT1920/204, p. 13.
144. NAA: M4435, 218.
145. Briscoe, 2010, p. 6.
146. Liddle, E, 1991, side B tape 1.
147. Liddle, M., 1991, side 1 page 1.
148. J. Neibour-Potts, interview, November 2018.
149. By Linda Wells.
150. Details in this section from NAA: A1, 1936/7846 and NAA: A1, 1927/2982 unless otherwise stated.
151. Haskins, 2009, p. 156.
152. Ibid.
153. Haskins, 2009, p. 163.
154. Haskins, 2009, p. 168.
155. Ibid.
156. NAA: A1, 1936/7846, p. 94.
157. Haskins, 2009, p. 168.
158. Austin 1991, p. 96.
159. NAA: A1, 1930/1542, p. 21.
160. Haskins, 2009, p.162; NAA: A1, 1936/7846, pp. 200–233.

161. NAA: A1, 1927/2982, pp. 179–181.
162. NAA: A1, 1936/7846, p. 233.
163. Ibid.
164. NAA: A1, 1936/7846, p. 234.
165. NAA: A1, 1936/7846, p. 230.
166. NAA: A1, 1927/2982, p. 387.
167. NAA: A1, 1927/2982, p. 383.
168. Haskins, 2009, p. 149.
169. NAA: A1, 1936/7846, p. 94.
170. NAA: A1, 1936/7846, p. 129.
171. NAA: A1, 1936/7846, pp. 95–96.
172. NAA: A1, 1936/7846, p. 85.
173. Austin, 1991, p. 58.
174. Austin, 1993, p. 85.
175. Austin, 1993, p. 86.
176. Ibid.
177. Ibid.
178. Ibid.
179. NAA: A1, 1936/7846, pp. 133, 136.
180. NAA: A1, 1936/7846, pp. 95–96.
181. NAA: A1, 1936/7846, pp. 126–129.
182. Details for this chapter come from NAA file A1, 1927/1106 unless otherwise stated.
183. NAA: A1, 1927/1106, p. 4.
184. National Archives of Australia, 'Sarah Breaden (Half Caste) Education of', p. 40.
185. Strehlow, 2015, pp. 55–64.
186. NAA: A1 1936/7846, p. 209.
187. Ibid.
188. NAA: A1, 1927/1106, pp. 42–45.
189. NAA: A1, 1927/1106, p. 104.
190. NAA: A1, 1927/1106, p. 10.
191. NAA: A1, 1927/1106, pp. 41–44.
192. NAA: A1, 1927/1106, p. 45.
193. NAA: A1, 1927/1106, p. 40.
194. NAA: A1, 1927/1106, pp. 40–41.
195. NAA: A1, 1927/1106, p. 34.
196. Photo of Sarah on her wedding day, courtesy of her daughter, Evelyn Atkinson.
197. NAA: A1, 1927/1106, p. 25.
198. Australian Human Rights Commission, 'Bringing Them Home: The National Inquiry into the Separation of Aboriginal and Torres Strait Islander Children from their Families,' <https://humanrights.gov.au/sites/default/files/content/pdf/social_justice/submissions_un_hr_committee/6_stolen_generations.pdf> (accessed 14 May 2020). Introduction.
199. NAA: A1, 1930/1542, p 6.
200. NAA: A1, 1930/1542, p. 21.
201. NAA: A3, NT1920/204, p. 33.
202. NAA: A3, NT1920/204, p. 31.
203. NAA: A3, NT1920/204, p. 30.
204. NAA: A3, NT1920/204, p. 28
205. NAA: A3, NT1920/204, p. 17.
206. Ibid.
207. NAA: A1, 1927/2982, p. 315.
208. NAA: 518, F241/6/11, p. 325.

209. NAA: 518, F241/6/11, p. 321.
210. Ibid.
211. NAA: A263, ALBUM.
212. NAA: 518, F241/6/11, p. 6.
213. Northern Territory of Australia, 1923, p. 7.
214. NAA: A1, 1927/2982, p.
215. NAA: A1, 1927/2982, pp.193–197.
216. NAA: A1, 1930/1542, p. 23.
217. Ibid.
218. NAA: A1, 1927/2982, p. 246.
219. Smith, 1988, side A, tape 1.
220. Smith 1988, side B, tape 1.
221. Smith 1988, side A, tape 1.
222. Liddle, M., 1981, p. 27.
223. 'School classes in police cell', *The Newcastle Sun*, 19 January 1935, p. 8.
224. NAA: A518, F241/6/11, p. 259.
225. Smith, 1988, side B tape 2.
226. NAA: A1, 1926/11559, p. 3.
227. Wade, 1979, pp. 12–13.
228. Smith, 1988, side A tape 2.
229. Ibid.
230. Ibid.
231. Wade, 1979, p. 14.
232. Smith, 1988, side B tape 1.
233. Ibid.
234. Smith, 1988, side A tape 3.
235. Smith, 1988, side B tape 1.
236. Ibid.
237. Liddle, M., 1991, p. 32.
238. Liddle, M., 1991, pp. 28–30.
239. Smith, 1988, side A tape 1.
240. Ibid.
241. Wade, 1979, p. 16.
242. Liddle, M., 1991, p. 30.
243. Ibid.
244. Wade, 1979, p. 15.
245. Smith, 1988, side B tape 2.
246. Ibid.
247. Smith, 1988, side B tape 5.
248. Wade, 1979, p. 16.
249. Wade, 1979, pp. 28–9.
250. PRG 1365/1/257, Jack Laver Collection, State Library South Australia.
251. PRG 1365/1/317, Jack Laver Collection, State Library South Australia.
252. NAA: A1, 1927/2982, p. 425.
253. NAA: A1, 1927/2982, p. 312.
254. Ibid.
255. NAA: A1, 1927/2982, p. 313.
256. NAA: A1, 1927/2982, p. 208.
257. Briscoe, 2010, p. 4.
258. NAA: A1, 1927/2982, pp. 229–230.
259. South Australian Museum.
260. Ibid.
261. NAA: A1, 1927/2982, p. 52.
262. NAA: A1, 1927/2982, p. 53.
263. NAA: A1, 1927/2982, p. 330.
264. Ibid.
265. NAA: A1, 1927/2982, p. 203.
266. NAA: A1, 1927/2982, p. 327.
267. NAA: A1, 1927/2982, p. 325.
268. Ibid.
269. Ibid.

270. NAA: A1, 1927/2982, p. 322.
271. Northern Territory of Australia, 1925, p. 8.
272. Details about Maggie Plenty in this section come from emails and phone calls with her daughter Jennifer Neibour Pott, unless otherwise stated.
273. Austin, T., *I Can Picture the Old Home So Clearly*, Aboriginal Studies Press, Canberra, 1993, p. 62.
274. Information and quotes about Maggie from email correspondence with Jennifer Neibour-Pott, February 2019.
275. Photos courtesy of Jennifer Neibour Pott.
276. Details about construction at Jay Creek from NAA: A1, 1927/2982 unless otherwise stated.
277. NAA: A1, 1927/2982, p. 31.
278. NAA: A1, 1927/2982, p. 177.
279. Ibid.
280. NAA: Series E1008.
281. NAA, A1, 1927/2982, p. 405.
282. NAA: A1, 1927/2982, p. 504.
283. NAA: A1, 1927/2982, p. 408.
284. Ibid.
285. NAA: A1, 1927/2982, p. 376.
286. Ibid.
287. NAA: A1, 1927/2982, p. 343.
288. NAA: A1, 1927/2982, p. 337.
289. Liddle, E., 1991, side B tape 1.
290. NAA: A1, 1929/5189 PHOTO 11D.
291. Madigan, 1932, p. 73.
292. NAA: A1, 1929/1329, p. 62.
293. 'Sergeant R. Stott's death: Sequel to railway accident', *The Adelaide Advertiser*, 7 May 1928, p. 17.
294. NAA: A1, 1929/1329, p. 68.
295. Madigan, 1932, p. 73.
296. NAA: A1, 1929/1329, pp. 3–4.
297. NAA: A1, 1929/1329, pp. 29–30.
298. PRG 1365/1/74, Jack Laver Collection, State Library South Australia.
299. The details pertaining to this chapter are from NAA: F125/2, unless otherwise stated.
300. Not real name.
301. NAA: A1, 1935/643, pp. 128.
302. Smith, 1999.
303. NAA: A1, 1930/1542, p. 21.
304. NAA: A1, 1927/2982, p. 52.
305. NAA: F125/2, pp. 157–8.
306. NAA: F125/2, p. 152.
307. NAA: F125/2, p. 140.
308. HREOC, 'Bringing Them Home'. pp. 140–141.
309. Attorney General's Department, 'Final Report Preface'.
310. HREOC, 'Bringing Them Home', pp. 5–6.
311. NAA: F125/2, p. 73.
312. NAA: A1, 1935/643, p. 31.
313. C. Donnellan, interview, Alice Springs, April 2019.
314. NAA: A1, 1936/7846, p. 265.
315. NAA: A1, 1936/7846, p. 136.

316. Liddle, E., 1991, side B tape 1.
317. Details in this chapter from NAA file F1, 1937/734, unless otherwise stated.
318. NAA: F1, 1937/734, p. 25.
319. Ibid.
320. Northern Territory of Australia, 'No. 9 of 1918', p. 1.
321. Ibid.
322. 'Divorce at Alice Springs', *Chronicle*, p. 43. https://trove.nla.gov.au/newspaper/article/92487511?searchTerm=emily%20geesing
323. Liddle, E., 1991, tape 2.
324. NAA: A1, 1937/734, p. 37.
325. Details from this hearing, from Centre for Indigenous Family History Studies 2015, Series F68, Item A19.
326. 'What is a half caste?', *The Advertiser*, 5 October 1937, p. 17.
327. NAA: A1, 1937/734, p. 16.
328. NAA: A1, 1937/734, p. 25.
329. NAA: A1, 1937/734, pp. 25–7.
330. Ibid.
331. NAA: A1, 1937/734, pp. 28–29.
332. Clarrie Smith, interviewed by Helen Chryssides, 1988. Tape 2, side A.
333. Details about Ida Standley in this section from Austin, 1993, unless otherwise stated.
334. PRG 1365/1/313, Jack Laver Collection, State Library South Australia.
335. NAA: A1, 1927/2982, p. 269.
336. PRG 1365/1/77 & PRG 1365/1/78, Jack Laver Collection, State Library South Australia.
337. NAA: A659, 1939/1/996, p. 445.
338. NAA: A659, 1939/1/996, p. 422.
339. NTAS: F92 Box A/B75 9/7/5
340. Ibid.
341. J. Neibour Pott, email communication, February 2019.
342. Nelson, *Australian Dictionary of Biography*.
343. C. Donnellan, interview, Alice Springs, April 2019.
344. Ibid.
345. Photo by Linda Wells.
346. Photo from Library & Archives NT, Conservation Commission of the Northern Territory, NTRS 3833 Photographs relating to Central Australia (CCNT Collection) ca 1855–ca1894, NTHP 50.
347. C. Donnellan, interview, Alice Springs, April 2019.
348. D. Stuart, personal communication, Alice Springs, April 2019.
349. Ibid.
350. I have chosen to cite oral history transcripts by the name of the person who told their story. Although this breaks with Harvard citation convention, it is more in line with oral histories as a democratising force in historiography, working on the principle that the story belongs to the person who told it.

References

Attorney General's Department, 2017, Royal Commission into Institutional Responses to Child Sexual Abuse, 'Final Report: Preface and Executive Summary', Attorney General's Department Canberra, retrieved 1 June 2020, https://www.childabuseroyalcommission.gov.au/sites/default/files/final_report_-_preface_and_executive_summary.pdf.

Austin, T. 1993, *I Can Picture the Old Home So Clearly*, Aboriginal Studies Press, Canberra.

Australian Human Rights Commission, 'The National Inquiry into the Separation of Aboriginal and Torres Strait Islander Children from their Families, Bringing them home', Australian Human Rights Commission, viewed 14 May 2020, <https://humanrights.gov.au/sites/default/files/content/pdf/social_justice/submissions_un_hr_committee/6_stolen_generations.pdf>.

Blackwell, D. & Lockwood, D. 1972, *Alice on the Line*, Rigby, Adelaide.

Briscoe, G. 2010, *Racial Folly: A Twentieth Century Aboriginal Family*, ANU Press, Canberra.

Bucknall, G. 2016, *Pioneers of the Old Track Oodnadatta: Alice Springs 1870–1929*, Occasional Papers 11, National Trust NT MCDS Branch.

Centre for Indigenous Family History Studies 2015 Series F68, Item A19, retrieved 11 September 2019, http://www.cifhs.com/.

Dallwitz, J. & Fazio, D. 1992, *White to black: Oodnadatta School 1892–1992*, Oodnadatta Aboriginal School, Oodnadatta.

Daly J. & L.2006, *Take a walk in Northern Territory's National Parks*, Take a walk publications, Brisbane.

Davidson, R. 1980, *Tracks*, Jonathan Cape, London.

Forrest, P. & Forrest, S. 2007, 'A hard and frugal life on the goldfields', *NT News*, 19 June.

Gibson, J., Potezny, V., Minervini, J. & Shaw, B. 1988, *Some Oodnadatta genealogies*, Aboriginal Heritage Branch & Dunjiba Community Council, Oodnadatta, SA.

Haebich, A. 2011, 'Forgetting Indigenous histories: cases from the history of Australia's stolen generations,' *Journal of*

Social History, vol. 44, no. 4, pp. 1033–46.

— 2015, 'Neoliberalism, settler colonialism and the history of Indigenous child removal in Australia', *Australian Indigenous Law Review*, vol. 19, no. 1, pp. 20–31.

Haskins, V. 2006, 'Beyond complicity: questions and issues for white women in Aboriginal history', *Australian Humanities Review*, no. 39–40.

— 2007, 'Domestic service and frontier feminism: the call for a woman visitor to "half-caste" girls and women in domestic service, Adelaide, 1925–1928', *Frontiers – A Journal of Women's Studies*, vol. 28, no. 1–2, pp. 124–164.

— 2009, 'From the Centre to the City: Modernity, mobility and mixed-descent Aboriginal domestic workers from Central Australia', *Women's History Review*, vol. 18, no. 1, pp. 155–175.

Herbert, Xavier. 1975, *Poor Fellow My Country*, Collins Australia, Sydney.

Hill, E. 1963, *The Great Australian Loneliness*, Angus & Robertson, Sydney.

Hogan, E. 2012, *Alice Springs*, NewSouth publishing, Sydney.

Holmes, K. 1990, *Alice Springs, the first 104 lots: a project to document the ownership and building history of the original township of Stuart, now Alice Springs, from 1888 to the present*, National Trust of Australia, Northern Territory.

Hyland, A. 2006, *Diamond Dove*, Text Publishing, Melbourne.

Inkamala, M. 2006, 'My Place', in J. Hutchinson (ed.), *The Milk in the Sky: Writing from the Centre*, Ptilotus Press, Alice Springs, pp. 117–118.

Jack Laver Collection, 1921–1926, Mixed material, PRG series, retrieved 21 September 2020, https://collections.slsa.sa.gov.au/fin d/jack+laver.

Kimber, R. 1986, *Man from Arltunga*, Hesperian Press, Western Australia.

— 1991, 'End of the bad old days: European settlement in CA 1871–1894', Occasional papers No. 25, State Library of the Northern Territory, Darwin.

Lee, G. 2011, *Cultural Landscape Assessment and Analysis of the Neale's Catchment and Algebuckina Waterhole*, retrieved 14 October 2019, file:///C:/Users/wellw/ Downloads/water-neales-catchment-andscape-2011-rep.pdf.

Library & Archives NT, Police Station Alice Springs, F255, Police journals, Officer-in-Charge, 1886–1956.

Liddle, E. 1991, 'Transcript of interview with Emily Liddle by Francis Good', NTRS 226, TS 660, Northern Territory Archives Service, Alice Springs.

Liddle, M. 1991, 'Transcript of interview with Milton Liddle by Josie Petrick', NTRS 226, TS 77,

Northern Territory Archives Service, Alice Springs.

Madigan, C.T. 1932, *Central Australia*, Oxford University Press, London

Moss, R. 2010, *The Hard Light of Day: an artist's story of friendships in Arrernte country*, University of Queensland Press, St Lucia.

National Archives of Australia: Department of External Affairs Melbourne; A1 1911/18824, Correspondence files containing documents relating to Establishment of Institution for Adequate Housing etc. of Half-castes in Northern Territory, 1910–1911.

— Department of Home and Territories, Central Office; A1 1930/1542, Correspondence Files Northern Territory, 1921–1924.

— Department of Home and Territories, Central Office; A1 1927/2982, Alice Springs Bungalow Central Australia File No. 1, 1914–1921.

— Department of Home and Territories, Central Office; A1 1927/1106, Sarah Breaden (Half Caste) Education of, 1925–1928.

— Department of Home and Territories, Central Office; A1, 1936/7846, Half Castes employed outside NT. 1. Suggested Appointment of Official Visitor. 2. Form of Agreement, 1925–1936.

— Department of External Affairs, Melbourne; A1, 1912/3519, Northern Territory. Marriages with Aboriginals. 1911–1912.

— Department of External Affairs, Melbourne; A1, 1911/9647, Northern Territory: Control of Police South of Barrow Creek, 1911–1911.

— Department of Home and Territories, Central Office; A3, NT1920/204, Correspondence files, annual single number series with 'NT' [Northern Territory] prefix, 01 Jul 1912–29 Sep 1925.

— Territories Branch, Prime Minister's Department; A518, F241/6/11, School facilities – Alice Springs, NT, 1913–1953.

— Medical Officer, Alice Springs; F125, 2, Enquiry: Freeman Case, 01 Jan 1934–31 Dec 1934.

Nelson, H., 'Standley, Ida (1869–1948)', Australian Dictionary of Biography, National Centre of Biography, Australian National University, http://adb.anu.edu.au/biography/standley-ida-8619, published first in hardcopy 1990, accessed online 9 April 2019.

Northern Territory Administration, *Report on the Administration of North Australia for the Year 1914–15*, retrieved 15 April 2019, https://aiatsis.gov.au/sites/default/files/docs/digitised_collections/remove/58957.pdf.

— *Report on the Administration of*

North Australia for the Year 1916-17, retrieved 14 April 2019, https://aiatsis.gov.au/sites/default/files/docs/digitised_collections/remove/58972.pdf.

— *Report on the Administration of North Australia for the Year 1922-23*, retrieved 15 April 2019, https://aiatsis.gov.au/sites/default/files/docs/digitised_collections/remove/59011.pdf.

— *Report on the Administration of North Australia for the Year 1925-26*, retrieved 14 April 2019, https://aiatsis.gov.au/sites/default/files/docs/digitised_collections/remove/59037.pdf

Northern Territory of Australia, 'No. 9 of 1918. An Ordinance Relating to Aboriginals', retrieved 22 September 2020, https://aiatsis.gov.au/sites/default/files/docs/digitised_collections/remove/72379.pdf.

O'Keefe, M. 2019, 'The healing songs', in J. Hutchinson (ed.), *Campfire Satellites: an inland anthology*, Ptilotus Press, Alice Springs.

Paterson, A. 2005, 'Early pastoral landscapes and culture contact in Central Australia', *Historical Archaeology*, vol. 39, no. 3, pp. 28–48.

— 2008, *The Lost Legions: Culture Contact in Colonial Australia*, Altamira Press, Lanham MD.

Pocius, D., 'Hardwicke Girls College', SA History Hub, History Trust of South Australia, accessed 11 September 2020, https://sahistoryhub.history.sa.gov.au/places/hardwicke-girls-college.

Reynolds, H. 1998, *This Whispering in Our Hearts*, Allen & Unwin, St Leonards.

— 2005, *Nowhere People*, Penguin, Camberwell, Vic.

Rowse, T. 1998, *White Flour, White Power: from Rations to Citizenship in Central Australia*, Cambridge University Press, UK.

Shaw, B. & Gibson, J. 1988, *Invasion and succession: an Aboriginal history of the Oodnadatta region & South Australia*, Aboriginal Heritage Branch & South Australia Department of Environment and Planning, Adelaide.

Shaw, B., Gibson, J., Ah Chee, F. 1987, *Wangkanyi: Aboriginal recollections of Oodnadatta*, Aboriginal Heritage Branch, Dept of Environment and Planning, Adelaide.

Shute, N. 1956, *A Town like Alice*, William Heinemann, Surrey, England.

Simpson, H. 1990, *Horrie Simpson's Oodnadatta*, Oodnadatta Progress Association, Oodnadatta.

Smith, C. 1988, 'Transcript of interview with Clarence Smith by Helen Chryssides', NTRS 226, TS 486, Northern Territory Archives Service, Alice Springs.

Spriggs, L. & Wauchope, E. 1979,

From Cleve on the Yadnane Plains 1879–1979, Cleve Centenary Committee, South Australia.

Stuart, J.M. 1858–1862, 'Stuart's Journals' John McDouall Stuart Society, retrieved 22 September 2019, http://johnmcdouallstuart.org.au/.

Stuart, J.M. 1815–1866 & Hardman, W. (ed.), 2012, *Explorations in Australia: the journals of John McDouall Stuart during the years 1858, 1859, 1860, 1861, & 1862: when he fixed the centre of the continent and successfully crossed it from sea to sea*, Cambridge University Press, UK.

Traynor, S. 2016, *Alice Springs: from Singing Wire to Iconic Outback Town*, Wakefield Press, South Australia.

Trenorden, E. 2019, 'Approaching Inland' in J Hutchinson (ed.), *Campfire Satellites: an inland anthology*, Ptilotus Press, Alice Springs.

Wade, A. 1979, 'Transcript of interview with Ada Wade by Vicki McDonald', NTRS 226, TS 348, Northern Territory Archives Service, Alice Springs.

Warumpi Band 1987, 'From the Bush,' track B6 on *Go Bush*, Parole Records, Vinyl LP.

Wauchope, E. & Hynes, T. 2008, *Standley*, Wudinna and Districts Telecentre, Wudinna South Australia.

White, P. 1960, *Voss*. Penguin, Harmondsworth.

Williams, B. 1999, *Kumenjayi's Country*, CQU Press, Rockhampton.

Yamma, F. and Piranpa 1999, 'Sanddune', track 5 on *Playing With Fire*, CAAMA Music, CD.

Young, M. & Dalton, G. 1991, *No Place for a Woman: The Autobiography of an Outback Publican*, Pan Macmillan, Australia.

www.ingramcontent.com/pod-product-compliance
Lightning Source LLC
Chambersburg PA
CBHW021057080526
44587CB00010B/280